AMERICAN
EVANGELICALS TODAY

AMERICAN EVANGELICALS TODAY

Corwin E. Smidt

ROWMAN & LITTLEFIELD PUBLISHERS, INC.

Lanham • Boulder • New York • London

Published by Rowman & Littlefield Publishers, Inc.
A wholly owned subsidiary of The Rowman & Littlefield Publishing Group, Inc.
4501 Forbes Boulevard, Suite 200, Lanham, Maryland 20706
www.rowman.com

10 Thornbury Road, Plymouth PL6 7PP, United Kingdom

British Library Cataloguing in Publication Information Available

The hardback edition of this book was previously cataloged by Library of Congress as follows:

Smidt, Corwin E., 1946–
  American evangelicals today / Corwin E. Smidt.
     pages cm
  Includes bibliographical references and index.
  1. Evangelicalism—United States—History—21st century. I. Title.
  BR1642.U6S65 2013
  277.3'083—dc23   2012045224

ISBN 978-1-4422-1729-4 (cloth : alk. paper)
ISBN 978-1-4422-1730-0 (pbk. : alk. paper)
ISBN 978-1-4422-1731-7 (electronic)

∞™ The paper used in this publication meets the minimum requirements of American National Standard for Information Sciences—Permanence of Paper for Printed Library Materials, ANSI/NISO Z39.48-1992.

Printed in the United States of America

To Paul Henry (1942–1993), esteemed colleague, engaging professor, and honorable public servant—Calvin College Professor of Political Science (1970–1978), Michigan state representative and senator (1978–1984), U.S. congressman (1984–1993), and author of *Politics for Evangelicals* (1974).

Contents

Preface to the Paperback Edition

SINCE THE PUBLICATION OF THE HARDCOVER edition of this book, American evangelicals have continued to be the focus of a good deal of scholarly analysis—as well as a great deal of media attention and comment. In terms of media, considerable coverage has been given to whether there has been a growing acceptance of same-sex marriages among evangelicals—particularly among young evangelicals—as well as within evangelical churches and denominations (e.g., Nazworth 2014; Stetzer 2014). There has also been a fair amount of media coverage related to evangelicals and climate change, with some evangelical groups even arguing that climate change is a "pro-life" issue (Valentine 2014). Media coverage of opposition to Obamacare, particularly in terms of opposition to the birth control mandates on employers, has frequently centered on evangelical organizations (e.g., Wheaton College) and businesses run by evangelicals (e.g., HobbyLobby). And some evangelical leaders and spokespersons have attracted media attention in their calls for a "pullback from politics," contending that political engagement by evangelicals has been hurting the purpose and mission of the church (King 2013; Deymaz 2014).

Unfortunately, however, the term "evangelical" as used in the media is often poorly defined. For the past several decades, many in the media have simply used the term "evangelical" either as a synonym for "any Christian believer, Protestant or Catholic, who feels strongly about his or her faith" (Swaim 2014) or simply as a designation for any (usually white) Christian who claims to be born-again. *Neither approach, as the present volume addresses in chapter 2, is a very helpful means by which to identity and understand just who should be considered evangelicals.*

Though scholars have generally been more careful than journalists in their use of the term "evangelical," they have nevertheless adopted different definitions to capture their subject matter. In this brief preface to the paperback edition, it is not possible to review all the various scholarly endeavors written about American evangelicals or survey the full range of media coverage given to American evangelicals that have occurred since the publication of the hardcover edition. Therefore, I will briefly examine a couple of noteworthy scholarly studies published shortly after the publication of the hardcover edition of the current volume—Molly Worthen's *Apostles of Reason: The Crisis of Authority in American Evangelicalism,* Lydia Bean's *The Politics of Evangelical Identity: Local Churches and Partisan Divides in the United States and Canada,* and Steven Miller's *The Age of Evangelicalism: America's Born-Again Years*—using them as a means by which to highlight some of the scholarly differences in defining who are evangelicals, the means by which they are studied, and the basis of comparisons made by which they are understood.

Briefly stated, *American Evangelicals Today* treats evangelicals as belonging to a religious tradition that, in many ways, constitutes a particular kind of religious subculture within American social life. Though this is not necessarily a highly unusual approach to understanding evangelicals, it is distinctively different, as will be evident below, from how a number of other scholars may choose to define evangelicalism. Sociologically, evangelicals are tied together through their particular religious affiliations, their various patterns of social interaction, and their overlapping social networks. Like members of other religious traditions, many of its members draw upon particular media sources that, in turn, shape and color the particular kinds of media messages they receive. Just as they do for other social groups, these factors serve to shape the way evangelicals view various issues, problems, and possible solutions. Nevertheless, not all evangelicals (or members of any other social group, for that matter) necessarily think and act alike. Rather, members tend to exhibit a *characteristic* way of interpreting and responding to the world—these are characteristic, but not defining, ways of responding, as the particular social, religious, and political characteristics of a group can change over time.

The present analysis of this volume draws primarily on survey research to reveal the social, religious, and political characteristics of evangelicals. Each of the data analysis chapters uses three major comparisons to better understand who evangelicals are and how they may have changed over time. First, evangelicals today are compared to members of other religious traditions (mainline Protestants, Black Protestants, and Roman Catholics) and the religiously unaffiliated. Accordingly, the question addressed in this section of each chapter is the extent to which evangelicals are similar to, or different from, those affiliated with other religious traditions. Then, the second section of each chapter examines change over time—the extent to which evangelicals may have changed in their thinking and behavior over the past forty years and whether such change is similar to, or different from, the change found among those affiliated with the other major religious traditions. Finally, each data analysis chapter examines differences among evangelicals in terms of their attitudes and behavior based on racial/ethnic differences, generational differences, educational differences, and religious differences—trying to assess the extent to which evangelicals exhibit cohesion in their thinking and behavior across such differences within the evangelical tradition.

How, then, does the present volume differ from the other scholarly studies noted above—and what is the significance of these differences? In addressing these questions, I seek to highlight what is distinctive about *American Evangelicals Today*, and how differences in one's definitions, methodologies, and analytical comparisons can sometimes result in complementary, but frequently divergent if not contradictory, findings about who evangelicals are and the characteristics they exhibit, as well as their religious, cultural, and political significance.

The Definitions Employed

Though each of the noted studies discuss American evangelicals, the nature of those captured by that label varies considerably across the studies. In particular, differences arise in terms of whether evangelicals are "members" of a particular religious tradition, are "members" of a particular religious movement, or represent something else—something less sociological in nature, as some definitions, noted below, move the study of evangelicalism away from being a sociological phenomenon to something like a characteristic mentality or even a particular age within American history. The reason why such differences in definitions matter is because they affect the assessment of how many Americans can be viewed as evangelicals (which will range from less than 10 percent to nearly 40 percent based on the definition employed). Such definitional differences also affect the resulting social, religious, and political characteristics evangelicals exhibit (for example, whether evangelicals are limited to whites only, or the extent to which evangelicals may share particular religious beliefs, or the extent to which they may be Republican in their partisanship), as well as their cultural significance. (Though the cultural significance of a group is not simply limited to its size, everything else being equal, generally the larger the group, the more culturally significant it is.)

The current volume treats evangelicals as members of a particular religious tradition and not as members of a particular religious movement. The defining character of a religious movement is different from the defining character of a religious tradition; movements seek change, whereas traditions seek to preserve and protect. As noted in chapter 2 of this volume, evangelicalism can be properly viewed sociologically as either a movement or as a tradition—but not as both simultaneously, as the social location of evangelicalism varies depending upon whether it is a movement or a tradition.

"Membership" in a particular religious tradition is based on one's report of affiliation with particular religious *denominations* and certain *nondenominational churches*, with the specific denominations comprising the evangelical, mainline, and Black Protestant traditions having been identified in previous studies (e.g., Kellstedt et al. 1996, 188–89; Steensland et al. 2000; Smidt, Kellstedt, and Guth 2009). This approach suggests, therefore, that evangelicals are found in certain specified denominations, but not in other denominations. In contrast, the religious movement approach suggests evangelicals are found within each of the major Christian faith traditions—including perhaps even the Roman Catholic Church (depending, in part, on the defining character of evangelicalism advanced by the analyst).

Therefore, in the analysis presented here, the basis of unity that evangelicals possess is their particular religious affiliation—not the specific religious beliefs they necessarily profess nor the particular religious behavior they may exhibit. As a result of their existing pattern of religious affiliation with particular denominations and local congregations, the ranks of evangelicals are not restricted to certain racial or ethnic groups: there are white evangelicals, black evangelicals, Hispanic evangelicals, Asian evangelicals, as well as evangelicals of other racial and ethnic groups. Neither are the ranks of evangelicals confined to those who willingly call themselves evangelicals. Affiliation is a sociological variable; identification is a psychological variable. Not all who affiliate with a denomination that is part of the evangelical tradition may choose to identify as an evangelical—but they nevertheless remain an evangelical in terms of their social (religious) affiliation.

In contrast, Molly Worthen is an historian focusing on intellectual history who defines evangelicalism as a religious movement in her book *Apostles of Reason: The Crisis of Authority in American Evangelicalism*—but a movement found only among certain white Americans. This can be inferred from her commenting that, though most African Americans are evangelicals by nearly every definition of evangelicalism based on religious beliefs, they refuse to classify themselves as evangelicals—and so their intellectual history needs to be examined in a separate volume. Nevertheless, by using self-definition as a means to differentiate between those who may hold similar religious beliefs, Worthen implies that self-definition as an evangelical is seemingly a minimal requirement for classification as an evangelical.

Moreover, Worthen's analysis seeks to recast the defining character of American evangelicalism; rather than being a movement defined by certain shared doctrines or politics, it is a movement defined by its struggle to reconcile "head knowledge and heart religion in an increasingly secular America." It is this struggle of "reason with revelation, heart with head, and private piety with the public square" that serves to create the crisis of authority within American evangelicalism noted in the title of her book.

Lydia Bean, a sociologist, also views evangelicalism as a religious movement in her book *The Politics of Evangelical Identity*—though at times she describes it as a religious tradition as well (see p. 10). In her introduction, she states that "Evangelicalism has always been a decentralized, trans-denominational movement based in self-governing local churches." Certainly, evangelicalism can be legitimately viewed as a religious movement. And it is certainly a decentralized movement, as no one denomination, organization, or person encapsulates and controls the movement, for as she notes: "This religious movement has no central control room, no lever . . . (to) pull to make all evangelicals think in a certain way."

Nevertheless, there are certain ambiguities related to her statement that evangelicalism is a "trans-denominational movement based in self-governing local churches." The difficulty relates to the use of "trans-denominational" with "self-governing local churches." The ecclesiastical structure of most denominations embodies one of three forms of church government—a congregational, a presbyterian, or an episcopal form of church polity—with only the congregational form being rightfully viewed as having local churches that are "self-governing." Local churches within most denominations are largely self-governing on a day-to-day basis, but they are not totally self-governing in nature—their actions fall under the oversight and potential disciplinary action of various denominational structures or agencies. Certainly, there are "self-governing" local churches that are part of the evangelical movement, but it is unclear from Bean's definition whether she wishes to restrict the boundaries of the evangelical movement only to self-governing local churches or whether she simply wishes to emphasize the decentralized nature of the evangelicalism—to suggest that evangelicalism is a trans-denominational movement based in local churches, with local congregations being relatively self-governing in nature.

Steven Miller does not provide a precise definition of evangelicals in his book *The Age of Evangelicalism: America's Born-Again Years*, only noting in a parenthetical aside that evangelicalism is "the label commonly given to the public expression of born-again Christianity." Accordingly, for Miller, there really are no evangelicals—as evangelicalism is simply a particular kind of public expression. Rather, this particular public expression was characteristic of a specific era of American history, and so his analysis seeks to shift our understanding of evangelicalism from that of being a particular ongoing religious subculture to a particular, and passing, era of American life.

The Methodologies Employed

All scholarly studies draw from some form of collected data—though the means by which such data are collected can vary greatly. For example, data can be collected through survey research, textual analysis, or participant observation—as well as various other means. Each methodological approach has its particular strengths and weaknesses, and the inferences that can be drawn from one's analysis vary according to the methodology employed.

The present volume draws its findings from analyses of national survey data, particularly the Pew Religious Landscape Survey of 2007, in which over 35,000 Americans were interviewed. Using this survey along with other survey data, the current volume seeks to better understand who evangelicals are, the extent to which they are religiously and politically distinctive, how they may have changed over time, and the differences among them. It is in this focus on divisions among evangelicals that the 2007 Pew Religious Landscape Survey comes predominantly into play, as this massive survey permits the analyst to ascertain racial and ethic, generational and educational, and even religious differences among evangelicals with far greater confidence than that associated with more standard surveys in which far fewer respondents are surveyed (typically ranging between 1000 and 1500 respondents). The strength of survey research is that it enables the analyst to make inferences to the population as a whole. On the other hand, the results of survey research are also shaped by the particular question wording employed, as different results can occur with altered question wording.

In contrast, Worthen is an historian who focuses on intellectual history, a field of study that traces the historiography of particular ideas of certain thinkers and how their ideas become diffused within a broader social network. Generally speaking, intellectual history is less concerned with social processes related to the promotion and adoption of ideas than it is with the particular pathway by which those ideas have been advanced (and possibly evolved) over time by means of particular leaders, thinkers, and/or popularizers that have led to such ideas becoming grounded within a particular body of people.

Though she traces a number of different ideas linked to American evangelicalism over a relatively large span of time, a central concern of the author is how, during the 1960s and 1970s, some popular authors advancing rather "dubious ideas" and possessing rather "weak credentials" were nevertheless able to play a major role in shaping and politicizing evangelical minds.

According to Worthen, the resulting shift in the prevailing framework of thinking that occurred within evangelicalism basically destroyed any remnants of evangelical progressivism that had earlier been present within the movement and enabled movement evangelicals during the 1970s and 1980s to align with movement conservatives within the Republican Party.

While tracing the dissemination of ideas can be a worthwhile endeavor, it can also be subjective in nature. This possible subjectivity becomes evident first in choosing whom to study, and then more fully when, reviewing the textual material of his/her talks or publications, the analyst selects one passage that moves to confirm a particular interpretation while ignoring or downplaying other passages that move away from such a confirmation. Likewise, the same subjectivity becomes evident when, confronted with a large amount of textual material that could be analyzed, the analyst chooses to examine certain texts while ignoring others.

Bean is a sociologist who engages in ethnographic research. The contentions of her book are drawn from data collected through participant observation she conducted among four congregations—two Baptist and two Pentecostal—over the course of one year spanning 2006 and 2007. These four congregations were matched on either side of the U.S.-Canadian border in Hamilton, Ontario, and Buffalo, New York. Bean argues that by comparing evangelicals in the United States with those in Canada, one can gain greater analytical leverage in terms of how evangelicalism is shaped by the different cultural contexts within which it operates.

Participant observation can certainly be an important and valuable approach to acquiring information about some topic at hand. This methodology approach can generate new observations and ascertain how different factors may be interrelated within the particular context being studied. However, because of the limited number of cases observed, it is hard to know just how generalizable the findings may be. This comment is not intended to dismiss the value of the insights which Bean may have obtained through her study, but rather to point to the difficulties in knowing just how applicable such insights gained through a comparison of the religious life of four congregations—two in Canada and two in the United States—may be to the much larger context of evangelical congregations on either side of the border.

The Comparisons Made

One can only understand the relative distinctiveness of a group in relationship to others. Hence, the basis of understanding typically stems from some form of comparative analysis. However, the bases of comparisons can vary greatly.

In the present volume, evangelical Protestants are compared and contrasted with those of other religious traditions in order to understand better
the extent to which evangelicals are distinctive—whether religiously, civically,
or politically. In other words, based on data gathered through survey research,
evangelical Protestants are examined in relationship to mainline Protestants,
Black Protestants, Roman Catholics, and the religiously unaffiliated.

Worthen is less concerned about comparing evangelicals with those outside the evangelical fold as she seeks to understand how particular ideas came
to be embedded within evangelical thought—and how "the evangelical imagination" influences evangelical action. In this regard, she is attentive to certain
religious differences among evangelicals and does not paint all evangelicals as
being alike. For example, she discusses the influence of ideas drawn from the
Reformed community on Wesleyan and Anabaptist groups within American
evangelicalism, and she examines the quest of more emotive evangelicals to
weight the head/heart balance in favor of the heart, as well as the quest of
other evangelicals to find more intellectual depth.

Bean's focus of comparison is the differences between evangelicals in
United States and Canada. In order to understand how evangelicalism became politicized in the American context, she "compared American evangelicals to a meaningful counterfactual: Canadian evangelicals, who share
their theological beliefs but not always their conservative politics." She argues
that "quantitative research has not explained how conservative politics" has
become "sacred and authentic" for American evangelicals nor shown "how
the *content* of local church life creates these effects." For Bean, it is the local
congregations that largely constrain how "rank-and-file evangelicals interpret
their tradition"; most political cues within congregational life come not from
ordained clergy but from a "broad base of volunteer *lay leaders*."

Concluding Comments

The present volume does not necessarily take a unique approach to defining
evangelicals, but it does engage in some unique analysis which helps us better
understand the relatively distinctive nature of American evangelicals and the
internal divisions within their ranks. First, evangelicals are compared to those
of specific other religious faith traditions rather than to all nonevangelicals
as a whole. When one group is compared to all other groups combined, far
greater differences typically emerge. But when analyzed in comparison to
those affiliated with other Christian faith traditions and the religiously unaffiliated, evangelicals do not necessarily look so distinctively different from
other Americans.

Second, the present volume assesses the extent to which evangelicals have changed over time—whether socially, religiously, or politically—versus the extent to which they are the same today as they were nearly a half-century ago. Evangelicals have changed in various important ways, but they have also remained the same in other ways. Some characteristics that evangelicals exhibit today are far less likely to remain in the future than other characteristics.

Finally, *American Evangelicals Today* systematically analyzes differences among evangelicals along four potential cleavages that might divide their ranks in terms of attitudes and behavior. To understand evangelical Protestants as being all the same, marching in some unified manner, pursing the same goals is a mistake. A full understanding of American evangelicals today requires an awareness of their general characteristics and the relative unity they exhibit, as well as the extent to which divisions are evident within their ranks—something which this volume seeks to provide.

Introduction

When Morning Gilds the Sky? Evangelicals in Contemporary American Society

THIS BOOK IS ABOUT AMERICAN EVANGELICAL Christians: who they are; what they believe and practice religiously; and the change and continuity evident among them both religiously and politically over the past quarter century. The study addresses the ways in which evangelicals might best be defined, analyzes how they differ from others and even among themselves in terms of what they think religiously, and examines how evangelicals apply their faith as they move out from their houses of worship into public life.

Of course, many may claim that they already know the answers to such questions, but much of what is common wisdom about evangelicals is based on journalistic images, caricatures, and shifting scholarly definitions of evangelicals. In fact, one scholar (Hart 2004, 16–17) has gone so far as to contend that any attempt to study evangelical Christians is simply doomed to failure in that the religious category "evangelicals" is basically a figment of one's imagination—being "a constructed ideal without any real substance" that "needs to be relinquished as a religious identity because it does not exist."

Despite this claim, evangelicals have continued to receive a great deal of journalistic and scholarly attention in recent years. Nevertheless, in studying evangelicals, both journalists and scholars have frequently employed, either knowingly or unwittingly, different definitional and measurement strategies that have resulted in a number of conflicting findings and interpretations. Some have emphasized religious beliefs (e.g., views of the Bible); others have focused on religious experiences (e.g., having had a born-again experience); others have used religious identifications (e.g., claiming to be an evangelical

Christian), while still others have adopted religious affiliation (e.g., being af-filiated with a denomination rooted in the evangelical Protestant tradition) as approaches to identify evangelical Christians. Moreover, there is little scholarly consensus as to whether evangelical Christians should be viewed simply as a collectivity of individuals, a religious movement, or a religious tradition.[1] These issues are no small matter, as one's particular definition and measurement approach shapes the findings and conclusions one draws about what evangelical Protestants are like. As a result, findings related to the demographic, religious, and political characteristics of American evangelicals are often inconsistent, if not contradictory.

Any study of American evangelical Christians in the first three decades following World War II would probably have been deemed as both an unin-teresting and unworthy endeavor. Public awareness of evangelical Christians was relatively low, as evangelicals were largely ignored by the media and scholars alike. Socially, evangelicals appeared to be relatively uneducated and located in the cultural backwaters of American society; religiously, they appeared to be a dying breed of traditionalists trying to preserve a doomed set of values; and culturally, evangelicals appeared to be old fashioned and anachronistic in a scientific era.

It was the candidacy and election of Jimmy Carter that prompted social scientists to lament the lack of empirical research that focused on evangeli-cals (e.g., Warner 1979; Hunter 1981). Still, public awareness of evangelicals increased, as Carter's campaign and presidency brought media attention to evangelicals. *Time, Newsweek,* and *U.S. News & World Report* all ran feature stories on evangelicals in 1976 or 1977, and a growing awareness of evangeli-cal strength led *Newsweek* in its October 25, 1976, issue to declare that year as "The Year of the Evangelical." Network television also contributed to this increased public awareness. During the course of his presidential campaign, network news broadcasts discussed Carter's religious commitment, and, fol-lowing his election, CBS produced a prime-time documentary about "born-again" Americans. Indeed, it was almost becoming fashionable to be "born again." A whole variety of public figures, including entertainment stars, professional athletes, and elected officials, claimed to be included within the ranks of the reborn.

Despite the fact that evangelicals had long been present within American society,[2] it was not until the late 1970s that George Gallup became the first pollster to try to identify evangelical Christians through survey research methodology.[3] Shortly thereafter the first book on American evangelicals based predominantly on survey research was published. It was James Davi-son Hunter's *American Evangelicalism,* and it drew heavily on Gallup's 1979 survey of evangelicals. Hunter described the primary task of his analysis as "examining the ways Evangelicalism accommodates, resists, and legitimates the forces of modernity" (Hunter 1983, 4). Subsequently, Christian Smith's *American Evangelicalism: Embattled and Thriving* was published, based on a national survey he conducted in 1996. Though this volume explored various characteristics of self-identified evangelicals, its particular focus was to assess "how contemporary evangelicals interact with and attempt to influence the secular culture and society they inhabit and how that shapes evangelical identity itself" (Smith 1998, 1). Surprisingly, to this day, these two books remain the only books based on survey research findings that provide a broad overview of evangelicals socially, religiously, and politically.[4]

Though both of these volumes sought to address important theoretical issues related to the continued presence of evangelicals within contemporary American life, neither was intended to be an introductory study that provided a general overview of who evangelicals are, what they believe, and how their faith shapes the level and nature of their engagement in civic and political life. Moreover, given the substantial gap in time since the publication of these two volumes, there is a need today for a more systematic analysis of evangelicals based on more recent data that provides a broader overview of their current social, religious, and political characteristics.

Possible Changes among American Evangelicals

Life is not static in nature; much has changed religiously, socially, and politically over the past several decades. The social and political landscape of America is substantially different today compared to that evident at the end of the Carter administration in 1979 (Hunter's 1983 volume)—or even at the time of Clinton's reelection campaign in 1996 (Smith's 1998 volume). Consequently, given the passage of time, the patterns related to evangelicals that were discussed in these volumes may no longer hold true.

First, evangelicals themselves may have changed in terms of their general demographic characteristics. In the late 1970s, evangelicals were found to be only moderately educated, trailing other religious traditions in terms of having graduated from, or even having attended, college. In fact, Hunter (1983, 55) noted that evangelicals were "most widely represented among the moderately educated, lower and lower middle-income, working-class occupations." But in his later study of evangelicals, Smith (1998, 76) reported that "on average, self-identified evangelicals have more years of education than fundamentalists, liberals, Roman Catholics, and those who are nonreligious," and that of all the religious groups analyzed, evangelicals had "made the greatest gains in intergenerational educational mobility." Certainly some change in educational attainment among evangelicals may well have occurred between these two surveys, but, given the relatively short interval in time between the two studies, it is much more likely that a substantial portion of the apparent increase in the levels of education found across the two studies was simply a function of the different operational strategies used to identify evangelical respondents. Consequently, though evangelicals may have changed in important ways since the last year of the Carter presidency, it is unclear to what extent, if at all, this is the case.[5]

Second, evangelicals may have changed religiously in some important ways as well. Several noteworthy changes have been occurring within American religious life over the past couple of decades, and these changes may have also affected evangelicals. For one, religious faith in America today is shaped less by the individual's social characteristics and more by their personal preferences and values. In this sense, religion in American life today is less rooted in the web of one's cultural or family heritage, becoming more a personal matter anchored in the private and subjective spheres of life. The presence of this growing individualism within American religious life poses, in turn, an important challenge to religious associational life and participation in public worship, as there is a growing tendency among Americans to be "believers but not belongers." Moreover, there has been a growth of religious diversity within American society—and particularly in terms of growing numbers of adherents to non-Christian faith traditions. As a result, the ways in which evangelicals may view and relate to those within the Christian faith tradition may have changed substantially over the past several decades—with the boundaries of "insiders" and "outsiders" shifting as a result.

Third, the social context may have changed the ways in which evangelicals choose to relate to public life. On the one hand, evangelicals may be entering a period of withdrawal from public life. Throughout American history, evangelicals have exhibited a cyclical pattern of political engagement and withdrawal, and more than a quarter century has now passed since the most recent wave of evangelical involvement in politics began. Organizations such as the Moral Majority and the Christian Coalition that once brought evangelicals to the polls are either in disarray or have been dissolved. And some evangelical leaders have even begun to question publicly the extent to which the political engagement of evangelicals has accomplished any meaningful political results and whether the church should simply return to "being the church." On the other hand, there has been growing competition for the votes of evangelicals (and other "religious voters"), as following the 2004 presidential election the Democratic Party launched a major effort to appeal more directly to "religious voters" who had largely perceived the Democratic Party as being unfriendly toward religion (Smidt et al. 2010, 68–72). This increased competition for evangelical votes could portend continued evangelical involvement in politics, though perhaps with less cohesive patterns of voting.

And, finally, evangelicals themselves may well have changed in terms of their particular political attitudes and priorities. Much has changed politically since the rise of the Moral Majority and the Christian Coalition. The Soviet Union has collapsed. Terrorist attacks on American soil have made "9/11" a household word. The United States has become embroiled in military action in the Middle East. Increased globalization has created a more competitive economic market and brought new challenges to American businesses and the American workforce. The housing market collapse and the economic downturn in the fall of 2008 have cost millions of Americans their jobs and have threatened many property owners with the loss of their homes. Given these important changes, have the political issues that propelled evangelicals to become politically involved changed and expanded over time? Are evangelicals today less tied to the advocacy of particular social issues than was true several decades ago? In other words, have the social issue concerns of evangelicals largely remained unchanged, or have evangelicals actually adopted a broader issue agenda so that now such matters as economic, environmental, and foreign policy concerns more fully rival social issues in their hierarchy of political priorities? And, if so, have evangelicals become less unified politically over the past several decades?

The Nature of the Present Analysis of Evangelicals

This volume analyzes American evangelicals today in terms of their social characteristics, their religious beliefs and behavior, and their attitudes and practices related to engagement in public life. Several important features of this volume serve to characterize the analysis. First, the analysis seeks to understand more fully the nature of contemporary evangelicals in the light of those characteristics exhibited by Americans affiliated with the other major Christian traditions. Hence, throughout the volume, evangelicals are compared to adherents of the other major Christian faith traditions in order to ascertain the extent to which evangelicals differ from other Christians.

Second, this study assesses the level of change that has occurred among evangelicals over approximately the past half century. The characteristics of evangelicals today will be compared to those among evangelicals more than four decades ago. It may be that substantial continuity exists in the religious practices, social characteristics, and political perspectives of today's evangelicals compared with evangelicals a number of decades ago. Or, perhaps, certain important changes may have occurred among evangelicals over that period of time as well. Regardless, where possible, this study seeks to assess the nature and level of change that has occurred among evangelical Protestants since the early 1960s.

Third, this study of evangelicals endeavors to assess differences among evangelicals themselves and the extent to which certain potentially important divisions may be evident within their ranks today. Failure to analyze such differences can blind analysts to important cross-cutting trends that may be occurring among different groups of evangelicals. Over the past several years, a variety of different commentators (e.g., Fitzgerald 2008; Gushee 2008) have discussed the emergence of a new generation of evangelicals, one less tied to evangelicalism's allegiance to Republican politics and more interested in pursuing social justice. Consequently, another important facet of this study is its effort to assess the extent to which such "new evangelicals" may be emerging among evangelicals today,[6] along with other assessments of the extent to which evangelicals may be divided among themselves today.

Fourth, this study examines evangelical Protestants in terms of their being "members" of a particular religious tradition. Generally speaking, scholars have not given sufficient attention to whether in American religious life evangelicalism is better viewed as a religious movement or a religious tradition. The nature of this distinction, and its implications, will be discussed more fully in chapter 2 of the volume. For this study, however, evangelicals will be analyzed in terms of their being associated with a distinct religious tradition within American religious life rather than their being affiliated with a particular religious movement that spans across each of the major Christian traditions found within America today.

Finally, this study is distinctive in that the analysis is primarily based on a recent national survey of a massive sample size—the Pew Religious Landscape Survey of 2007. This random survey of over 35,000 Americans (N=35,556) is particularly advantageous given the desire to analyze differences within the ranks of evangelicals, as over 9,000 evangelicals were interviewed in the Religious Landscape Survey. Most national surveys today are done by major newspapers, television networks, or particular interested parties; these types of surveys typically want to secure some quick assessment as to where the American public opinion rests related to the particular "issue/topic of the day." In order to accomplish these surveys quickly and cheaply, only about 1,000 people are usually surveyed. Such surveys, however, are problematic when one wishes to engage in any subgroup analysis within a particular religious tradition.[7] Obviously, the massive size of the Pew Religious Landscape Survey offers the opportunity to engage in far more refined subgroup analyses, providing much greater confidence in the validity of the resultant findings obtained.

Divisions among Contemporary American Evangelicals

Though there are a number of potentially important divisions that may separate evangelicals religiously and politically (e.g., in terms of gender or region of residence), four potentially important cleavages will be examined in this study. These potential divisions relate to racial, generational, educational, and theological differences. Though some commentators have suggested the emergence of a new generation of evangelicals, other analysts have suggested that important theological divisions exist within evangelicalism that move evangelicals in different directions socially and politically. And, finally, important cleavages may exist among evangelicals based on educational differences within their ranks. Though these purported divisions are likely to be interrelated empirically,[8] they are analytically distinct and will be addressed separately.

Racial and Ethnic Differences

Evangelical Protestants, like most other religious traditions in the United States, are overwhelmingly white (see table 3.4). Nevertheless, Hispanics[9] are a growing constituency within American evangelical Protestantism, and there are approximately as many black members within evangelical Protestant churches as there are Latinos.[10] What unites these white, black, and Hispanic evangelicals is their religious affiliation. Nevertheless, it is unclear just how much religious, social, and political unity is exhibited by evangelicals across these racial and ethnic categories. In fact, some (e.g., Greeley and Hout 2006, 72) contend that race "directs" the impact of religion politically, as the relationship between religious beliefs and partisanship depends on the believers' differing racial ancestries.

However, most analyses of racial and ethnic differences among evangelicals suffer from the problem of a limited number of respondents within the non-white categories of evangelicals. The massive size of the Pew Religious Landscape Survey, however, offers the opportunity to engage in far more refined subgroup analyses, providing much greater confidence in the validity of the resultant findings obtained. In particular, this massive survey allows analysts to compare with far greater confidence the similarities and differences between African American evangelicals and other evangelicals (both white and Hispanic)—as well as the similarities and differences between African American evangelicals and those African Americans affiliated with Black Protestant churches.[11]

Generational Differences

The notion that important generational differences may exist among members of a society has a long-standing history within the social sciences. Whereas birth cohorts are typically examined by demographers in terms of decades coinciding with the census years, generations are discerned somewhat more subjectively and typically encompass a span of fifteen to twenty years (Dillon 2007, 528). The basic idea behind assessing generational differences rests on the understanding that particular factors or events (e.g., different patterns of social relationships, distinctive national and international events experienced, the introduction of new technology, or even different patterns of child-rearing) can produce a distinctive kind of shared experience that generates a certain commonality or proclivity among members of one generation within society that serves to mark them off from members of other generations (Dillon 2007).

For example, those Americans born before 1929 were socialized in a much different political context than those Americans born after World War II. Those born prior to 1929 lived during the Great Depression and the Second World War, while those born after 1946 lived through neither such experience. The social realities of members of the "Greatest Generation" (Brokaw 1998) or "Silent Generation" were dramatically different from those of the "Baby Boom Generation" (i.e., those born between 1946 and 1964), as the Baby Boomers experienced economic stability following the war and a society undergoing rapid social change (e.g., the end of segregation, the expansion of education opportunities, the sexual revolution, women's liberation, the anti–Vietnam War movement). More recently, Generation X has come of age in an era where individualism appears to be the dominant value, where affluence had expanded (though unequally realized), and where consumerism has become rampant. And, finally, social analysts are now examining generational differences in terms of America's newest generation—namely, Millennials, who only attained voting age after the turn of the millennium.[12]

Though generational analyses have a long history in the social sciences, it is far from an exact science. By using the particular year in which one is born to divide members of American society, the analyst introduces an "element of false precision," through setting exact boundaries between the end of one generation and the beginning of another. Yet creating such particular cutting points is necessary in order to carry out any analysis that compares one generation of respondents to another. Moreover, regardless of where the year-of-birth boundaries are set, there likely remains a host of differences in attitudes, values, behaviors, and lifestyles even within a particular generational cohort. Not all members of a designated generation will necessarily think or act alike; rather, members of different generations are simply more likely to exhibit some greater tendency to think in a particular fashion or some greater proclivity to behave in a certain manner.

Though some analysts have now begun to talk about the presence of "new evangelicals" within American life, these analysts could well mean different things by this designation, as the alleged emergence of such "new evangelicals" need not be tied to generational differences. Nevertheless, some commentators have clearly suggested that there is a linkage between the two in that, when they discuss the presence of "new evangelicals," they do so in terms of generational differences. For example, David Gushee has noted that there is "definitively a generation division . . . [with] young evangelicals attracted to a broader [issue] agenda" than older evangelicals (quoted in Goodstein 2008).

As a result, this volume will examine generational differences among American evangelicals today in an effort to discern whether there are distinctive differences between younger and older evangelicals religiously, socially, and politically. Given the fact that young evangelicals have grown up during a time in American society when there was not only greater public recognition of evangelicals but when such recognition has been associated with greater negativity to their presence (e.g., Putnam and Campbell 2010, 509), it may be that the viewpoints of younger evangelicals diverge in significant ways from those held by older generations of evangelicals. Hence, throughout the volume, the views of evangelicals who are part of the millennial generation will be compared and contrasted with the views of older evangelicals—and the views of evangelicals within these generational categories will be compared and contrasted with the corresponding generations found within the other religious traditions.

Educational Differences

Though religious communities seek to instill their particular faith within their members, inevitably differences arise among them in terms of the extent to which such beliefs and practices are adopted and, if adopted, the intensity with which they are held or practiced. This variation can generate in-group tensions among members of the tradition, particularly when these differences may be reinforced by social differences.

One such social difference that might generate and reinforce divergent religious beliefs and practices within a religious tradition is one's level of educational attainment. Increased educational attainment has long been viewed as contributing to an erosion of religious beliefs and practices—whether through the acquisition of new knowledge or due to increased exposure to secular perspectives across one's lifetime as a result of higher educational attainment (Johnson 1997; Skerkat 1998). Initial scholarly findings generally confirmed that higher education both weakened religious beliefs (Feldman and Newcomb 1969; Hunter 1983) and increased apostasy (Caplovitz and Sherrow 1977; Wadsworth and Freeman 1983; Hadaway and Roof 1988)— suggesting that important differences may well exist between evangelicals who are college educated and those who are not.

However, more recent studies have generally been rather inconsistent in their findings related to the extent to which educational attainment necessarily shapes religious beliefs and practices. For example, there are a variety of studies that reveal that increased educational attainment is related to increased attendance at religious services (e.g., Petersen 1994; Johnson 1997) and that this positive relationship holds true across all major religious traditions in America (Sacerdote and Glaeser 2001). Still, there is other recent research that generally confirms earlier findings that higher educational attainment tends to soften religious beliefs and generate more tolerant views of other religions (Pascarella and Terenzini 2005; Mayrl and Oeure 2009).

Thus, it is unclear to what extent differences in educational attainment necessarily serve as a major source of cleavage among evangelicals or whether exposure to competing theories and worldviews necessarily weakens or strengthens their religious faith. It is possible that a college education typically exposes students to alternative frameworks of interpretation and understanding. Yet it is also true that not all majors, nor all colleges and universities, do so to the same extent. And even if there is exposure to such alternative perspectives, one must still choose to engage these theories intellectually in order for such ideas to liberalize—with some research suggesting that this kind of critical engagement with ideas is relatively rare among college students (Clydesdale 2007). Moreover, a number of scholars (Smith 1998; Beyerlein 2004; Woodberry and Smith 2008) have argued that evangelicals, unlike their fundamentalist predecessors, have not sought to remove themselves from the world around them but see advanced education as an opportunity to engage a pluralistic culture without surrendering their theological viewpoints. From this perspective, engaging the world (and its institutions of higher education) need not so much "preclude a robust orthodox faith" as it "offers opportunities to test and strengthen it" (Massengill 2008, 546). As a result, it is unclear whether college-educated evangelicals differ at all from their non-college-educated counterparts in terms of their religious beliefs and practices.

Theological Differences

While some see important generational differences among evangelicals, other analysts point to theological differences evident within their ranks. Here the division among evangelicals is posited to be less generational in nature and more based on differences between evangelical traditionalists and evangelical modernists.

These theological differences may have social bases (e.g., being linked to generational differences), but the presence of these theological differences is not viewed to be a function of age differences per se. Rather, this division among evangelicals is based on changes transpiring within American religious life itself. During the latter half of the twentieth century, there has been a "re-structuring of American religion" (Wuthnow 1988) that has led to the emergence of two different religious groups within most religious traditions (Green 2010). As people re-sort themselves into congenial theological environments, religion has been largely "restructured" into two distinct camps with opposing worldviews, fostered by competing religious institutions and leaders.[13] Old religious traditions have been polarized by theological, social, and cultural conflicts into a "conservative," "orthodox," or "traditionalist" faction on one side, and a "liberal," "progressive," or "modernist" one on the other.[14]

These competing camps are characterized by alternative belief systems, different religious practices, and adherence to rival religious movements. Although critics are rightly skeptical about extreme statements of the restructuring theory or its related notion of "culture wars," evidence for a milder version of such divisions is convincing, especially in older American religious institutions. The press frequently reports on battles between traditionalists and modernists that have continued in almost every major Protestant body, as well as in the American Catholic Church. Although rooted in theology and practice, these struggles also produce opposing moral, social, economic, and political perspectives. To be sure, "culture war" theorists overstate the consequent polarization, both within religious institutions and among the mass public, as there are "centrists" in the religious battles just as there are "moderates" in the political wars. But the religious divisions they identify may well influence politics, if only because both religious and political elites are polarized, thus shaping the cues presented to the public (Guth et al. 1997; Fiorina, Abrams, and Pope 2005).

This perspective then suggests that there may be a division among evangelicals (as well as members of other faith traditions) between traditionalists and modernists (or non-traditionalists more generally).[15] These differences relate to divergent religious beliefs and practices within their ranks. In particular, divisions between these two different groupings of evangelicals may be evident in the holding of differing views on the source and nature of religious authority, different views of the truth and salvific nature of non-Christian faiths, different views related to the formation of the earth and the emergence of humankind, as well as varying levels of participation in corporate worship and other group activities.

Outline of the Volume

The next chapter of the volume reviews the history of the evangelical tradition within American public life. The discussion aims to illuminate both the continuity of important major defining characteristics of American evangelicals and to recognize the important role that evangelicals have played in American life historically. Thus, the chapter seeks to place evangelicals in contemporary American religious life within a larger historical perspective as a means to better understand the historical bases that undergird some of the particular beliefs and practices associated with their religious expression and engagement with public life.

Chapter 2 is more analytical and methodological in nature. First, the chapter assesses the strengths and weaknesses associated with different approaches to defining evangelicals as well as the consequences that flow from their adoption. In addition, the chapter provides various analytical distinctions to be used as a guide for the subsequent discussion contained in the remainder of the book and provides the theoretical framework within which the term "evangelical" is defined in this study. Finally, the chapter discusses the primary data sources that will be used in the analysis of the volume.

The third chapter examines the size and social characteristics of evangelical Protestants within American society. It first assesses the relative proportion of evangelicals today and whether there is any evidence of growth in the proportion of evangelicals within American society over the past several decades. Second, the chapter examines the social characteristics of evangelicals and analyzes them in light of the social characteristics exhibited by adherents of the other major Christian traditions and by the religiously unaffiliated. Finally, the chapter examines the social characteristics of contemporary evangelicals over time in an effort to ascertain whether any of these particular characteristics may have changed in important ways (e.g., in terms of their relative level of education).

Chapter 4 examines the theological beliefs and religious practices of evangelical Protestants. Evangelicals are compared to Christians found in other faith traditions, as well as to the religiously unaffiliated. In addition, the chapter begins to analyze differences among black, Hispanic, and white evangelicals as well as between black evangelical Protestants and blacks within the Black Protestant tradition, and between Hispanic evangelicals and Hispanic Catholics. Finally, the chapter examines the extent to which religious traditionalists and modernists may be evident within the ranks of evangelicals today and the extent to which these religious differences may be related to generational and educational differences within their ranks.

The fifth chapter analyzes the "social theology" of contemporary evangelicals. Social theology constitutes a set of beliefs that link theology to public affairs—namely, those particular perspectives that serve to interpret and express the way(s) in which one's more specific religious beliefs are related to public life. Though related to one's theological perspective, one's social theology is not necessarily a direct product of one's theology, but it is related more to one's notions of the locus of moral authority, the nature of society, and the context within which the theological is mediated into politics.

Chapter 6 examines the civic life of evangelicals. Just as participation in religious organizational life does not encompass all of religious life, neither is public life limited to political life. The means by which citizens choose to address collective problems need not be through governmental institutions. Whereas political life seeks to influence "the selection of governmental personnel and/or the actions they take," civic life reflects "publicly spirited collective action," nonremunerative in nature, that is not directly guided "by some desire to shape public policy" (Campbell 2004, 7). Given their social theologies, evangelical involvement in public life may not, despite appearances, be centered on politics but more on the broader parameters of civic life.

Chapter 7 analyzes American evangelical Christians in terms of their issue positions, their ideological and partisan orientations, and their electoral behavior with regard to their voting turnout and presidential vote choices. The data are examined to assess whether the cohesion exhibited by evangelicals differs significantly from that exhibited by other religious groups and to ascertain whether or not there is any evidence to suggest that important changes may be taking place within their ranks (e.g., in terms of whether evangelicals are beginning to adopt political stands across a broader range of issues confronting American society or whether evangelicals are becoming more unified in the political stands that they take).

The final chapter addresses issues related to the change and continuity found within the ranks of American evangelicals over the past half century. It first examines certain issues related to what serves as the center of being an evangelical in that the core of evangelical Protestantism must continue to be largely evident for there to be any meaningful link between some future manifestation of the evangelical tradition and its past. The chapter then assesses the current divisions found among evangelical Protestants today and what they may suggest about the future viability of evangelicalism as a religious tradition. And, finally, the chapter concludes with a discussion of what changes are likely to occur within American evangelicalism over the course of the next fifty years and how such changes are likely to shape the ability of American evangelicalism to remain a vibrant force within American religious life decades from now.

1

Oh God, Our Help in Ages Past? The Evangelical Tradition in American Religious Life

A S NOTED IN THE INTRODUCTION, evangelical Protestantism is defined and examined in this study in terms of affiliation with a particular religious tradition.[1] But if evangelical Protestantism constitutes a religious *tradition*, then it must exhibit some extended history within American religious life in order for it to be deemed a major religious tradition. As this chapter will attempt to demonstrate, evangelicalism has constituted a significant force defining and shaping the contours of American society and culture since the eighteenth century. And during the nineteenth century, evangelicalism actually constituted the dominant religious expression in America (Coleman 1980, 20), with its ethical and interpretative system permeating American culture to such an extent that it has been argued that "the story of American Evangelicalism is the story of America itself in the years 1800 to 1900" (McLoughlin 1968, 1).

Even today, evangelicalism continues to be an influential force in American life, though, to be sure, it can no longer be considered *the* central shaping force, as a variety of forces exist and contribute to the molding of contemporary life. Nevertheless, evangelicalism remains an important contributing factor—both directly through contemporary evangelical involvement in public life and indirectly through its historical legacy.

Subsequent chapters will analyze the connection between current religious beliefs and practices of American evangelicals and their civic and political attitudes and behavior. This chapter, however, will focus on the evangelical tradition in American history. The legacy of this tradition helps to define the nature of American evangelical Protestantism today and influences the way in which evangelicals become involved in contemporary public life. This legacy of over two centuries provides evangelicals with a variety of historical responses by which they have related to American social and political life. These different historical responses can, in turn, be used to justify different modes and levels of contemporary involvement in public life as well as provide various interpretative "myths"[2] of American history that can be used by religious and political leaders to motivate and substantiate the character of evangelical engagement in public life.

Nearly three decades ago, Leonard Sweet (1984a, 1) argued that there were three indisputable facts with regard to the evangelical tradition in America: it is important, it is understudied, and it is diverse. Though the second fact may no longer hold true, one could possibly add two other facts related to the evangelical tradition. The first is that it is disputed. And the second is that, because this legacy is both diverse and disputed, it is not easily summarized.[3]

Nevertheless, engaging in an analysis of this tradition provides an important perspective on American evangelical Protestants today. Such an analysis reveals the deep and varied historical roots that have served to nourish and establish the evangelical tradition and that can serve to feed and strengthen different patterns of public involvement among evangelicals. Therefore, despite the limitations inherent within any summary of such a long and varied tradition, a discussion of its broad contours can help place the analyses found in later chapters within a broader, and important, historical perspective.

The Roots of the Evangelical Tradition

Religion can be interpreted as entailing qualities related to both the mind and heart. On the one hand, religion involves the holding of certain beliefs, adherence to particular religious doctrines, and/or professing certain confessions of faith that together serve to embody the cognitive components of one's religious faith. On the other hand, religious emotions or experiences can serve to "validate" the authentic nature of those beliefs existentially in the lives of the adherents of those particular systems of beliefs. However, finding the right balance between these cognitive and affective aspects of religion is an ongoing process within religious communities. Too much emphasis on doctrine can lead to dead formalism; too much emphasis on experience can lead to heterodoxy and a lack of religious knowledge, a limited depth of religious understanding, or diminished comprehension of the historical continuity of one's religious tradition.

In some ways, evangelical Protestantism can trace portions of its heritage back to Martin Luther and the Reformation, as Luther argued that an experience of faith was central to salvation, and this insistence "generated an enduring sense that personal experience was the *sine qua non* of authentic Christianity" (Krapohl and Lippy 1999, 17). But evangelical Protestantism's more immediate roots were nourished by the Pietistic movements that emerged during the first half of the eighteenth century on the European continent. These movements protested against the religious formalism within the state churches, as Pietists engaged in a search for a "true religion of the heart" (Noll 2001, 10).

In America, this emphasis on the importance of personal experience, "something marked by affective or emotional expression," was one of the hallmarks of the First Great Awakening, a "sporadic series of revivals" that occurred during the late 1730s and 1740s (Krapohl and Lippy 1999, 18). The First Great Awakening constituted neither a well-organized nor a chronologically discrete event,[4] but reflected a gradual and pervasive turn to religion during the second quarter of the eighteenth century. And though it grew out of Puritanism, the Awakening was also heavily influenced by the Pietistic movements on the continent (Kincheloe 1980). However, the awakeners so fundamentally altered the substance of certain elements within the Puritan heritage that, in the end, these same elements came to stand opposed to Puritanism at many key points (Brauer 1976, 18).[5] Thus, in the wake of the First Great Awakening, both Puritanism and American society were left markedly changed (Noll 1977, 35).

Basically, the Awakening represented a reassertion of orthodox Protestant theology with its emphasis upon the "holiness of God, the sinfulness of mankind, and the futility of seeking salvation through any means but the freely offered grace of God in Jesus Christ" (Noll 1983, 101). The controversy generated by the First Great Awakening was whether the emphasis should be on converted individuals or on the concept of a Christian society (Noll 1983, 102). In response to a Puritan synthesis that had affirmed both a personal and a corporate covenant, the awakeners opted unreservedly for the reassertion of individual salvation through Jesus Christ.

A second important modification was the reinterpretation of the concept of conversion (Brauer 1976, 19). For the awakeners, conversion was a radical break in the life of the converted believer—with the death of the old man and the creation of the new man. As such, conversion represented a profound and shattering experience that transformed the total life of the person. This new emphasis represented a seemingly subtle, but important, change from the older Puritan notion of conversion—with the new understanding being more subjective and individualistic in nature than the older understanding (Brauer 1976, 19–21; Brauer 1978, 241).[6]

Historians now consider the First Great Awakening to be a major turning point in American history. Several different factors have been cited as contributing to its lasting significance. First, the Great Awakening represented the first colony-wide movement, and it provided Americans with their first truly national experience. Consequently, according to McLoughlin (1982, 175), most historians now consider the Great Awakening "as the starting point of a distinctively American identity."

Second, the Great Awakening helped to foster a particular kind of relationship among the various churches—denominationalism. During the revival, the use of the word "denomination" came into vogue to describe other organizational expressions of Protestant faiths found in America (Hudson 1961, 33). Rather than viewing one's neighboring churches as outside the fold of the true church of Christ, Christian leaders now began to talk "as seldom before, about the church of Christ, 'variously denominated'" (Carpenter 2004, 37).

Third, historians have also emphasized that the social side of the religious awakening constituted a rebellion on the part of "commoners" against the prevailing structures of society (e.g., Isaac 1974; Stout 1977). Awakeners challenged the idea that the clergy and traditional lay magistrates had authority because of their position or education and, in its place, they emphasized the new man—reborn in the Spirit and living out the converted life (Brauer 1976, 26). Thus, the Great Awakening unleashed a type of individualistic, democratic impulse that initiated a movement away from the prevailing organic view of society (Brauer 1978, 242; McLoughlin 1982, 176). Moreover, the religious cooperation evident in the First Great Awakening helped prepare Americans for the necessary political and military cooperation of the political revolution that was to follow only several decades later. In fact, McLoughlin (1977) has gone so far as to claim that the Great Awakening constitutes "the key to the American revolution."[7] And Marty (1977) has spoken of "two revolutions," with the first constituting an internal and spiritual revolution that made American religion evangelical (the Great Awakening) and the second constituting an external and political revolution that made American society republican (the American Revolution).

Fourth, the Great Awakening also facilitated the movement toward religious disestablishment. Certainly, the Awakening helped to create a sharp distinction between the church and the world (Noll 1983, 103), as many awakeners promoted a "pure" church membership to be composed of only truly converted believers. For awakeners, the church could no longer be viewed as inclusive of all members of society; as a result, a foundation was laid for the separation of church and state given the awakeners' distinction between converted and non-converted members of society.

Finally, the stress and centrality given to conversion by the awakeners represented a continued, yet growing, subjectivization of Protestantism. Beginning with the First Great Awakening, this growing subjectivization culminated in revivalism becoming "the predominant way of building and sustaining church life in the United States" (Brauer 1982, 148). If individuals did not automatically enter into church membership by being part of the corporate entity, then it was necessary to persuade them of their need for membership. To this end, it was thought that the primary problem related to religious persuasion was one of will rather than intellect and, therefore, the appeal was made to changing people's hearts rather than their minds. Thus, neither the Awakening nor subsequent revivalism called individuals to "reflection and decorum but to feeling and action" (Noll 1977, 42).

The Great Awakening of the 1740s injected an evangelical element into American religious life, but it did not succeed in transforming American Protestantism into a thoroughly evangelical religion. The full flourishing of evangelical Protestantism did not occur until later. Consequently, the First Great Awakening was "more successful at ending Puritanism than inaugurating evangelicalism" (Noll 2001, 193).

The Second Great Awakening

The successful outcome of the Revolutionary War, in the face of seemingly overwhelming odds, strengthened a belief in the covenantal notion of Americans being a chosen people. In addition, for many, it also suggested that American independence had been won in order that the nation might accomplish some greater task. Still, despite these general public sentiments, many church leaders perceived neither the country nor the church as being ready to respond to the task. American society itself was exhibiting considerable strain, and the American church was experiencing a decline in influence.

In the aftermath of the Revolutionary War, the success on the battlefield had given way to major social and political divisions within the country. Acts of violence and fear were evident (e.g., Shays' Rebellion, the Alien and Sedition Acts), and these divisions within American society became further evident in the efforts to ratify the Constitution of 1787 and in the subsequent emergence of the Federalist and anti-Federalist parties. Between 1780 and 1820, the American people had become fascinated with the revolutionary idea that political sovereignty rested with the people. This idea that the people— common people—were sovereign created a serious crisis of authority within American society, and it ultimately contributed to a second revolution—a social and explicitly democratic revolution, symbolized in the election of Jefferson to the presidency. In a complex cultural process that gained momentum from a variety of sources, people began to organize against "the authority of mediating elites, of social distinctions, and of any human tie that did not spring from volitional allegiance" (Hatch 1982, 64). This rejection of a hierarchical and ordered society generated demands for fundamental reforms in politics, law, and religion.

The time following the Revolutionary War was a relatively bleak period of time in the history of American Christianity.[8] By the advent of the 1790s, clerics lamented both the lack of vitality evident within their churches and the public immorality evident throughout society as a whole. Not only had attendance at Sunday worship services declined and membership lagged, but Sunday had become, in various parts of the country, largely a day of "riot and drunkenness" (Olmstead 1961, 55). Seemingly, everywhere throughout the country, morality had declined and discipline lagged.

Moreover, various new challenges now confronted the churches. First, the non-establishment clause of the First Amendment made religious affiliation and participation voluntary in nature,[9] and this voluntary status of religion had revolutionary implications. Not only were churches, if they were to have members at all, required to persuade people to join voluntarily, but they were confronted with the need to develop strong commitments among their members in order both to ensure adequate financial contributions to the churches and to implement the establishment of a moral society through voluntary means (Hudson 1961, 69).

Second, with the attainment of independence, it had become a constitutional principle that laws had to be based upon the consent of the governed. As a result, any religiously based moral order could only be secured to the extent that a majority of citizens could be persuaded to voluntarily adopt those laws that God had designed for the well-being of the larger community.

Third, by the early 1800s, it was clear that, as a result of the westward migration of the American people, the balance of political power and the destiny of the nation were shifting to the frontier communities. Any forging of a Christian society, therefore, rested upon the ability of the churches to make an impact upon a frontier society. Yet ministers were few and churches even fewer on the western frontier. The challenge was not simply sending ministers; it entailed the conversion of countless persons who were unchurched. Furthermore, it seemed that the conditions of the frontier were far more conducive to behavior based on more primitive instincts than religious piety—as the concerns linked to basic survival appeared so great as to leave relatively little time for any cultivation of the spiritual dimensions of life.

When the new century dawned in 1800, probably no more than 10 percent of the American people were members of congregations (Handy 1977, 162).[10] Thus, the churches confronted these formidable tasks within a society that was undergoing considerable strain. Churches desired to stem the tide of moral decay and spiritual lethargy, win new converts, form new congregations, strengthen religious commitments, and translate faith into actions that moved toward the fulfillment of God's end in society. What was needed, therefore, was a dynamic, vital faith—a faith that could appeal to the heart as well as the mind.

The signs of spiritual renewal were forthcoming in the Second Great Awakening. Scattered signs of renewal began to appear in New England and in the South already in the 1790s (Handy 1977, 163–66). People began to take a fresh interest in religious matters; converts were added, and new congregations were formed.

The patterns of renewal evident in the Second Great Awakening varied considerably—from the more orderly awakenings of New England to the excitement of the frontier camp meetings. Though there were real differences between the revivals of the East and those of the frontier, both contributed to a resurgence in, and a realignment of, Protestantism in the new century— with evangelicalism emerging as the dominant strain within nineteenth-century Protestantism (Handy 1977, 171). In fact, this realignment was so pervasive that the terms "evangelical" and "Protestant" could virtually be used interchangeably until at least the Civil War (Marty 1970, foreword).

Associated with the Second Great Awakening was the development of a "democratic theology" (Hatch 1980).[11] The revolutionary idea of the sovereignty of the people had created a serious crisis of authority within American society. In an egalitarian society, political elites could no longer speak authoritatively for the people, and, as the implications of this idea were being worked out, it took little imagination to begin to question both the social function of the clergy and any claim they might make in terms of their right to interpret the scriptures for others (Hatch 1982, 65). Thus, during the First Great Awakening, it was the authority of those clergy who had not had a conversion experience that was brought into question, but during the Second Great Awakening, the authority of all clergymen was largely brought into question.

Consequently, the Second Great Awakening entailed a movement toward an "egalitarian religion"—a revolutionary movement within the church that attempted to put the laity on an equal plane with the clergy. It was democracy at work in religion (Mathews 1969, 35). According to McLoughlin (1982, 187), this movement rested, at least in part, upon the need of Americans "for a God who was directly available to serve their needs and solve their problems, to inspire them with faith in themselves and hope for the millennium regardless of their status, family background, or educational attainment." In doing so, it contributed to the waning of deferential politics and the waxing of egalitarian democracy.

This "democratic revolution" in American Protestantism can be seen in at least two ways. First, it fostered the emergence of those religious faiths that placed less stress upon an educated clergy. Before the Second Great Awakening, the ministry had been reserved primarily for those having completed theological studies. During the Second Great Awakening, however, church growth occurred predominantly in those denominations that did not require an educated clergy (e.g., Baptist, Methodist, and Disciples of Christ churches) and in which revivalism was strongest (Handy 1977, 195–96; Hatch 1980).

Second, this "democratic revolution" fostered the emergence of a populist hermeneutic. Though the leaders of the Reformation promoted popular translations of the Bible, they did not view the laity as being adequately able to understand the scriptures apart from ministerial guidance. Revivalists of the Second Great Awakening, however, stressed a Bible devoid of authoritative interpretations grounded in established theological interpretations. The maxim "no creed but the Bible" reflected not only the Protestant principle of *sola Scriptura*, but the growing emphasis upon private judgment as the final court of scriptural interpretation as well. Thus, after 1800, views of biblical interpretation and democratic values were moving in the same direction— mutually reinforcing such ideas as volitional allegiance, self-reliance, and private judgment (Hatch 1982, 74).

Finally, it should be noted that this movement toward hearing the voice of the people in religion clearly encouraged a more literal interpretation of scripture. Without theological training, competency in Old and New Testament languages of Hebrew and Greek, or appreciation for church tradition, readers were left with few tools with which to interpret scripture (Hatch 1980; Marsden 1982). Not too surprisingly, therefore, common people and uneducated clergy tended to understand and view scripture in terms of its "face value." After all, did not scripture state that the simple truth of the Gospel was given to the relatively uneducated because its truth tended to confound the wisdom of the wise?

Thus, during this period of time, evangelical Christianity was not characterized by ascetic withdrawal or spiritualistic contemplation. Rather, it was largely "activist, pragmatic, and oriented toward measureable results" (Askew and Spellman 1984, 82). "Saved for service" was a popular evangelical emphasis—with converts being enlisted to carry on the tasks of revival, to seek converts, to build churches, and to do works of benevolence among the people (Handy 1977, 173).

Much of the activity associated with the Second Great Awakening focused upon establishing a moral order based upon the new social and political conditions. Under the new strains imposed by independence and intellectual turmoil, the American people were busily attempting to impose order upon their society (Mathews 1969, 33). Not only religious but political leaders as well repeatedly warned that the success of the American experiment rested on the character of the American people.

During these years, church leaders began to emphasize the services of religion to the American republic (Maclear 1959, 55).[12] Though monarchies and despotic governments might rule by coercion, a free republic was dependent solely on mass moral restraint. The safety and prosperity of the republic rested upon public morality and piety, and both political and religious leaders throughout the country agreed that such virtues should be diffused and inculcated among the common people and taught regularly to each generation (McLoughlin 1982, 184).

The justification, and general point of agreement, for this vision among Protestants was the basic and familiar theme that, without religiously based moral standards, society would collapse (Handy 1971, 35–36). So while an institutional separation of church and state was generally accepted and at times strongly defended, Protestants could, and did, reject any notion that religion and morals could be separated from public life and public well-being.

A whole new nation and culture was being created—and needed to be shaped properly. Educational institutions needed to be established, social reforms accomplished, and public opinion molded and mobilized. As early as 1796, voluntary societies had been formed to accomplish such purposes (Hudson 1961, 82). And by sometime after 1812, evangelicals had largely turned to "voluntary societies as a way of promoting public morality" (Noll 2001, 196). These voluntary societies were interdenominational in character and were not structurally tied to the churches. By concentrating on a single objective, these societies could enlist the broadest support while avoiding divisive theological issues (Askew and Spellman 1984, 86). These groups, organized to accomplish selected benevolent purposes, provided effective channels for quick, concerted action without either compromising denominational differences or violating the principles of the First Amendment (Handy 1977, 173).

During the Second Great Awakening, Americans began to form an extraordinary number of such voluntary societies—with over 350 societies being formed in Massachusetts alone between 1810 and 1830 (Moorhead 1984, 73).[13] Societies were formed to promote domestic and foreign missions, build evangelical colleges, abolish slavery, support temperance, and further a host of other causes. This organizing process had reached such proportions by 1820 that a large number of national organizations, known later to historians as the Evangelical United Front, had been formed to shape the culture of the young republic. In fact, such societies had become so widespread that one commentator of the period claimed that "matters have come to such a pass that a peaceable man can hardly venture to eat or drink, to go to bed or get up, to correct his child or kiss his wife" without the guidance of one and possibly more benevolent societies (Singleton 1975, 554–55).

Thus, linked to the Second Great Awakening was the establishment of what contemporaries termed "a benevolent empire" that embodied "an interlocking network of voluntary associations, large and small, local, national, and international, to implement its varied purposes" (Howe 2007, 130). The motivation behind the formation of these voluntary societies was, at least in part, the search for new forms of social cohesion (Moorhead 1984, 73). Yet the goal was not establishment of some kind of cohesion for its own sake, but rather the creation of a particular kind of America (Hammond 1979, 206). The Evangelical United Front did not constitute, nor did it work for, a united front theologically; instead, it represented a united front socially for the purposes of eliminating evil everywhere. It was a united front seeking the creation of the perfectly just society—for shaping America into what Marty (1970) has called the "Righteous Empire."

It is perhaps in the field of public education that the Protestant concern for the advancing of morality and civilization can best be seen. During this period of time, both pastors and educational leaders believed that public schools could serve as an integral part of the effort to create a moral, and Christian, society (Tyack 1966, 455). For example, while Horace Mann (1796–1859) and other educational leaders were determined that public schools should be nonsectarian, they were also determined that such schools should inculcate those general moral and religious teachings upon which most Protestants agreed (Handy 1977, 179). Religion and civilization were seen to be partners.

Consequently, despite differences in doctrine and polity, Protestants could support public education because they saw it as a means for moral education. When the city of New York took over the Protestant Public School Society in 1842, for example, it did not constitute some kind of victory for secularism but rather a triumph for a kind of nondenominational Protestantism: "An evangelical consensus of faith and ethics had come so to dominate the national culture that a majority of Protestants were willing to entrust the state with the task of educating children, confident that education would be 'religious' still" (Smith 1967, 687). Protestants became ardent supporters of public elementary education because public educational institutions could seemingly be trusted to play an important role in the molding of a Christian society—and it was during this period of time that the drive for universal, compulsory, free public elementary education was won (Handy 1977, 179).

By the end of the Second Great Awakening, American religious life had become realigned (Handy 1977, 196). The period of time from the Revolution to the Civil War witnessed an unprecedented expansion of evangelical

Protestant Christianity. During this time, there was both a dramatic increase in religious affiliation and an increasing growth in the influence of religion on American culture (Noll 2002, 166).

Still, this increase in religious affiliation occurred more predominantly within some, rather than other, denominations. Just prior to the Revolutionary War, more than half of those attending church went to Congregational, Presbyterian, and Anglican worship services, and they generally supported the legal establishment of their churches (Sweeney 2005, 62). By 1850, however, these denominations contained fewer than 20 percent of churchgoers, while evangelical churches dominated the landscape. By the midpoint of the nineteenth century, those attending Baptist and Methodist churches alone now numbered over half of all religious attenders in the country (Sweeney 2005, 62). Both Baptists and Methodists gained influence, in part, because they saw individual experience as paramount religiously (Krapohl and Lippy 1999, 19).

In fact, it is estimated that Methodists comprised less than 3 percent of the church population in 1776, but swelled to nearly 35 percent in 1850 (Noll 1994, 117). Thus, almost out of nowhere, and over a relatively short period of time, Methodism had become America's largest denomination, having first topped the charts as the country's biggest denomination in 1844 (Sweeney 2005, 65). It was their method of outreach that helped propel them to such a prominent position in such a relatively short period of time, as the Methodists adopted the use of circuit riders to reach communities on the frontier. These circuit riders covered large expanses of territory in order to preach to ordinary folk, and their efforts "helped implant in American Protestantism the notion of individual choice in matters of salvation" (Krapohl and Lippy 1999, 19).[14]

The Second Great Awakening, and revivalism more generally, served to give American Christianity a particular populist and democratic cast (Hankins 2008, 16). As the "common man" rose in power and prominence, the consequence was "the displacement from power of the uncommon man, the man of ideas" (Hatch 1984b, 75). Instead, in revivals, the audience is treated as sovereign (Hatch 1984b, 73) in that the audience chooses which preachers have authority and legitimacy on the basis of who can best stir their hearts and minds. Thus, educational attainment or theological sophistication has not generally bestowed the mantle of authority on preachers within the evangelical tradition, but rather authority is conferred more through an ability to communicate effectively with the masses (Hankins 2008, 16). This distinctively democratic feature of American religion helps to explain, in part, the relative religious vitality of American religious life.

Though they differed in many particulars, there was a core of common characteristics that served to provide unity to American evangelicalism at the time. First, evangelicals "were determined Protestants who took with particular earnestness the historic Protestant attachment to Scripture" and who "shared a conviction that true religion required the active experience of God" (Noll 1994, 129). Flowing from this common characteristic was "a bias ... against inherited structures and institutions," as no structure or institution "could communicate the power of God's presence as adequately as Scripture and personal Christian experience" (Noll 1994, 129–30).

It was during the early 1800s, then, that evangelicalism became the dominant religious expression within American religious life. Yet even such a statement does not convey its significance during this period of time. In reality, evangelicalism no longer simply represented one religious expression among a variety of others; rather, for the most part, it simply constituted American Christianity at the time.

The Civil War to Post–World War I

Ahlstrom (1972, 823) has argued that no aspect of American religious history "is more in need of summary and yet so difficult to summarize as the movements of dissent and reaction which occurred between the Civil War and World War I." Seeking to summarize the history of evangelical Protestantism during this period of time is a challenging task. All one can really do is highlight some important developments that transpired within the evangelical tradition during this time span.

With its emphasis on revivalism, the prevailing nature of evangelical Protestantism during the nineteenth century did not entail a focus on ascetic withdrawal or spiritualistic contemplation. Rather, it was one of civic engagement, and it was Charles Finney (1792–1875) who popularized a millennial vision that forged the previously formed benevolent societies into a larger mass movement that held that the kingdom of God could be advanced and secured by human action. This postmillennial eschatology suggested that human effort could help usher in the Kingdom of God and that the millennium rested upon a growing Christian perfectionism, both individually as believers and collectively as a society. Thus, already by the mid-1800s, Christian perfectionism was emerging as "one of the central themes of American social, intellectual, and religious life" (Synan 1971, 28).

Tied to such perfectionist thought was the goal of personal Christian perfection. With roots evident in the revival of 1857–1858,[15] the Holiness movement emerged organizationally following the Civil War, when the National Camp Meeting Association for the Promotion of Holiness (and other Holiness associations) came into existence. At its inception, the Holiness movement resided primarily within the Methodist church,[16] and it embodied an "attempt to recover Wesley's original second-blessing eradication doctrine of sanctification" (Menzies 1975, 85). John Wesley, the founder of Methodism, contended that there were two distinct operations of grace to be experienced: justification, which occurred at the time of one's conversion, and then, subsequently, sanctification, which was a blessing that could ultimately bring perfection. During the early decades of the nineteenth century, this emphasis upon perfection, or "holiness," helped to attract many to Methodism. But by the last third of the century, as worship grew more formal and restrained in many Methodist churches, a Holiness movement began to flourish not only within but increasingly outside the Methodist church.

Tied to this perfectionistic thought were also a variety of reform movements—each designed "to perfect" American life. Such reform movements related to such issues as women's rights, the abolition of slavery, prohibition, and political reform (Synan 1971, 28), with the greatest effort toward the reform and perfection of American society being the American Civil War itself.

However, during this period of time, American society was also experiencing a number of dramatic and fundamental changes that spawned other religious movements as well. Industrialization and urbanization were changing the character of the nation, economic power was increasingly becoming concentrated in the hands of the few, and immigration was bringing increasing numbers of non-Protestants to the American shores.

These changes prompted social critics to subject almost every American institution to a searching scrutiny. Increasing industrialization and urbanization created new social and economic problems that private organizations were seemingly ill equipped to handle. With the concentration of economic power in the hands of the few, businesses flourished while many workers were paid little, living lives of poverty and squalor in urban slums. And, finally, the increasing number of Catholic, Jewish, and unchurched immigrants not only threatened the dominance of Protestantism generally but also seemingly threatened the very religious and moral consensus of the country itself.

In response to these changes, there emerged within evangelicalism a strong liberal element that increasingly took a stance that stressed the incorporation of modern assumptions and paradigms within the Christian tradition (Hutchison 1976). This element tended to stress the findings of history, linguistic scholarship, and comparative religion, and it became convinced that the Bible contained both historical errors and scientifically untenable conceptions. As a result, these theological liberals generally downplayed God's revelation of "Himself" and emphasized man's discovery of God, downplayed the fixed nature of revelation in the Bible and emphasized God's continuing nature of revelation in the world, downplayed the personal revelation of God in Jesus Christ and emphasized God's general revelation in nature and history, and downplayed God's transcendence from the world and emphasized God's immanence within the world.

Moreover, associated with this more liberal theological stance was an emphasis upon a social gospel. Advocates of the social gospel argued that the moral and social ills of society were largely the product of social, political, and economic realities over which individuals had little, if any, control. Consequently, social gospel advocates largely rejected revivalism as a basis for societal reform; rather, they argued that it was structural conditions that precipitated the social maladies of the day and that these social structures needed to be changed.[17]

While the more liberal wing of Protestantism was emphasizing political means to solve social problems, interest in political action among revivalist evangelicals diminished, but did not disappear. Revivalist evangelicals still championed social concerns—though largely in the form of private charity. During this period of time, evangelicals moved from a largely "Calvinistic" perspective that saw politics as an important means to advance the Kingdom to a more "pietistic" perspective that viewed politics as little more than a means to restrain evil (Marsden 1980, 86). Or, in terms of another theological perspective, evangelicals moved largely from a postmillennial[18] to a premillennial[19] position in their eschatological perspectives (Moorhead 1984).[20]

Actually, the social gospel movement drew, in large part, on the same perfectionist thought that produced the Holiness movement (Synan 1971, 58). Both groups assumed that human beings could be perfected. Where they diverged was over the issues of the perfectibility of society, as those in the Holiness movement contended that such perfection of society would occur only with the second coming of Christ and the advent of the millennium while those within the social gospel movement eventually shifted to a notion that the progress of civilizations, particularly through achievements derived from science and education, would bring an increasingly enlightened and civilized world.

Yet, while one can discern movement toward polarization within evangelicalism during the latter part of the nineteenth century, a spectrum of theological positions still remained. In fact, Handy (1955) has identified at least five different theological parties at the turn of the century: modernists, evangelical liberals, conservative evangelicals, conservatives, and fundamentalists. Indeed, this latter part of the nineteenth century was still a time in which Dwight Moody, a major progenitor of fundamentalism, could easily "maintain cordial relations with members of both emerging parties in American Protestantism" (Marsden 1980, 32–33) and in which "liberal and evangelical leaders . . . were still quite willing to join forces in order to achieve larger aims" (Wacker 1985, 52).

The passing of evangelical cultural dominance by the early decades of the twentieth century, however, was also accompanied by several significant religious developments that continue to have far-reaching effects even today. Two such developments should be briefly noted. First, African American churches and denominations began to form prior to the Civil War, and the post–Civil War era brought new opportunities for these churches. Actually, this emergence and development of the black church might well have allowed for the expansion of the cultural reach of evangelical Protestantism in America, as most black Americans who attend African American denominations and congregations share many of the same religious beliefs and moral values of evangelical Protestants. Prior to the Civil War, evangelicals were among the early, and important, leaders in the fight against slavery. Yet other evangelicals at the time either tolerated or defended the institution. And though black and evangelical Protestants shared (and continue to share) many theological beliefs, their styles of worship differed and, during much of the nineteenth century and into the twentieth century, many white evangelicals frowned on aspects of African culture that were retained in the worship of many black Christian churches. Finally, given that many white evangelicals tended to be supportive of a social and political status quo that marginalized African Americans, many African American Protestants have generally held differing viewpoints politically than those held by many evangelical Protestants. Thus, for various historical reasons, the ties between black Protestants and evangelical Protestants are not as close as their shared beliefs and values might lead one to expect (Noll 2001, 14).

The second important development was the emergence of Pentecostalism, which originated during the early days of the twentieth century from emphases on Christian "holiness" that had long existed in several Protestant bodies. However, beginning at the turn of the twentieth century, Pentecostalism began to emphasize the experience of "speaking in tongues" as a mark of the Holy Spirit and a sign that the world was entering the latter days just prior to the second coming of Jesus Christ. In the decades that followed, the relationship between Pentecostals and other Christians was frequently turbulent, marked as much by disdain, skepticism, and mistrust as by charity, acceptance, and mutual understanding. Even as late as three decades ago, Pentecostals remained highly marginalized both religiously and socially, well outside the "mainstream" of American life. Nevertheless, in the post–World War II years, Pentecostalism made important inroads within American religious life. Not only did Pentecostal denominations join associations such as the National Association of Evangelicals, but other Spirit-filled movements emerged outside the historic Pentecostal denominations—namely, the charismatic renewal movement within mainline Protestant churches and within the

Roman Catholic churches. Moreover, Pentecostalism's influence has hardly been confined to American society; with its emphasis on the direct work of the Holy Spirit, it has become a major force within Christianity globally in the twentieth century (Noll 2001, 16).

The 1920s to the 1950s

The real disappearance of social involvement among evangelicals can be traced largely to the period between 1900 and 1930. It was the reaction to the social gospel found within the emerging fundamentalist party that signaled the major reversal in evangelical social and political involvement (Marsden 1980, chapter 10). Though the social gospel, at least in its classic formulation by Rauschenbusch, did not specifically state that it was impossible to ascertain the validity of religious beliefs, it did adopt the pragmatist position that it was impossible to determine their validity until the nature of actions that flowed from them could be determined. On the other hand, evangelicals contended that truth could be known directly and that God cared as much about religious beliefs as about human actions—though the two were never seen as totally separate (Marsden 1980, 92). The danger that evangelicals saw in the social gospel was not that it endorsed social concern or social action, but that its particular theological formulation seemingly threatened both the status of biblical revelation and the importance of the gospel message.

Only in the 1920s, then, did American Protestantism truly become polarized.[21] The more conservative theological parties within many of the major denominations sensed that they were on the brink of losing control of their denominational bodies; as a result, they launched a strong attack on modernist forces. It was in these struggles of the 1920s that those in the theological middle were forced to cast their lot with one of the two sides; consequently, Protestantism became, at least for a period of time, divided into two camps—the modernist and fundamentalist camps.

During this period of time, the term "fundamentalism" came to denote a movement of a somewhat diverse group of conservative Christians engaged in an anti-modernist campaign. While roots of the fundamentalist movement existed prior to the controversies of the 1920s (Sandeen 1970), fundamentalism represented "a mosaic of divergent and sometimes contradictory traditions and tendencies" (Marsden 1980, 43) that coalesced in response to the social and political, but primarily religious, conditions evident in the United States in the early part of this century. In essence, this movement constituted a militant, antimodernist faction of evangelicalism opposed to "both modernism in theology and the cultural changes that modernism endorsed" (Marsden 1980, 4).

Fundamentalism constituted a popular movement, but only after World War I did it become a self-conscious and nationally organized movement (Carpenter 1980; Marsden 1980). As a social movement, fundamentalism developed largely at the "grass roots" level among the laity and not in seminaries or other institutions of higher learning, emerging from a network of interpersonal and interinstitutional relationships (Marsden 1980, 61–62).

Because modernists generally explained life and much of religion in terms of natural developments, fundamentalists responded by placing greater emphasis upon the supernatural. Given that modernists stressed the subjective nature of historical truth, fundamentalists responded by stressing the divinely guaranteed verbal inerrancy of scripture and by making adherence to this doctrine a test of denominational purity.

The classical formulation of the inerrancy position was published in 1881 by Hodge and Warfield, two orthodox Calvinists teaching at Princeton Seminary. Basically, the inerrancy position argues that the scriptures are errorless in all their elements and affirmations. This emphasis on the verbal inerrancy of scripture was obviously related to the Protestant principle of *sola Scriptura*, though evangelicals had previously emphasized the infallibility[22] of scripture as the basis for *sola Scriptura*. But, in response to subjectivism and higher criticism in interpretation, the Princeton theologians had moved to a more specific position to defend the truth of scripture—namely, inerrancy. The purpose of scripture, supposedly, was to communicate a "record of truth." And if truth constituted an objective statement of fact (in which the subjective element was almost, if not totally, eliminated), then the inspiration of scripture had to be of such a nature that the Holy Spirit, while not mechanically dictating, inspired the authors to select correct words.

This particular doctrine of biblical inspiration became an identifying characteristic of fundamentalists in their campaign against modernist forces. The denominational struggles of the 1920s centered on the authority of scripture. For fundamentalists, the basic issue was a theological one in that it related to the nature of the inspiration and truth of the Bible. German higher criticism[23] seemed to challenge the inspiration of scripture, and subjectivism seemed to challenge the truth of scripture. But for fundamentalists, truth by its very nature was eternal and objective, and God's truth, as revealed in scripture, was propositional in form and inerrant in detail.[24]

Moreover, in the late 1800s, a new form of premillennialism—dispensational premillennialism—had gained growing acceptance among certain segments of the evangelical community. Dispensational premillennialism both contributed to the emergence of the fundamentalist movement and helped to characterize it (Sandeen 1970; Marsden 1980; Weber 1983). As a system of biblical interpretation, dispensationalism was highly dependent upon the doctrine of biblical inerrancy and required a high degree of literalism in interpretation (Marsden 1980, chapter 6).

According to dispensationalists, Christ's Kingdom will not be realized in this age nor will it be realized through human efforts; rather, such a Kingdom is to be entirely realized in the future, is totally supernatural in origin, and is completely discontinuous with the present age. Within this framework, the present age is the age of the Holy Spirit and the true church is a spiritual, not an institutional, church. This true church is composed of the faithful remnant who are "separate and holy" from the world. And through the lens of the dispensationalist interpretation of scripture, the vast majority of the institutional church would become apostate during the period of the last dispensation.

The viewpoint that the world was growing increasingly, and irreversibly, worse not only marked an important change from the dominant tradition within American evangelicalism, but it also fostered less emphasis on institutional reforms within society. Previously, revivalism had been coupled primarily with postmillennial views because of its emphasis upon being "saved for service." But if the world was a "wrecked vessel," then the saving of individual souls from eternal damnation became the primary, if not sole, end of Christian activity. Thus, a major element in the fundamentalist movement was the subordination of all other concerns to the saving of individual souls through conversion (Marsden 1980, 43).

Earlier, some evangelicals and conservatives had warned that an overemphasis on social concerns would ultimately undermine concern for right beliefs and the salvation of souls. And now advocates of the social gospel not only rejected revivalism as a basis of societal reform but were also inclined to understand that the Kingdom of God could be realized on earth through the progress of civilization. This understanding of how the Kingdom of God was to be realized contrasted sharply with premillennialist dispensationalist expectations, with the result that the difference between the social gospel and the revivalist gospel became increasingly clear and distinct.

In the face of growing differences in religious beliefs, fundamentalists moved to oust modernists from the major denominations, and when their efforts failed, many fundamentalists withdrew and regrouped. The dispensational interpretation of scripture summoned Christians to separate themselves from apostasy wherever it may be found. Moreover, dispensationalism contended that, in this last period of time before the second coming of Jesus Christ, the vast majority of humanity, along with much of the institutional church, would become apostate. For the fundamentalists following their denominational defeats, this expectation had become a reality. Dispensationalism, therefore, summoned Christians to separate themselves by forming fellowships of true believers (the faithful remnant) awaiting the imminent return of Christ, as the world was living through its final days before Christ's return. Thus, whereas American Protestantism was broadly evangelical in nature prior to the 1900s, evangelical Protestants largely disappeared from public view during the next half century—particularly in the aftermath of the Scopes Monkey Trial in 1925 (Ammerman 2009, 55).

This separatist impulse had other ramifications as well. Given that their efforts to reverse the liberal trends within the major denominations had apparently failed, fundamentalists shifted their attention to evangelism and institution building (Carpenter 1984a, 4). Rather than persisting in such denominational struggles, they began to develop their own institutional base from which they could pursue their major goal—namely, the proclamation of the evangelical gospel (Carpenter 1980, 73).

Building upon their sense of identity and Christian devotion, fundamentalists began to create and operate within independent denominations, congregations, and Bible institutes. Likewise, they began to invest themselves in building a myriad of social and religious institutions.[25] As radio became the nation's favorite pastime, fundamentalists established radio broadcasting as a major component of their network of institutions. In fact, while the various programs of the old-line denominations were experiencing difficulties during the 1930s, the fundamentalists' array of Bible schools, summer Bible conferences, religious periodicals, and evangelist and missionary agencies prospered (Carpenter 1980).

Fundamentalism constituted a popular movement, not merely a mentality (Carpenter 1980, 64). It had its own ideology to promote (i.e., inerrancy and dispensationalism), and it had its own program to pursue (i.e., worldwide evangelism) (Carpenter 1980, 74). It was a movement that both spanned denominations and existed outside denominations—particularly when the anti-evolution movement, composed of many people with little or no interest in fundamentalist doctrinal concerns, became linked with the fundamentalist movement (Marsden 1980, chapter 18).

Thus, fundamentalism was far from a defeated party in the denominational struggles of the 1920s. Moving outside the older denominational structures, it created its own institutions, fostered its own leadership, and developed its own particular self-identity, which enabled fundamentalists to distinguish themselves from other religionists. Thus, in a little more than a decade after the denominational battles, fundamentalists had created a base of growing institutions that largely paralleled those of the older denominations (Carpenter 1997).

Yet, in reality, this fundamentalist movement still remained loosely organized. Whatever common spirit may have served to bind fundamentalists together, it assumed few commonly shared institutional manifestations.

Instead, a radical pluralism prevailed. The array of mission boards, religious periodicals, denominations, laymen leagues, radio programs, and Bible institutes created by fundamentalists represented, at best, an amorphous collectivity—a smorgasbord of different organizational endeavors. Power, influence, and authority were radically dispersed.

Consequently, between the mid-1920s and the early 1940s, the character of fundamentalism changed rather dramatically (Marsden 1975). In the early 1920s, fundamentalism had been a movement within the mainstream of American Protestantism seeking to maintain theological "orthodoxy" as they understood it and a movement aspiring to shape American culture as well. By the 1940s, however, the locus and vision of fundamentalists had shifted. Though they still aspired to shape American culture, fundamentalists were now largely located outside the mainstream of American Protestantism. And though the "fundamentals" of the Christian faith were still stressed, fundamentalists now frequently emphasized practice as well as doctrine by using the practice of separation as a "doctrinal" test of Christian fidelity.

Still, fundamentalism was internally conflicted as it struggled with two competing desires: the desire to separate itself from a culture perceived to be apostate and the desire at the same time to save that very same culture for Christ (Carpenter 1984a, 4). Their desire for separation had made fundamentalists insular and defensive. Yet much of the driving force behind the fundamentalist movement was their desire for revival and the preservation of the evangelical foundations of American civilization, but the separatist and dispensationalist impulses found among fundamentalists stood in tension with their desire to save America through revival.

By the early 1940s, fundamentalists had established a variety of institutional structures with a base of popular support, and so the desire to seek once again to win America by revival grew stronger within the movement. It was this desire for revival that led many fundamentalists to seek fellowship and cooperation with those evangelicals who did not share all of their premillennial dispensational beliefs.[26]

Thus, beginning in the early 1940s, a new movement took place within fundamentalism that repudiated both the temperament and the theological and cultural excesses[27] associated with fundamentalism (Quebedeaux 1974, 3, 12; Carpenter 1984a, 1984b). This movement was given formal expression by the creation of the National Association of Evangelicals (NAE). Though the NAE had been formed by "progressive" fundamentalists, this fact did not become clearly evident even to NEA adherents until the break between Billy Graham and separatist fundamentalists in 1957. As a result, the term "evangelical" was increasingly employed in order to differentiate themselves from both separatist fundamentalists and theological liberals.

While the NAE was called together largely by moderate fundamentalists, they sought to be inclusively evangelical. The American evangelical tradition constituted a large and varied mosaic of which fundamentalism represented one segment. And in order to join in common cause with these other evangelicals, fundamentalists who joined the NAE dropped one of their own tests of fellowship—premillennialism (Carpenter 1984b, 267). That these moderate fundamentalists even initiated the call for such an organization points to some significant religious developments that had transpired over the previous decades—including fundamentalism's interdenominational base, its penetration of other theological traditions, and its development of paradenominational institutional foundations (Carpenter 1984b, 259). These changes enabled those forming the NAE to presume national evangelical leadership and provided them with a foundation on which they could attempt to build a broadening coalition.

The 1950s to the Present

Following the Scopes trial, most social commentators assumed that "the era of Protestant hegemony had ended . . . and that cultural authority has definitely passed to science and secular institutions" (Brint and Schroedel 2009, 4). Moreover, there was growing discussion and acceptance within the academic world that the processes of modernization (including those of economic development, increased urbanization, and ever widening levels of education) invariably would lead to increased secularization within society; from this perspective, religion reflected little more than some dying vestige of the past—doomed to decline in importance and perhaps even disappear with the passage of time. And patterns of increased college and university education among the young, movement to the cities and suburbs, and rapid technological developments all suggested that the religious mooring of American society was shifting.[28] And, to the extent that religion did not disappear, its residue supposedly would largely be confined to the subjective realm, becoming little more than a private matter largely devoid of any public consequence.

But even if the secularization thesis did not fully hold true, the theological stance of the evangelicals seemed, to many observers, far too simplistic—if not archaic. To critics, evangelicals all too often presented Christianity as a series of simple answers to complex questions. Nevertheless, already by the early 1960s, there were signs of rapid growth among evangelicals (Fowler 1982, 1), and during the 1960s and 1970s, virtually the only denominations experiencing membership growth were evangelical denominations—with growth rates often exceeding the rate of the nation's population growth (Roof

1982, 168; Hout, Greeley, and Wilde 2001; Chaves 2004, 33). Thus, by the mid-1970s, evangelical Protestantism seemingly enjoyed greater vitality and more resources than at any time since the Second Great Awakening (Sweet 1984b, 32).

During this period between the 1950s and the mid-1970s, one would be hard pressed to overestimate the importance of the role that Billy Graham played within American evangelicalism. In fact, perhaps no other person has had more of an effect on twentieth-century Christianity (Long 2008, xiii). Graham was a public revivalist in the evangelical tradition and the "personal pastor" to many presidents during the latter half of the twentieth century (Gibbs and Duffy 2007). Through his radio programs and televised religious crusades held across numerous American cities (and across the world) during these years, Graham personified American evangelicalism for the American public. His organization was not tied to any particular denomination, but worked instead directly through independent parachurch organizations (Hatch and Hamilton 1995, 400). Though Graham stressed personal conversion, he downplayed doctrinal and denominational differences within American Protestantism as, in conducting his crusades, he worked in cooperation across the full spectrum of Protestant churches. His harshest critics typically were Christian fundamentalists, in that Graham had abandoned fundamentalism's separatist ways (Long 2008, xiii). But his cooperative approach also led "most American fundamentalists out of their sheltered enclaves into broader fields of fellowship and activity" (Hatch and Hamilton 1995, 401).

In so doing, Graham helped to foster "a grass-roots ecumenism" that regarded "denominational divisions as irrelevant rather than pernicious" (Hatch and Hamilton 1995, 401). Thus, whether it was due to the perceived moral decline of American culture or to Graham's fostering of a Christian fellowship that transcended confessional boundaries, distinctions between fundamentalists and neo-evangelicals declined in importance.[29] And, through his ties to presidents and other major political leaders and his public adoption of "cautiously progressive positions on . . . issues like civil rights, poverty, and the nuclear arms race," Graham in many ways made "it easier for evangelicals to return to the public square" (Hatch and Hamilton 1995, 400–401).

Moreover, the vitality that was evident within evangelical Protestant denominations during this period of time contrasted with the apparent languishing, if not decline, of "mainline" Protestant denominations. Theologically, these latter institutions tended to stress nurturing more than conversion (Roof 1982, 173). In addition, mainline churches tended to assume that the processes of change made the "modern mind" unreceptive to traditional religious symbols and doctrines. As a result, many churches "willingly relinquished their creeds, rituals, pieties, and beliefs to accommodate new social attitudes" (Sweet 1984b, 33).[30]

Moreover, mainline Protestant clergy were often at the forefront of countercultural protest and tended to express theological and political views that were far different from most members of their congregations (Hadden 1969; Guth et al. 1997). Even sympathetic critics contended that mainline denominations had become so bureaucratic in nature, so removed from the aspirations and spiritual needs of those in the pews, and so subject to theological faddism that they had become ineffective (Marty 1982, 159; Coleman 1980, 36–37). Thus, a crisis of identity and authority was seemingly evident within the mainline denominations (Coleman 1980, 36–39; Roof 1982, 172–74; Sweet 1984b), while, at the same time, evangelicalism's sense of identity and trust in biblical authority seemingly provided the bases for its ascendency.

Still, the cultural upheavals during the 1960s and 1970s left many evangelical Protestants feeling besieged. Both American society and the American political system appeared to be losing their moral bearings. The sexual revolution of the 1960s, along with the feminist and gay rights movements growing out of the decade, challenged basic cultural understandings among evangelicals (Brint and Schroedel 2009, 4). And the 1963 decision of the Supreme Court that reciting prayers in public schools was unconstitutional, along with its decision in 1973 to legalize abortion, only further contributed to an understanding that American society and public life was losing its moral bearings.

These various cultural changes, along with a number of court decisions and disappointments related to the Carter administration, led to the formation of a number of Christian Right organizations in the late 1970s and early 1980s that sought to mobilize conservative Protestants more broadly. These organizations focused on issues that appealed to many evangelicals, and their efforts helped to create both a public identity for evangelicals and a political narrative that served to foster political action among them. As with other movements tied to identity politics, these Christian Right organizations "emphasized the valuable qualities and central importance of a group unfairly marginalized by the dominant powers in society" (Brint and Schroedel 2009, 5), and their leaders promoted a narrative outlining what was wrong with American culture and what evangelicals could, and must, do about it (Ammerman 2009, 61).

Moreover, because the cultural isolation of the evangelical community had begun to erode following World War II, evangelicals linked to the Christian Right were able to increase their political clout by "finding common cause (politically) with other conservative religionists whose theologies might have kept earlier generations apart" (Ammerman 2009, 59). A variety of factors contributed to the diminishing of this cultural separateness, including, but not limited to, the sense of national unity and purpose related to the country's engagement in World War II, the growing levels of education and increased geographical mobility among evangelicals, the diffusion of national televised programming, and the celebration of the nation's heritage during the American bicentennial.

Following World War II, many long-standing religious antagonisms also began to diminish and change. In particular, the old discord evident between Protestants and Catholics diminished significantly.[31] In the wake of the secularizing and cultural changes occurring within the country, many Americans across different faith traditions found common cause in a variety of political endeavors—whether working together to resist the advancement of abortion rights, to protect the traditional family, to combat a perceived decline in public morality, or to resist efforts to restrict religion's presence in the public square. The various changes that had occurred within and outside evangelical Protestantism following World War II enabled evangelical Protestants to forge political alliances with Roman Catholics, Mormons, orthodox Jews, and others in ways that would not have been possible only a half century earlier.

Still, despite these changes taking place within American religious life, evangelical Protestantism had, in some ways, remained much the same over this period of time. As did evangelicals in the past, evangelical Protestants typically continued to insist that conversion was the first step in the Christian life (Coleman 1980, 73). For evangelicals, sin is seen to be rooted in human nature. However, though sin may be rooted in our human condition, salvation is possible by responding to God's offer through Christ—in other words, by making a "decision for Christ" (Fowler 1982, 2)—because the "essence of evangelical commitment to Christ" is that such a decision be "undertaken voluntarily, consciously, and responsibly by the individual for himself or herself" (Howe 2007, 128). Evangelical Protestants in the latter half of the twentieth century continued to emphasize, as their predecessors did, the personal nature of sin and the individual need for salvation.

This individualistic emphasis within evangelicalism continues to have important ramifications related to the structural nature of evangelical Protestantism. Whatever constitutes the nature of the common spirit that serves to bind evangelicals together, it has never assumed, and continues not to assume, any unified institutional arrangements (Hatch 1984b, 76). A radical pluralism exists within evangelicalism; organizational structures remain largely fragmented, with power and influence within evangelicalism being highly dispersed. This radical pluralism can be largely attributed to evangelicalism's "democratic structure." By emphasizing personal experience, evangelicalism tends to diminish the significance of the sacraments, the authority of the church's hierarchical structures, and the significance of doctrinal complexities (Ahlstrom 1975, 270). Similarly, it has fostered personal interpretations of scripture, personal followings of different evangelical leaders, and personal financial support of different evangelical institutions.[32]

During the latter half of the twentieth century, evangelical Protestants persisted in their affirmation of the truth and authority of the scriptures. Evangelicals continued to hold that God not only revealed Himself directly through the divine event in Jesus Christ but also directly though His divine word—the Holy Scriptures. Although the biblical authors wrote and spoke in different styles and from particular historical perspectives, their message is seen as divine and not human. Thus, for contemporary evangelicals, the scriptures do not represent a word about God but constitute the word of God.

Yet, while the Bible is accepted as the basis of religious authority among evangelicals, views related to the nature of that authority may vary somewhat among them. Many evangelicals continue to insist upon the doctrine of biblical inerrancy, while others favor a position of infallibility (Smidt 1989). But regardless of which position is adopted, all contemporary evangelicals continue to "hold firmly to traditional supernaturalist understandings of the Bible message" (Marsden 1984, xi). Thus, any differences in positions among evangelicals concerning the specific nature of biblical authority take place within a context in which such evangelicals acknowledge the authority of the Bible and endeavor to live and worship by its commands (Fowler 1982, 3).

Despite these commonalities and continuities, contemporary evangelicalism exhibits a considerable amount of diversity (Sweet 1984a, 84; Smith 2000, 13–15). Certainly, evangelical Protestantism has always exhibited a substantial level of diversity in that it has encompassed historic "peace church" denominations, which emphasize passive resistance, as well as denominations that embrace standards for discerning "just war" circumstances. It has encompassed Pentecostal congregations and denominations that emphasize the continuity of the apostolic church with the contemporary church in terms of the gifts and manifestations of the Holy Spirit as well as more fundamentalist congregations and denominations that mark the present dispensation of God's grace as markedly different from that present in the apostolic church. Thus, though they generally share a commitment to the authority of the Bible, the need for personal salvation, and sharing the Good News related to Jesus Christ, there has always been considerable theological diversity within the ranks of evangelicals.

Nevertheless, the diversity within American evangelicalism has become even more obvious over the past several decades (Noll 2001, 222). The growth of the charismatic movement and its presence within evangelical denominations along with the decline of denominational loyalties and the growth of nondenominational congregations have contributed to even greater diversity within evangelical Protestantism. The unifying presence of Billy Graham is no longer as strong as it once was. His influence has largely diminished now that, with advancing age, he is no longer active in evangelism, and new leaders and new concerns have emerged. All of this has helped to create "a more pluralistic evangelicalism than has ever existed in American history" (Noll 2001, 222).

Other changes have occurred as well. Some of these changes may be "understood collectively as a shift away from the theological toward the relational" (Hatch and Hamilton 1995, 402). In part, this may be a consequence of broader cultural changes in which image is replacing text as the major means of communication—a change that serves to undermine the "historic Protestant reliance on the written word" (Noll 2001, 24). Thus, whereas fifty years ago evangelicals centered on the propositional truths of scripture, today they are increasingly focused on the experience linked with worship—whether it is liturgical or charismatic in nature (Hatch and Hamilton 1995, 402).

Overall, therefore, evangelicals occupied a different place in American culture and society at the close of the century than they did at mid-century (Ammerman 2009, 60). They had clearly become more visible, regardless of whether or not their numbers had grown proportionately to the size of the American population. No longer did national journalists ponder, as was evident when Jimmy Carter ran for the presidency in 1976, what being "born again" signified religiously. Certainly, the influx of evangelicals into American electoral politics in the latter quarter of the century brought considerable visibility as well as political significance to their ranks, though their "wedding of religious piety and social activism" was in clear continuity with earlier, and most, periods of American history (Ammerman 2009, 54). And rather than removing themselves from public life and settling within their faith communities, evangelicals had entered the halls of power and were found among the elites of American society (Lindsay 2007).

Conclusion

Contemporary evangelical Protestantism is based upon a fairly continuous and unified tradition within American Protestantism. While evangelicalism has undergone considerable change over the past several centuries, contemporary evangelicalism continues to represent a particular form of Protestantism and a general form of Christianity. Thus, the evangelical tradition has been shaped by a variety of religious movements and forces with differing religious emphases (e.g., Puritanism, pietism, revivalism, fundamentalism), but at its core evangelical Protestantism is distinguished by the general tendency of its members to affirm that personal salvation is obtained through Jesus Christ, to call individuals to conversion by turning from their old selves to being "a new creature in Christ," and to hold the Bible to be the final authority concerning all matters of faith and practice. Beyond these particular characteristics, evangelical Protestantism remains highly diverse, and within its parameters a variety of more specific religious beliefs and themes are expressed.

To view evangelicalism as having a historical tradition suggests that evangelicalism should not be viewed so much as a categorical group designating a number of individuals meeting certain stipulated, and rather arbitrary, criteria (e.g., "born-again" Christians or "conservative Protestants"); rather, it may be better viewed as a social group manifesting an organic character bound together by social ties and organizational alliances. Evangelicals draw upon a certain common heritage, and they exhibit certain common tendencies. Evangelicalism may be composed of many separate and strikingly diverse pieces, but it nevertheless displays an overall pattern, maintains an identity, and looks back to its origins with a large measure of sympathy and respect (Ahlstrom 1975; Marsden 1984).

If one's perspective is limited to the past fifty years, evangelicalism appears to be a relatively new religious movement that emerged out of fundamentalism several decades ago and whose roots can be traced to a highly distinct religious subculture outside the mainstream of American religious life. However, if viewed from a perspective that covers the past several centuries, contemporary evangelicalism can be seen as embodying a deeply rooted religious tradition, and historically speaking, as standing within the mainstream of American religious life. Contemporary evangelicalism can be viewed, therefore, as being deeply rooted in American life. The continuing hallmark of American Protestantism has been the emphasis upon direct experience rather than religious knowledge (Albanese 1981, 109). To treat contemporary evangelicals, therefore, as merely a by-product of a particular stage of cultural evolution or of certain social-psychological forces is to fail to take evangelicalism seriously as constituting an authentic religious tradition (Stackhouse 1982, 52). And since evangelicalism has been very influential in shaping the general ethos of American culture, failure to grasp its inner content and general contours is likely to produce little more than a marginal understanding of contemporary evangelical involvement in public life.

The evangelical tradition within American religious life provides two different visions upon which contemporary evangelicals can draw. Both visions stress (1) that spiritual change is first necessary to alter the human condition in any fundamental manner, and (2) that social and political change, without spiritual change, only provides small bandages for gaping wounds. One vision is associated with fundamentalism and leads away from social and political involvement, despairing of any significant social and political improvement. From this perspective, we are living in the last age, the millennium will only begin after Christ's return, the forces of darkness will continue to grow stronger until Christ's return, and the focus of Christian activity should be limited to the saving of individual souls from eternal damnation.

However, there is an older, and deeper, vision from which today's evangelicals may draw. This is the custodial tradition in which religion serves to sustain a democratic republic and holds that public officials have a "custodial responsibility for the spiritual as well as the physical well-being" of members of the body politic (Wacker 1984, 22). For many Americans, including evangelicals, this tradition draws upon the idea of a covenanted nation that places importance upon America being a "city on a hill" and national obedience to God's laws, not only as private individuals, but also in matters of public policy. According to this older tradition, moral issues are exceedingly practical issues, as moral virtue underpins civic virtue, and republics depend on moral self-restraint in order to thrive.[33] As a result, the success or failure of the nation is seen to be directly related to the preservation of its moral heritage. It is not too surprising, therefore, that a significant portion of evangelicals could remain relatively apolitical under conditions of religious pluralism as long as a basic moral consensus prevailed. But, with the perceived breakdown of traditional morality, many evangelicals became politically active in an effort to save the nation from what they believed was certain destruction if the American people persisted in breaking their covenantal obligation.

Finally, the relative vitality of evangelicalism within American culture may well spring from values that are mutually shared across the two related, but different, spheres of life. In fact, some analysts contend that "evangelical religion and American politics are so interconnected that the threads of causation are all but impossible to follow" (Balmer 1999, 59). Evangelicals have both shaped and been shaped by the style and content of public discourse, and evangelicals have both determined and reflected cultural trends in American life (Balmer 1999, 60).

Other analysts, however, have gone so far as to contend that evangelicalism and the unfolding of modernity exist in a symbiotic relationship with each other, as evangelicalism constitutes "the characteristic Protestant . . . way of relating to modernity" (Marty 1981, 9). Certainly, evangelicalism in America emphasizes the individual and a personal faith, is relatively experiential in its orientation and style of worship, is highly pragmatic (e.g., in terms of its emphasis on audience size, its use of technology), focuses its attention more on common people than the elites of society, and is very "free market" oriented in terms of "religious competition." And these characteristics of American evangelicalism are also reflected in basic prevailing American values, as American culture tends to emphasize individualism over community, experience over reflection, pragmatism over ideology,[34] and free market over state-controlled economies. Since American politics has always "been as much about moral convictions and a sense of (national) destiny" as it has been about matters of economic policy, the debate over "which moral convictions and sense of destiny will guide the nation" is likely to be one that will "remain at the heart of American politics." As a result, evangelicals will likely remain as discussion partners in that public debate (Ammerman 2009, 66).

2

Seek and You Shall Find?
The Bases of Analyzing Evangelicals Today

THOUGH EVANGELICALS HAVE LONG BEEN present within American society, it is only within the last several decades that any effort has been made to identify evangelical Christians in national surveys. Subsequently, scholars have produced a wealth of studies related to evangelical Christians based on survey research, though these studies have analyzed American evangelicals "using different measures of belief, behavior, and belonging, [sometimes] even within the same report" (Hackett and Lindsay 2008, 499). Thus, despite the fact that there has been considerable journalistic and scholarly discussion of the role of evangelicals in American public life, just who are to be included within the ranks of evangelicals and what serves as the basis for their inclusion are far from being clear; the label remains somewhat of a contested term.

This chapter examines the analytical issues related to the study of evangelicals today. It raises a number of points related to the conceptualization of just who should, and should not, be classified as evangelicals, and it analyzes various measurement approaches to do so. The chapter also identifies the major sources of data employed in this study, as one survey alone is not likely to ask all the kinds of questions our current study seeks to address; different surveys are needed to be employed to address more fully the questions raised. Hence, this chapter also seeks to ascertain whether, given the measurement strategy adopted, the various surveys employed necessarily capture relatively identical "evangelical respondents." It does so by examining whether the evangelical respondents found in each survey exhibit relatively identical social characteristics, religious beliefs, and religious practices across the surveys employed.

Who Are Evangelicals?

Just who should be labeled as an evangelical today? What serves as the basis of unity for those gathered together under that label? And what is the nature of the grouping of individuals included under that label—does it constitute simply a categorical group of individuals brought together in the mind of the analyst, or does it represent a social group of some type in which members exhibit certain patterns of social interaction? While these questions are relatively simple to raise, the answers are far more difficult to discern—and are largely dependent upon one's starting assumptions related to the defining nature of religion and what particular facets of religion are most likely to shape human behavior outside the religious context. Let us examine briefly the various issues related to conceptualization of evangelicals and the different analytical approaches that might be adopted to identify evangelical Christians, before settling on the particular approach that will be utilized for the remainder of this study.

Issues Related to Conceptualization

Three distinct, yet interrelated, issues confront the analyst when seeking to define just who should be classified as evangelicals. The first issue relates to whether religion generally (and evangelicals more specifically in the context of this book) constitutes primarily a cognitive or a social phenomenon. On the one hand, beliefs are central to any understanding of religion. As Stark and Glock (1968, 16) put it, "theology, or religious belief, is at the heart of the faith," as religion embodies the "fundamental beliefs, ideas, ethical codes, and symbols associated with a religious tradition, including what others call a theology or belief system" (Wald and Calhoun-Brown 2007, 26). Yet, while religious beliefs are central to all religious faiths, just how important are such beliefs to understanding human behavior outside the religious context? Some would argue that religious beliefs have important social consequences in that "people act politically, economically, and socially in keeping with their ultimate beliefs" (Swierenga 1990, 154). Yet not all who hold the same religious beliefs necessarily behave in the same fashion. Such differences in behavior among those holding the same beliefs may be explained, in part, by the fact that not all who embrace such beliefs do so with the same level of intensity. And, according to theories of cognitive consistency, those for whom religious beliefs are highly salient should feel greater pressure to bring their behavior into congruence with their religious convictions than those for whom such beliefs are less salient (Hoge and de Zulueta 1985). Thus, within this cognitive framework of analysis, beliefs are viewed to be the critical link between religion and behavior, with their effects being understood to be rather "immediate" and direct, the product of internal cognitive processing (Wald and Smidt 1993, 32).

On the other hand, religion is frequently viewed as a social phenomenon. From this perspective, religion is expressed through affiliation with a local church, a specific denomination, or even a religious tradition. Thus, one's social behavior may be less a function of specific religious beliefs than the result of particular patterns of social interaction and memberships in distinctive social networks. For example, as we shall see later, many black Protestants may hold a substantial number of identical religious beliefs to those of white evangelical Protestants, yet they do not necessarily share similar political attitudes or vote in the same way.

As a member of a social group, individuals tend to share certain common experiences that derive from their group affiliations and, by means of their differing patterns of association and interaction, members of different religious groups may receive disparate kinds of information, experience different levels of social acceptance, and be exposed to varying interpretations of social and political events—thereby acquiring divergent social and political attitudes and behavior (even while holding identical religious beliefs). However, these experiences and interactions are not necessarily uniform across all members of a social group, and consequently the particular attitudes and behavior linked to group membership are not uniformly acquired or expressed. Thus, it is not the uniformity of holding certain beliefs or exhibiting certain actions that define a social group, but rather their *greater tendency* to think or act in particular ways.

So the first issue relates to whether one posits religious beliefs and cognitive processing to be the primary shaper of human behavior or whether one views patterns of social interaction and communication, friendship networks, and social constraints as the more important means by which human behavior is governed. Do patterns of religious beliefs shape patterns of affiliation, or do patterns of affiliation shape patterns of religious beliefs? Actually, both are likely to occur, as there is much reciprocal causation within social life. But in defining religious groupings, the analyst is forced to choose between one or the other as the primary causal process. For example, when one is determining which individuals are to be classified as Catholics (or evangelicals, or any other religious grouping), should one consider as Catholics only those who subscribe fully to certain specified church doctrines, or should one also consider as Catholics those who attend Mass with some regularity even if they do not necessarily subscribe to all church doctrines?

The second issue, somewhat intertwined with the first, relates to whether evangelicals constitute simply some categorical designation of individuals whose "unity" as a collectivity is strictly the function of some stipulated criteria employed by the analyst—or whether evangelicals should be viewed instead as a social group that exhibits a certain level of social cohesion. For example, people with brown eyes represent a categorical group; their unity as a group reflects nothing more than the analyst's decision to differentiate them from people with eyes of other colors. People with brown eyes do not generally choose to interact with each other in some systematic, or regularly scheduled, fashion; nor would we anticipate that people with brown eyes necessarily share particular social or political attitudes that markedly differentiate them from others whose eyes are some other color. Rather, whatever unity is possessed by people with brown eyes is a function of the categorization process of the analyst who brings them together as "members" of the same group. In a similar fashion, some have defined evangelicals as constituting born-again Protestants. In doing so, the analyst implicitly suggests that evangelicals exhibit, as a constructed category of specified individuals, no social unity—as the basis for the unity of the category is simply the analyst's arbitrary decision that all sharing the designation of evangelicals must report a particular kind of religious experience to be included under the label.

Social groups are different from categorical groups in that social groups are linked together in a web-like fashion by interconnecting patterns of social interaction resulting in the exhibition of a certain level of social cohesion.[1] The point here is simply that categorical and social groups are different in nature—with the former exhibiting a certain level of unity based on the criteria prescribed by some analyst, while the other exhibits a certain level of social cohesion based, in part, on social relationships among members of the group. So, are evangelicals little more than some categorical group who share in certain common religious characteristics stipulated by the analyst, or are they a social group who exhibit certain patterns of social interaction and display certain commonalities in their social and/or political beliefs and behavior? Again, the analyst must decide the nature of the unity that defines those who fall within the umbrella of the label "evangelical."

Let's assume for the time being that evangelicals comprise something more than a categorical group and represent a social group of some type. Of course, holding that evangelicals constitute a social group does not specify the particular kind of social group it comprises. Thus, the third issue relates to whether evangelicals are better conceptualized to be individuals tied to a particular religious movement or individuals affiliated with a particular religious tradition.

Should evangelicals be viewed basically as "members" of a particular religious movement? Social movements seek change, and religious movements seek change within religious life and institutions. Some religious movements operate within a particular religious tradition (e.g., the movement to return to the Latin Mass within the Catholic Church), while other movements often cross denominational boundaries and occasionally even transcend religious traditions (e.g., the charismatic movement is found within both Protestantism and Catholicism). In seeking religious change, organizations may be created within the movement to accomplish certain ends, and over time, facets of the religious movement and its associated organizations may become institutionalized and perhaps even transformed into a religious tradition itself. After all, Protestantism today may be considered a religious tradition, though initially it represented simply an effort by various reformers who sought religious change within the Catholic Church.

Some analysts view evangelicalism as a religious movement that transcends most, if not all, Protestant denominations and that possesses certain tendencies that may even find expression within the Catholic Church as well.[2] It is fairly commonplace to see evangelicals as being defined in terms of a religious movement—this is particularly true among religious historians and theologians. Many different references could be marshaled to substantiate this claim, but, for present purposes, perhaps the following two citations may suffice: (1) evangelicalism is "a movement of spiritual renewal which is grounded in certain theological convictions" (Weber 1991, 14); (2) evangelicalism is "a broad and identifiable movement stretching back to at least the revivals of the eighteenth century" (Kyle 2006, 11).

On the other hand, many social scientists treat evangelical Protestants as a religious tradition by virtue of being affiliated with a distinct set of religious denominations and congregations that are interrelated in some historical and organizational fashion and whose "members" exhibit relatively similar beliefs and behaviors (Kellstedt and Green 1993; Kellstedt et al. 1996; Steensland et al. 2000). Religious traditions have somewhat different tendencies than religious movements: movements seek change, while traditions try to protect and retain the established core principles and values that are historically part of the tradition. Typically, those who adopt the religious tradition approach view evangelical Protestantism as one of the major religious traditions present within American religious life today.[3]

In the end, however, evangelicalism can be viewed as either a religious movement or a religious tradition, and evangelicals can therefore be treated, on the one hand, as those who are linked to a particular religious movement or, on the other hand, as those who are affiliated with a particular religious tradition. However, while these two approaches are intertwined, each conceptualization emphasizes different tendencies and captures different segments of American society. If viewed in terms of those associated with a religious tradition, then evangelicals are found in certain denominations but not in others, whereas if viewed as those associated with a religious movement, then evangel-icals are present within most, if not all, Protestant denominations and perhaps even within the Catholic Church itself. While either analytical approach may be adopted, the analyst who seeks to be consistent in his or her analysis and discussion is forced to adopt one approach as opposed to the other.

Measurement Approaches

One's choice with regard to these starting assumptions about evangelicals is inherent to the various measurement approaches used in survey research to identify such respondents, even though they are rarely discussed by analysts.[4] Little attention is typically given to the particular implications of employing one, as opposed to some other, set of questions used to classify evangelicals. Consequently, the starting point of much of the confusion about the nature of evangelicals, their distinctive characteristics, and their relative size within American society is linked to the choice about whether identifying evangeli-cals through survey research should be based on (1) adherence to distinctive religious beliefs, (2) claims of a particular religious experience, (3) affiliation with specific denominations and congregations, or (4) self-identification in terms of association with a particular religious movement. Each approach captures somewhat overlapping, but nevertheless relatively different, seg-ments of American society.

Defining Evangelicals by Religious Beliefs

Not surprisingly, some scholars have focused their emphasis on identify-ing evangelicals in terms of the expression of distinctive religious doctrines or beliefs. For example, the historian David Bebbington (1989, 2–17) is frequently cited for his definition of evangelicals in which he stipulates four major qualities that define evangelicals: biblicism, a high view of the authority of the Bible; cruicentrism, a focus on the atoning work of Christ on the cross; conversionism, the belief that human beings need to be converted; and activ-ism, the belief that the gospel needs to be expressed in effort. However, while helpful in specifying certain distinctive emphases of evangelical religious perspectives, such a listing (1) suggests that all evangelicals hold identical core religious beliefs, (2) leaves unanswered whether those who may subscribe to most, but not all, of the four specified beliefs are nevertheless to be considered evangelicals, and (3) implies that evangelicals represent little more than a cat-egorical group unified simply by the stipulated criteria employed.

Let us consider these issues in relationship to the approach that the Barna Research Group uses to denote which respondents in their surveys are to be included as "evangelicals," as Barna basically follows the logic of Bebbington's approach. For respondents to be classified as an evangelical, Barna requires that they first indicate that they have made some type of personal commitment to Jesus Christ that is still important in their life today and then, secondly, that they believe that they will go to heaven when they die because they have confessed their sins and have accepted Jesus Christ as their personal Savior. Then, after meeting this two-fold requirement, respondents must still indicate agreement with seven other criteria in order to be labeled an "evangelical": (1) saying their faith is very important in their life today; (2) believing they have a personal responsibility to share their religious beliefs about Christ with non-Christians; (3) believing that Satan exists; (4) believing that eternal salvation is possible only through grace, not works; (5) believing that Jesus Christ lived a sinless life on earth; (6) asserting that the Bible is accurate in all that it teaches; and (7) describing God as the all-knowing, all-powerful, perfect deity who created the universe and still rules it today (Hackett and Lindsay 2008, 503–4). Only those who meet these specified criteria are then classified as evangelicals.

While this approach creates a grouping of respondents who share these particular, identical religious beliefs, the resultant grouping of respondents reflects basically a categorical, rather than a social, group. Such so-called evangelicals do not necessarily share any historic commonality or social unity. Anyone who meets these criteria is placed in an "evangelical" category (including those who are Roman Catholics, Eastern Orthodox, or Latter-day Saints by religious affiliation). But social groups (whether they are religious or not in nature) are *not* defined by all members holding the same beliefs; rather, in everyday practice, social (including religious) groups are defined mostly by affiliation, *not* by uniformity of belief. Not all Democrats or Republicans hold identical political beliefs; nor do all Catholics or Mormons hold identical religious beliefs. As a result, many of Barna's "evangelicals" are unlikely to recognize each other as fellow members of the same religious group. Nor is the resultant group likely to exhibit much social and political cohesion— given that many African Americans are likely to meet these stipulated criteria. Consequently, by this definitional approach, evangelicals would appear to be rather divided politically, as there is likely to be little similarity in the political attitudes and behavior between white and black evangelicals so defined.

Defining Evangelicals as "Born-Again" Christians

At times, evangelicals have been referred to as "born-again" Christians. Certainly, as noted in Bebbington's definitional criteria, evangelicals (tend to) believe in conversionism—namely, that human beings need to be converted.

Yet, in terms of survey research, the question used to measure this character-istic frequently asks whether the respondent has had some kind of relatively intense conversion experience that marks a spiritual turning point in one's life—rather than whether the respondent actually holds a belief that human beings need to be converted. This shift from belief to experience most likely can be attributed to the fact that Gallup (1979), in his initial national survey of evangelical Christians, used an affirmative response to such a question as one of his defining requirements in order to be classified as an evangelical.[5] Subse-quently, the born-again question has become one of the most commonly used measures in survey research for identifying evangelicals.

However, while evangelicals may claim that one must be "born again" in order to be saved, many evangelicals do not claim that they have had any type of a sudden Saul/Paul conversion experience, as, in its broadest sense, to be "born again" is simply to confess and to repent from one's sinful nature and to accept Jesus Christ as one's personal Savior (Poloma 1982, 243).[6] This ac-ceptance of Christ as one's personal Savior and Lord need not occur through some instantaneous conversion experience; it can also occur so gradually that one is unable to pinpoint any specific time in which one made such an acceptance of Jesus Christ as one's personal Savior. As a result, both specific and gradual born-again experiences can signify an important transformation in the life of the individual.[7]

Still, the use of "born-again" questions is an inadequate measure for identi-fying evangelicals. First, the measure is too narrow for capturing evangelicals. Given the widespread association of born-again language with the notion of having experienced some particular spiritual turning point in one's life, born-again terminology tends to be used largely in some, but not other, segments of evangelical Protestantism, as evangelicals from more confessional tradi-tions are less likely than those from more pietistic traditions to understand the conversion experience in terms of a specific identifiable point in one's life (Smidt and Kellstedt 1987). Confessional evangelicals claim they have made a personal commitment to Jesus Christ—even though they may not have had a specific born-again experience. Hence, having an instantaneous born-again conversion experience is a rather narrow defining criterion for being an evangelical. Moreover, such born-again measures capture too wide a swath of religionists to be properly labeled as evangelicals, as even some people of non-Christian faiths claim to be born again by having had some relatively in-tense religious experience that marked a spiritual turning point in their lives.

Finally, in an effort to identify evangelical respondents, the question is sometimes posed as "Do you consider yourself to be a born again or evangeli-cal Christian?" Though the question seemingly poses being "born again" and being an "evangelical" as synonymous in nature, two distinct phenomena are actually being assessed in one question. For example, the Exploring Religious America Survey[8] asked Christians in two separate questions: (1) whether they would describe themselves as evangelicals, and (2) whether they would describe themselves as born again. Among those who labeled themselves born again, less than half (38 percent) also described themselves as "evangelical Christians," and among those who willingly described themselves as evangelical Christians more than one in four (27 percent) did not describe themselves as born again. Thus, neither claiming a born-again experience nor identifying as being "born again" captures the evangelical segment of the American population with any sufficient degree of accuracy.

Defining Evangelicals by Religious Affiliation

When linking religion to public life, journalists and social scientists have frequently treated religion primarily as a social, rather than a cognitive or experiential phenomenon. As a social phenomenon, religion is frequently expressed through affiliation with a local church, a specific denomination, or a religious tradition. Thus, Catholics are defined by their affiliation with the Roman Catholic Church—not whether they stand in conformity to the distinctive theological teaching of the church or whether they have had certain religious experiences.

But given the multiplicity of congregations and denominations in the United States, survey researchers must sift through the scores, if not hundreds, of specific denominational affiliations reported and classify them into a manageable number of categories. Obviously, researchers can use different schema to classify these highly varied responses,[9] and the choices they make will affect the results. The key question for analysts, then, is this: "What is the most useful classificatory scheme for these reported denominational affiliations?"[10]

Over the past several decades, scholars have increasingly used the concept of religious tradition to classify adherents based on their denominational affiliations, as religious traditions constitute "a useful and increasingly popular conceptualization of religious belonging" (Layman 2001, 60). Accordingly, respondents are classified as evangelicals based on their affiliation with particular denominations and nondenominational congregations.[11] Given the hundreds of different denominations found in the United States, the use of a much smaller range of religious traditions categories is employed to organize the vast array of reported denominational affiliations, with respondents typically placed within one of the following categories: evangelical Protestants, mainline Protestants, Black Protestants, Roman Catholics, Jews, and the religiously unaffiliated.[12] However, this concept of religious tradition has not only been used because of the parsimony of its categories, but it has been increasingly employed because it has proven to be a relatively powerful predictor of a variety of social and political attitudes and behavior (Kellstedt et al. 1996; Kohut et al. 2000; Layman and Green, 2005; Guth et al. 2006; Green 2007; Green et al. 2007).

Defining Evangelicals by Religious Self-Identification

Rather than asking respondents for their denominational affiliation and then classifying those respondents affiliated with particular denominations as being part of the evangelical Protestant tradition, some researchers have simply asked respondents a series of self-classification or self-identification questions to ascertain whether the respondent willingly defines himself or herself as an "evangelical Christian"[13] (with other options typically being a fundamentalist Christian, a Pentecostal or charismatic Christian, a progressive Christian, and so forth). Sociologist Christian Smith (1998) used identification with religious movements as the conceptual and measurement centerpiece for his work on contemporary evangelicalism.

This self-identification approach is probably best viewed as capturing those respondents who see themselves as part of a particular religious movement (in this case the evangelical movement) rather than as being affiliated with a broader religious tradition, as movements do not have formal memberships per se. Movements are made up of many different organizations, and no single organization can encapsulate a movement. Moreover, many who see themselves as part of a movement are not formal members of any particular movement organization that serves to comprise that larger movement (e.g., many may self-identify as environmentalists even though they are not a member of any specific organization seeking to address environmental concerns). Consequently, when analysts study "movement membership," they frequently do so in terms of identification with that movement (a psychological phenomenon).[14]

However, the use of such religious movement labels within survey research has been somewhat problematic. First, most options provided survey respondents tend to be associated with movements on the more conservative, rather than liberal, end of the theological spectrum. More theologically liberal movements are harder to specify, though labels such as liberal-progressive, "neoorthodox," ecumenical, and even "mainline" have been used. Precise identification with liberal theological movements at the mass level is difficult, in part, because such movements often originated in seminaries and have been the province of elites. Moreover, while some Protestant movement terms may apply to Catholics (Welch and Leege 1991), other language may be better suited to capture the ebb and flow of movements within the Catholic Church.

Moreover, the referents of movement labels are much more amorphous than some denominational label ("charismatic," for example, is less concrete than "Southern Baptist" or "Bethel United Methodist Church"). As a result, when respondents are presented with labels related to various religious movements (e.g., fundamentalist, evangelical, charismatic) and then are asked whether they consider themselves to be a member of such a movement, respondents can assign whatever meaning he/she desires to the particular label advanced (since what embodies the charismatic movement is less evident than what constitutes either a specific congregation or a specific denomination).[15]

When evangelicals are defined in relationship to a movement (and not in relationship to affiliation with specific denominations), it is likely that self-identified evangelicals will be found across many religious traditions. Accordingly, some members of mainline Protestant denominations as well as some members of Roman Catholic parishes will self-identify as evangelicals. Conversely, many who are members of what might be labeled evangelical denominations will not personally claim the label to describe themselves religiously.

Implications

It is widely recognized, though all too easily forgotten, that the choice of one's analytical and measurement approach can significantly affect one's findings. For example, the estimated proportion of evangelical Protestants within American society varies considerably by the approach adopted. Given these different definitional approaches, estimates of the size of the adult evangelical population within American society have ranged from less than 10 percent to well over 40 percent (Hackett and Lindsay 2008, 499). Roughly speaking, evangelical Protestants constitute almost half of the population when measured in terms of claims to be "born again," about a quarter of the population when measured in terms of denominational affiliation, about one-seventh when defined in terms of religious self-identification, and less than one-tenth of the population when specified in terms of Barna's list of beliefs. Similarly, the political characteristics of those falling within the evangelical Protestant category will vary greatly by the approach adopted. Because many more African Americans fall into Barna's evangelical category than when using other ways of classifying evangelicals,[16] his reported proportion of evangelicals voting Democratic in an election is far higher than when evangelicals are defined in terms of self-identification or religious affiliation.

Evangelical Protestantism as a Religious Tradition

For the purposes of this book, evangelicals will be understood as "members" of a particular religious tradition—namely, evangelical Protestantism.[17] Those who are part of a particular religious tradition exhibit a *characteristic* way of interpreting and responding to the world that is evident *among people who are affiliated with a set of religious bodies* that are interrelated in some historical and organizational fashion. Religious traditions "place limits on what any given individual or groups of individuals can do within the tradition and still remain within it"; as a result, religious traditions "shape and construct individuals and cultures" and "are not merely constructed by them" (Queen 2002, 91).

Several implications are embedded in such a definition.[18] First, given that a religious tradition denotes some characteristic, but not uniform, way of interpreting and responding, not everyone within a religious tradition necessarily thinks alike. Nevertheless, as a whole, members of a particular religious tradition tend to exhibit certain characteristics that differentiate them from those associated with other religious traditions.

Second, such characteristic patterns are viewed as being linked to people who *are affiliated* with particular religious bodies that exhibit some historical and organizational linkages. In other words, the concept of religious tradition, as defined here, is understood to be both a religious and a sociological category. Members of a religious tradition are linked together socially, whether through patterns of social interaction, networks of social memberships, weak forms of social ties, or the institutions of which the members may be a part. At the core, members are tied together through relatively regular patterns of social interaction. At the outer limits, members of a religious tradition are linked only weakly through relatively infrequent patterns of social interaction, where characteristic ways of interpreting and responding to the world reflect more cultural residues of earlier periods in which greater integration was evident.

Third, membership within a religious tradition is distinct from being some religious traditionalist within that tradition. Each religious tradition has its traditionalists, but not all within a religious tradition are traditionalists. For example, among Roman Catholics, there are traditionalists who subscribe to papal infallibility, to the restoration of the Latin Mass, and/or to the maintenance of restricting the priesthood to celibate male clergy; on the other hand, there are Catholics who do not subscribe to papal infallibility, who embrace the liturgical changes rooted in Vatican II, who favor permitting priests to marry, and/or who favor allowing women to become priests. Obviously, not all who are part of a religious tradition necessarily think and act alike, as some people may be part of a tradition without necessarily responding in a traditional manner.

Fourth, religious traditions have a historical legacy. The various characteristic ways of thinking and responding associated with a religious tradition develop over time. Religious traditions are not born overnight; they develop and become rooted. Nor do religious traditions bloom and wither within a short span of time. Religious traditions, by definition, have some historical standing.

Fifth, as noted previously, religious traditions are different from religious movements. Traditions can change, albeit slowly. At any point in time, the beliefs that define a tradition, while rooted in a common past, can be modified by present-day factors. In contrast, a social or religious movement seeks change—either to recapture the past or to transform the future. Some religious movements transcend or span across different religious traditions (e.g., the charismatic movement), while others arise within religious traditions (e.g., the movement to restore the Latin Mass within the Roman Catholic Church). There may arise, for example, evangelical movements that are closely tied to, or evident within, the evangelical tradition. But the two are not the same thing. In short, a religious movement is only a segment of the tradition (or a segment that spans across several traditions). A religious movement does not (nor can it) encapsulate the tradition, but it can seek to steer the tradition in a particular direction. Thus, the evangelical tradition is generally much more diverse and less cohesive than any particular evangelical movement that may seek to guide and shape the tradition.

Finally, members of a religious tradition may, or may not, even perceive themselves to be part of a particular religious tradition and thereby self-consciously identify as a member of that tradition. For example, it may be that there are many who, by virtue of their denominational affiliation (or even religious beliefs), are evangelical Protestants but, when asked, do not perceive themselves to be evangelical Protestants. Moreover, individuals may adopt particular religious identities that, by virtue of their denominational affiliations, stand outside the religious tradition linked to their specific denominations. For example, when survey respondents are given a list of religious labels from which they are to choose those that apply to them personally, there may be those who choose to label themselves as evangelicals even though they may be part of mainline Protestantism or Catholicism by virtue of denominational affiliation.

Because many Protestants affiliated with "evangelical" denominations do not necessarily identify as evangelicals, some analysts have championed the use of "conservative Protestantism" to designate members of the religious tradition (e.g., Woodberry and Smith 1998; Greeley and Hout 2006).

However, affiliation and identification are two analytically distinct phenomena; thus, there is no reason to expect that all, or even most, affiliates of an "evangelical" religious tradition (a sociological phenomenon) would identify with a religious movement label (a psychological phenomenon). Moreover, such a discrepancy between a scholar's classification and a respondent's recognition or acceptance of such a designation is not unique to religion. For example, a scholar might well choose to classify someone as a political conservative based on his/her ties with certain political organizations (e.g., the Christian Coalition) even if such a respondent would not, if asked, identify as a political conservative.

Moreover, the label "conservative Protestantism" is even more problematic than that of "evangelical Protestantism." Not only is it unclear whether "conservative" is a theological or a political designation (the two are often conflated), but the term itself is ahistorical, suggesting that characteristics that seemingly define the tradition currently are inherent to the tradition itself rather than some characteristic that may change with time (thereby precluding, for example, any recognition of the fact that, less than a century ago, evangelical Protestants were among the leading social reformers within American public life). Furthermore, the "conservative Protestant" label can easily encompass groups such as Latter-day Saints and Jehovah's Witnesses, which, though "conservative" in some sense, fall outside the evangelical Protestant tradition on almost every social, theological, and organizational indicator.

The Data Sources Employed

For this study, the Pew Religious Landscape Survey will serve as the primary source of the data presented in this volume. This survey, which was conducted from May 8 to August 13, 2007, was a national survey of Americans in which more than 35,550 respondents participated. Clearly, the massive size of the number of respondents to the survey offers some distinct advantages when examining subgroups within American society. Whereas many national surveys today draw upon fewer than 1,500 respondents, the Pew Religious Landscape Survey captures more than 9,450 evangelical Protestants alone. This substantial number of evangelicals surveyed allows for the examination of important segments of the evangelical community without confronting the problem of basing one's analysis of such subgroups on a limited number of cases—which creates problems related to the representativeness of the small number of respondents captured in such subgroups.[19] Accordingly, the Pew Religious Landscape Survey is ideally suited to analyze differences that may be evident between and among white, black, and Latino evangelicals.

Though the Pew Religious Landscape Survey will serve as the major survey on which the findings of this book will be drawn, two other surveys conducted at roughly the same time will be used periodically to supplement these Pew data.[20] This is because surveys are limited in the number of questions they can ask, and, as a result, valuable supplementary information may be available in surveys outside the Pew Landscape Survey. These two additional surveys employed are the Henry Institute National Survey on Religion and Public Life and the Fifth National Survey of Religion and Politics conducted by the University of Akron Survey Research Center. The former survey was a national survey of 3,003 Americans conducted from April 9 to May 10, 2008, while the latter survey was a national survey of 4,000 Americans conducted during the spring months of 2008. Both of these two surveys were conducted prior to the presidential election in 2008, with respondents then being re-surveyed in the days immediately following Election Day. More important, these two national surveys employed the same measurement approach to identifying evangelical respondents as did the Pew Religious Landscape Survey. Consequently, though the latter two surveys were conducted about six to twelve months later than the Landscape Survey, it is anticipated that evangelical Protestant respondents in each of these three different surveys will exhibit relatively identical religious and social characteristics, despite the fact that these surveys were in the field at somewhat different points in time and were conducted by three different survey organizations.

In order to assess the relative comparability of the results obtained by these three different surveys, a comparative analysis was done first in terms of the social characteristics of the respondents associated with each survey. Table 2.1 compares respondents in these three surveys in terms of their race, gender, age, education, and marital status. Clearly, the three surveys are relatively similar in the resultant distribution of respondents falling within each of these categories. Generally speaking, only relatively small, marginal differences are found across the three surveys in terms of the respondents' sociodemographic characteristics, as the percentages associated with each category of the different variables are within 1 to 3 percentage points of each other.[21] Overall, therefore, these results provide some assurance that the three surveys captured relatively similar kinds of respondents.

Of course, the major question is whether the evangelical respondents captured by each of the surveys are basically the same kinds of people who exhibit similar characteristics or whether the evangelicals captured by each survey are relatively different kinds of respondents. Since the Religious Landscape Survey involves such a large sample size, can we have any confidence that evangelical respondents captured in the other two surveys involving a much smaller sample size are similar to those captured in the Religious Landscape

TABLE 2.1
Characteristics of Respondents across Surveys Employed

	Pew Forum Religious Landscape Survey, 2007 (%)	Henry Institute Religion and Public Life Survey, 2008 (%)	University of Akron Religion and Politics Survey, 2008 (%)
Race			
White	71	71	69
Black	11	10	11
Hispanic	12	13	12
Other	6	7	7
Gender			
Male	48	48	49
Female	52	52	51
Age			
18–34	30	30	31
35–50	32	31	30
51–65	23	23	21
66+	15	16	17
Education			
Non–High School Graduate	14	14	13
High School Graduate	36	36	33
Some College	23	24	27
College Graduate	16	13	17
Post-College Graduate	11	13	11
Marital Status			
Married	54	54	59
Living with Partner	6	*	*
Divorced	10	10	10
Separated	2	2	2
Widowed	8	7	7
Never Married	19	26	21

* – not a response option

Survey? Hence, table 2.2 analyzes the evangelical Protestant respondents found in each survey in terms of several sociodemographic and religious characteristics.

Given the data presented in table 2.2, it would appear that the evangelical respondents captured by each of the three surveys do mirror each other both socially and religiously. Though the respondents in each of the three surveys

TABLE 2.2
Characteristics of Evangelical Respondents across Surveys Employed

Sociodemographic and Religious Characteristics	Pew Forum Religious Landscape Survey, 2007 (%)	Henry Institute Religion and Public Life Survey, 2008 (%)	University of Akron Religion and Politics Survey, 2008 (%)
Gender			
Male	47	48	47
Female	53	52	53
Age			
18–34	26	23	28
35–50	33	32	31
51–65	24	24	22
66+	17	20	20
Frequency of private prayer			
Once a day or more	79	75	79
Once a week or more	14	13	10
Once a month or more	3	6	2
Less than once a month*	4	3	7
Never	1	3	3
Church Attendance			
Weekly	59	59	58
Once or twice a month	15	18	18
Few times a year	23	17	21
Never	4	6	2

* – "Occasionally" rather than "Less than once a month" is option provided in University of Akron National Survey of Religion and Politics

can be weighted in such a manner that the gender and age composition of the survey respondents would reflect the population as a whole in terms of these characteristics, such weighting of the total sample does not guarantee that the gender and age composition within particular subgroupings across each of the surveys would necessarily be equivalent in such social characteristics. Nevertheless, the data reveal that the gender and age composition of evangelicals across each of the three surveys are remarkably comparable in nature.

The same is true religiously; there is a remarkable level of comparability across the three surveys in terms of the religious practices of evangelicals. In table 2.2, evangelicals are compared in terms of their religious practices in terms of both a private religious behavior (frequency of private prayer) and a public religious behavior (frequency of church attendance). As the table reveals, the levels of frequency of private prayers (e.g., reporting that they pray daily) and the levels of frequency of church attendance (e.g., reporting that they attend church weekly) among evangelicals across each of the surveys are basically identical in nature.

Based on this analysis, it would appear that the evangelicals captured by each of the three surveys are rather identical in nature. This gives us greater confidence that, when needed, one can shift from one survey to another in terms of analysis without much fear that the answers provided by evangelical respondents in one particular survey would depart significantly from responses that would have been provided, had they been asked, by evangelical respondents in the other surveys. Thus, even though the Religious Landscape Survey, given its overall sample size, captures a much larger number of evangelical respondents, the evangelical respondents in the other two surveys basically reflect the same characteristics as evangelical respondents in the Religious Landscape Survey.

3

Let the Weak Say I Am Strong? The Size and Social Characteristics of Evangelicals

---

In the immediate years following World War II, religious institutions flourished in the United States. In fact, there was even discussion that a religious revival might be occurring.[1] However, much of this religious vitality was directly related to changes in American family life at the time. Soldiers were returning from war, and they were either entering or reentering married life. This increase in married life was coupled with the subsequent birth of the Baby Boom generation; with the birth of these children, many parents were attending church more faithfully.[2]

Nevertheless, though most churches and denominations saw increased religious attendance and participation during the 1950s, there were growing signs during the 1960s and 1970s that important religious changes were transpiring within American society. In particular, there appeared to be growing evidence that evangelical Protestant churches were experiencing greater vitality than their mainline Protestant church counterparts.[3] By the 1980s, a powerful resurgence in evangelical fervor appeared to be well under way across the country, coupled with an apparent languishing of mainline Protestant denominations, as membership within evangelical churches was growing while membership in mainline churches was declining.[4]

This chapter examines the relative size and social characteristics of evangelicals today. The first portion of this chapter assesses whether the alleged distinctive religious qualities of evangelical Protestants are, in fact, captured through our measurement approach of defining them in terms of their denominational affiliations. After demonstrating the validity of this classification scheme for identifying evangelical Protestants, the second portion of the chapter assesses the proportion of Americans who are affiliated with evangelical Protestant denominations and churches today and then examines the proportion present several decades ago. The chapter then analyzes the social characteristics of evangelicals—particularly in relationship to the social characteristics exhibited by those affiliated with other religious traditions. And, finally, the chapter examines how some of the social characteristics of evangelicals in America may have changed in important ways over the past several decades.

Assessing the Characteristic Qualities of Evangelical Protestantism

As was noted in the conclusion of chapter 1, evangelical Protestantism is, at its core, a tradition within the Christian faith whose members typically affirm personal salvation through Jesus Christ, call individuals to conversion by turning from their old selves to being "a new creature in Christ," and regard the Bible to be the final authority concerning all matters of faith and practice. Beyond these particular points, evangelical Protestantism remains relatively diverse in that, within its boundaries, a variety of more specific religious beliefs and themes are expressed.

Do those so defined as evangelicals by this denominational affiliation approach exhibit the qualities that serve to distinguish evangelical Christians? Table 3.1 addresses this question by assessing whether those so operationally defined as evangelicals exhibit these important qualities of evangelicals— namely, their predilection to hold high views of biblical authority, their proclivity to believe that Jesus is the only way to salvation, and their propensity to claim the label "evangelical" to describe themselves religiously.

It should be noted that this validation assessment is based on data drawn from the Henry Institute National Survey on Religion and Public Life and not on the Pew Religious Landscape Survey. This was done for several reasons. First, as will be discussed below, it had a measure of biblical authority that better differentiated among competing perspectives on the nature of biblical authority. Second, it included a question not found in the Pew Religious Landscape Survey that affirmed salvation through Jesus Christ. And, finally, it had a measure that tapped self-identification more narrowly as an evangelical—something not available in the Landscape Survey.[5]

However, prior to engaging in this validation effort, it is first necessary to discuss why the biblical measure contained in the Religion and Public Life study constitutes a more appropriate way to differentiate among respondents in terms of their views of the nature of biblical authority. It will be recalled that it is the evangelical emphasis on the Bible as the ultimate religious authority that helps, along with several other factors, to distinguish evangelical Christians from other Christians. However, while the Bible is accepted as the basis of religious authority among Protestants, the nature of that authority may be viewed somewhat differently among those who adhere to high views of the authority of scripture.

Several different positions related to biblical authority can be identified that, while related, are analytically distinct. Generally speaking, evangelicals generally adhere to one of three different positions: an infallible, an inerrant, or a literal view of the Bible. Those who subscribe to an infallible view of scripture believe that the Bible is the inspired Word of God and that it is true in all that it teaches. As such, it is the word of God to humankind—but it is not literally *the* words of God. The Bible contains a divine message, but that message is expressed in human terms. Thus, scripture is seen to be the inspired Word of God that comes to the church mediated through the words of human writers. Those who adhere to biblical infallibility argue that the authors of the biblical books were inspired by God to be authors of His message. However, such writers were not mere stenographers of a message dictated by God; rather, there was an interplay between divine and human authorship within the biblical texts that reveals different styles of writing and composition.

From this perspective, scripture is infallible in that it does not deceive humans concerning matters of salvation. It is not, however, intended to be an encyclopedia of information on every human topic; one does not go to the Bible necessarily to answer "philosophical questions or to gain accurate information concerning history, science, geography, or astronomy" (McKim 1985, 93). It isn't that scripture does not contain information about such topics, but that the nature of the information provided is governed by the purpose of God's revelation.

Obviously, views concerning the nature of scriptural authority affect the principles by which it should be interpreted. For example, evangelicals who subscribe to biblical infallibility tend to argue that, given its particular purposes, the Bible should be viewed as a religious document. Accordingly, naturalistic accounts of creation, such as the poetic account of creation in Genesis 1, may reveal truths about creation, but such accounts are not to be understood either as a precise, literal account of the creation process itself or as a general "scientific" statement concerning the specific, sequential nature of that process. Consequently, those who adhere to the infallibility of scripture stress that the revelational truths contained in the creation story pertain to the truths that God is the creator of the universe, that humans are created in the image of God, and that humans are to act as stewards of God's creation. Accordingly, evangelicals who subscribe to biblical infallibility hold that

Genesis 1 is a true account, but they are likely to stress the revelational, rather than the "scientific," nature of that account.

The inerrancy position is more stringent than the infallibility position. The inerrancy position posits that the Bible, at least in terms of the original documents, is totally without error in all its statements whether they relate to religious faith, historical events, or natural occurrences. Biblical inerrantists are more prone than infallibilists to stress that the account of creation in Genesis 1 is a true account—not only religiously but also scientifically. Many inerrantists would recognize that the term "day" discussed in the account does not necessarily refer to a twenty-four-hour span of time (as the account is poetic and God is eternal and exists outside the dimension of time). However, such inerrantists might well insist that the creation sequence is true in terms of the natural history of matter and that many, if not most, scientific accounts of the origins of the universe can be harmonized with the account of Genesis 1.

Finally, biblical literalism is a specific principle of interpretation related to biblical inerrancy.[6] The position of inerrancy does not necessarily require a literalist interpretation. For example, though a biblical literalist would, by definition, adhere to a belief in a historical, six-day creation, a biblical inerrantist need not necessarily do so.[7]

Most surveys of religion typically include a question on biblical authority that taps literalism and inerrancy together (captured by the response "The Bible is the inerrant Word of God and should be interpreted literally").[8] Such a measurement approach, however, largely ignores the more long-standing, and less restrictive, view of biblical authority as being infallible, to which many evangelicals subscribe. Moreover, the conventional survey questions tapping views of biblical authority typically offer only one alternative to the view that the Bible is the Word of God—namely, that it is a book of myths and legends.[9] This is also problematic in that, culturally speaking, Americans generally hold a high regard for the Bible. Consequently, when provided with only one alternative to viewing the Bible as the Word of God (i.e., it is a book of myths and legends), the overwhelming majority of Americans reject such an option. What is needed, therefore, are more culturally acceptable options for giving respect to the historic place of the Bible in American cultural life, without "forcing" respondents to subscribe to a notion that the Bible is necessarily the Word of God.

Given the problems associated with the conventional measure of biblical authority, the Henry Institute National Survey on Religion and Public Life used a question on biblical authority in which respondents were given three simple options: (1) the Bible is the true Word of God, (2) the Bible is a book of wisdom and history, and (3) the Bible is a book of myths and legends. Certainly, anyone who may hold "high views of scripture" would consider the Bible to be more than simply a book of wisdom and history—let alone a book of myths and legends. As shown in table 3.1, when the options are posed in this manner, evangelical Protestants are the most prone of all the religious traditions to respond that the Bible is "the true Word of God," as nearly all evangelicals responded in such a manner. Black Protestants ranked a little behind evangelicals in terms of their tendency to see the Bible as the Word of God (86 percent versus 76 percent, respectively), while only a bare majority of mainline Protestants and Roman Catholics responded that they viewed the Bible in such a manner. Less than one-quarter of the religiously unaffiliated did so. Thus, these data suggest that when evangelicals are designated by means of their religious affiliation one does indeed find that they exhibit the distinguishing quality of adhering to a "high view of scripture" that is associated with evangelical Protestantism.

In addition, it was noted that evangelical Protestantism is an expression of Christianity that affirms personal salvation through Jesus Christ. But, given that the person and life of Jesus stand at the center of the Christian faith, one would anticipate that many Christians, regardless of their particular Christian tradition, would likely affirm the traditional Christian understanding that salvation comes through the life, death, and resurrection of Jesus Christ.

TABLE 3.1
Assessing the Expected Religious Characteristics of Evangelical Protestants

	Evangelical Protestant (%)	Mainline Protestant (%)	Black Protestant (%)	Roman Catholic (%)	Unaffiliated (%)
View of the Bible					
True Word of God	86	55	76	55	22
Book of wisdom and history	12	42	22	39	38
Book of myths and legends	3	4	4	7	40
Believe Jesus is the only way to salvation	88	64	89	65	32
Word "evangelical" describes one's religious perspective fairly/ very well	52	20	35	22	11

Source: Henry Institute Survey on Religion and Public Life, 2008

Note: Entries show percent agreeing with statement

Nevertheless, if our measure does capture evangelical Protestants, then those classified as evangelicals should overwhelmingly affirm such an understanding.

The Henry Institute survey also contained a question that asked respondents whether or not they agreed with the statement that "Jesus is the only way to salvation." As can be seen in table 3.1, almost all (88 percent) classified evangelical Protestants so agreed, as did a similar level of Black Protestants (89 percent). Also, not surprisingly, differences in subscription to this understanding across the four Christian traditions are less than that which is evident in terms of views related to biblical authority. Nevertheless, important differences remain across the religious traditions, and those who are classified as evangelicals through our assignment process also overwhelmingly exhibit this distinguishing quality of evangelical Protestantism.

The final validating criterion employed in table 3.1 is self-definition as an evangelical. As noted in the introduction to this book, self-definition as an evangelical is not a defining quality of being an evangelical, though one would expect evangelical Protestants to be more likely than those from other religious traditions to adopt the label to describe themselves religiously. Moreover, given that evangelical Protestantism is both a religious movement that spans religious traditions and a religious tradition itself, one might also expect there would be some in other religious traditions who would likely claim the label "evangelical."

These expectations are also met. The denominational affiliation measure used to capture evangelical Protestants captures those respondents who are most prone to adopt the label to describe themselves religiously, as more than half of our classified evangelical Protestants claim that the word "evangelical" describes their religious perspective either "fairly well" or "very well." In contrast, only a little more than one-third of Black Protestants, and one-fifth of mainline Protestants and Catholics, do so.

In addition, if our adopted measure for identifying evangelical Protestants is a valid measure, one would anticipate that, among those classified as evangelical Protestants, there should be an increased willingness to adopt the label "evangelical" as their frequency of church attendance increases. This is because an understanding of the meaning of religious terms (such as the word "evangelical") would likely be greatest among those who are most engaged in religious life, as such greater involvement is likely to bring with it an increased familiarity with the religious language used in such settings. And, in fact, this is the case (data not shown). The percentage of evangelical Protestants who adopt the label "evangelical" to describe themselves religiously increases monotonically from 41 percent among those who attend church a few times a year or less, to 49 percent among those who attend church on a monthly basis, to 71 percent among those who attend church on a weekly basis.

The Relative Size of American Evangelicals

Having validated that the classification system employed captures those who exhibit the defining qualities of evangelical Protestantism, we can now move to an examination of the size and social characteristics of evangelical Protestants. As noted in chapter 1, America has had a predominantly Protestant heritage, and evangelical Protestants have long been present within American society. But the question remains: Just how large a segment of the American population do evangelical Protestants represent?

For purposes of the analysis presented in table 3.2, Americans are divided into six broad categories of religious affiliation; the categories include three Protestant traditions (evangelical Protestant, mainline Protestant, and Black Protestant), the Roman Catholic tradition, and the religiously unaffiliated, with all other remaining religious traditions combined into one general ("other") category. As the data reveal, America continues to remain a largely Protestant nation, though Protestantism's statistical dominance is substantially less today than a century ago. Only fifty years ago, Protestants constituted nearly two-thirds of the American people (see table 3.3). Now, however, the three Protestant categories together encompass only slightly more than a majority of the American people (51.3 percent).

Of the various religious traditions in America today, evangelical Protestants comprise the largest religious tradition within American society. With a little more than one-quarter of American people (26.3 percent), evangelical Protestants outnumber mainline (18.1 percent) and Black Protestants (6.9 percent) combined. Even though the numbers of Catholics have been expanding through the influx of Hispanic immigrants, evangelicals continue to represent a somewhat larger portion of American society than do Roman

TABLE 3.2
Relative Frequency of Religious Traditions in America Today

Religious Tradition Affiliation	Percentage of Population (%)
Evangelical Protestant	26.3
Mainline Protestant	18.1
Black Protestant	6.9
Roman Catholic	23.9
Unaffiliated	16.1
Other	8.7
Total	100.0
(N)	(35,556)

Source: Pew Forum Religious Landscape Survey, 2007

Catholics. The religiously unaffiliated, according to the massive Pew Religious Landscape Survey, now constitute roughly a little more than one out of six Americans (16.1 percent), with the vast diversity found within the remaining "other" religious affiliations representing less than one-tenth of all Americans.

However, as noted earlier, there were indications that evangelical Protestant churches were growing during the 1960s and 1970s, while mainline Protestant churches were languishing. During this same period of time, analysts also noted a growth in the percentage of religiously unaffiliated (Glenn 1987) and that this lack of religious affiliation tended to be greatest among the younger age cohorts (Glenn 1987; Roof and McKinney 1987, 155). To what extent, then, has evangelical Protestantism grown over the course of the past several decades? And has evangelical Protestantism grown despite both the apparent growth in the number of religiously unaffiliated and the influx of other non-Christian religions linked to more recent waves of immigration to the United States?

Table 3.3 addresses these questions. Recall that evangelical Protestantism is defined here in terms of affiliation with particular denominations within the Christian faith. As a result, in order to make valid comparisons over time, it is necessary to find earlier survey data that employed rather detailed denominational affiliation measures that enable analysts to assign respondents to their proper religious tradition. Most studies prior to the late 1980s rarely employed these detailed denominational measures; fortunately, however,

TABLE 3.3
Relative Frequency of Religious Traditions over Time

Religious Tradition Affiliation	Percentage of Population		
	1964 (%)	1996 (%)	2007 (%)
Evangelical Protestant	22.0	26.9	26.3
Mainline Protestant	30.4	18.0	18.1
Black Protestant	11.0	8.1	6.9
Roman Catholic	25.8	22.7	23.9
Unaffiliated	4.3	17.5	16.1
Other	6.5	6.7	8.7
Total	100.0	99.9	100.0
(N)	(1975)	(4037)	(35,556)

Sources:

1964: Anti-Semitism in the United States

1996: University of Akron, Second National Survey of Religion and Politics

2007: Pew Forum Religious Landscape Survey

there is one study—the Anti-Semitism Study of 1964—that did so. These data allow us to make a fairly reliable assessment of change in patterns of religious tradition affiliation over time. In addition, data from 1996, drawn from the Second National Study of Religion and Politics,[10] are also presented; these data are included as a means to assess whether changes in affiliation moved consistently in the same direction over time.

Clearly, over the past forty years, there have been several important changes in the way in which the American people report affiliation with different religious traditions. The percentage of evangelical Protestants clearly grew between 1964 and 1996, whereas the percentage of mainline Protestants declined substantially over the same period of time.[11] Over the course of these three decades, the relative percentage of Roman Catholics and Black Protestants declined only slightly, while those of "other religions" increased slightly. During the same period of time, however, the proportion of the American people who claimed no religious affiliation grew substantially—more than tripling over the three-decade period.

On the other hand, between 1996 and 2007, changes in religious affiliation were only marginal in nature. This relative stability in religious tradition affiliation over the course of the decade is due either to (1) the rather short interval of time being examined, or (2) the fact that the particular social forces that had been at work shifting patterns of religious affiliation between the 1960s and 1990s had largely run their course. Regardless of what may be the case, there has been relatively little change in the aggregate distribution of the religious affiliations of Americans between 1996 and 2007.

Overall, therefore, evangelical Protestants today comprise a plurality of Americans, though their numbers constitute substantially less than a majority of the American people. Their numbers have grown over the past forty years, but this growth has leveled off over the past decade or two. Still, though they do not constitute a majority of the American people, they nevertheless represent an important segment of the population; their numbers alone help to enhance their cultural, social, and political significance within American society.

The Social Characteristics of American Evangelicals

Not only does the relative size of a group provide important information about a group's social significance, so too do their social characteristics. Are evangelicals located more predominantly within certain segments of American society than other segments? And, with their growth in numbers over the past several decades, have the social characteristics of evangelical Protestants changed in important ways as well?

Table 3.4 presents data pertaining to the racial, gender, age, and marital composition of evangelical Protestants in relationship to those found among mainline Protestants, Black Protestants, Roman Catholics, and the religiously unaffiliated.[12] And these data reveal that the social composition of evangelical Protestants differs in some important ways from other religious groups within American society.

Race

First, evangelical Protestants tend to be somewhat racially diverse, though less so than among Roman Catholics and the religiously unaffiliated. About four out of five evangelicals are white (81 percent), with the remainder distributed across a variety of racial and ethnic groups.[13] Around 6 percent of evangelicals are black, with slightly more being Hispanic (7 percent). Another 2 percent of evangelicals are drawn from Asians, while the remainder (4 percent) is drawn from various other racial groups.

Thus, evangelicals stand between the other major religious traditions in terms of their racial diversity. Black Protestants and mainline Protestants are the most racially homogeneous religious traditions, with more than 90 percent of their members falling within one particular racial category. On the other hand, Roman Catholics and the religiously unaffiliated are somewhat more racially diverse in composition than evangelical Protestants. However, the greater racial diversity of Catholics stems largely from the high concentration of Hispanics within their ranks, as nearly one-third (29 percent) of all Catholics today are Hispanics. The religiously unaffiliated exhibit the highest concentration of Asians, the largest percentage of blacks outside the Black Protestant tradition, and the greatest proportion of Hispanics outside the Catholic tradition. Thus, in terms of racial diversity, evangelical Protestants stand between the greater homogeneity of Black Protestants and mainline Protestants, on the one hand, and the greater diversity of Catholics and the religiously unaffiliated, on the other.

Gender

Given their greater longevity, there is a higher proportion of women than men within American society. In addition, it has long been recognized that, as a group, women tend to be more religious than men. As a result, one would anticipate that each major religious tradition (other than the religiously unaffiliated) would contain a higher concentration of women than men. And, as can be seen from table 3.4, this is the case.

However, in comparison to other religious traditions, evangelicals tend to have a *lower* percentage of women within its ranks than those in other religious traditions. Stated somewhat differently, evangelical Protestantism seemingly does better in attracting and/or retaining male adherents than the other major religious traditions. In fact, of all the religious traditions

TABLE 3.4
Social Characteristics by Religious Tradition

	Evangelical Protestant (%)	Mainline Protestant (%)	Black Protestant (%)	Roman Catholic (%)	Unaffiliated (%)	Total Population (%)
Race						
White	81	91	2	65	73	71
Black	6	2	92	2	8	11
Hispanic	7	3	4	29	11	12
Asian	2	1	*	2	4	3
Other	4	3	1	2	4	3
Gender						
Male	47	46	41	46	59	48
Female	53	54	59	54	41	52
Age						
18–34	26	22	32	28	43	30
35–50	33	30	31	34	31	32
51–65	24	27	23	23	17	23
66+	17	21	14	15	7	15
Generational Composition						
Millennials	11	10	17	12	21	18
Generation X	30	26	29	34	37	25
Baby Boomers	36	37	35	34	31	37
Silent	23	28	19	20	11	20
Marital Status						
Married	59	57	33	58	46	56
Living with Partner	5	5	6	7	10	6
Divorced	11	11	12	8	9	10
Separated	2	2	4	2	2	2
Widowed	9	11	11	8	4	8
Never Married	14	15	34	17	28	19

Source: Pew Forum Religious Landscape Survey, 2007

* – less than 1%

examined in table 3.4, evangelical Protestants come closest to reflecting the American population in terms of gender composition (53 percent of evangelicals, and 52 percent of the American people, are female). Particularly noteworthy in terms of their deviation from the population parameters are Black Protestants and the religiously unaffiliated. Among the former, nearly three in five—59 percent—are females, while among the latter nearly three in five—59 percent—are males.

Age and Generational Cohort

Evangelical Protestants also differ from members of other religious traditions in terms of their age composition (see table 3.4). As a group, evangelical Protestants tend to be younger than mainline Protestants, but older than Black Protestants. Evangelical Protestants most closely approximate Roman Catholics in age, though Catholics tend to be somewhat younger than evangelical Protestants. However, it is the religiously unaffiliated who exhibit the largest percentage of respondents within the youngest age category, as more than two-fifths of the unaffiliated (43 percent) report being less than 35 years of age.

Because subsequent chapters will analyze generational differences in order to ascertain whether a "new generation of evangelicals" may be emerging, evangelical Protestants are compared here to those affiliated with the other major religious traditions in terms of generational differences. The generational categories employed here are discussed in the introductory chapter, and based on this generational analysis, nearly three-fifths of all evangelicals (59 percent) fall within the Baby Boomer and Silent categories—trailing only mainline Protestants in the percentage of affiliates found within these two generations. Millennials constitute about one-tenth of all evangelical Protestants (11 percent), approximately the same proportion found among mainline Protestants (10 percent) and Catholics (12 percent). But millennials constitute about one-sixth of all Black Protestants (17 percent) and one-fifth of all of the religiously unaffiliated (21 percent).

Marital Status

Another basic demographic variable of social significance relates to marital and fertility patterns. Traditionally, the typical American family structure has been viewed largely in terms of a husband being the breadwinner and the wife as the homemaker. Over the past several decades, however, there have been serious challenges to this traditional notion of the family structure. Expanding roles for women, increased divorce rates, and alternative lifestyles have each challenged these traditional views of family life. Yet, for many evangelicals, the traditional, nuclear family is still viewed as the ideal, with the biblical concept of the marriage being defined as heterosexual in nature and lifelong in commitment (Roof and McKinney 1987, 156).

Do evangelicals, then, differ from non-evangelicals in terms of their marital patterns? The data presented in table 3.4 suggest that they do. Nearly three-fifths of all evangelicals surveyed reported that they are currently married; as such, they are slightly more likely to do so than those in the other religious traditions. Moreover, evangelicals are the least likely of the major religious groups analyzed to report that they have never been married.

Nevertheless, it is not clear whether these differences in marital status stem from differences in lifestyle commitments or simply from age differences found within the different traditions. Since singles are most likely to be found among the young and the widowed among the old, it may be that these differences in marital status reflect little more than age differences present among those within each of the different traditions.

In order to ascertain better whether it is age or lifestyle differences that account for these differences in marital status, the relationship between religious tradition and marital status is analyzed while controlling for the age of the respondents. These data are presented in table 3.5, and they suggest that there are indeed lifestyle differences between young evangelicals and the young in other religious traditions. First, among those between 18 and 34 years of age, evangelical Protestants are far more likely to report being married than those found in any other major religious tradition analyzed.[14] Second, regardless of the age category analyzed, evangelical Protestants are the least likely to report never having been married at some point during their life.

Family Size

Simple social patterns can carry with them important implications. For example, the fact that young evangelicals are more likely to be married than their counterparts in other religious traditions has implications for the long-term growth of evangelicals based simply on the greater likelihood of offspring being produced within married families. It is true that the presence of children is now no longer as closely tied today to conventional marital patterns as was true in the past. Still, despite these changes, child-bearing and child-rearing still occur more frequently within, rather than outside, marital commitments.

Over time, the size of the membership of any religious group is dependent upon two major factors: its level of natural growth and its net level of gains or losses resulting from switching between religious groups. Given that

TABLE 3.5
Marital Status by Age Cohort (controlling for religious tradition)

	Evangelical Protestant (%)	Mainline Protestant (%)	Black Protestant (%)	Roman Catholic (%)	Unaffiliated (%)	Total Population (%)
Ages 18–34						
Married	47	42	21	42	31	39
Never Married	38	43	63	40	49	44
Ages 35–50						
Married	67	68	41	68	60	65
Never Married	10	10	30	11	17	13
Ages 51–65						
Married	67	65	40	67	57	64
Never Married	4	8	17	7	10	8
Ages 66+						
Married	50	47	28	49	44	47
Never Married	1	3	5	4	6	3

Source: Pew Forum Religious Landscape Survey, 2007

"most faiths are able to hold the loyalty of a majority of the children born to members" (Roof and McKinney 1987, 157–58), the higher the level of births among members of a religious group, the greater the potential for numerical growth. Consequently, table 3.6 presents the mean number of children under 18 years of age reported by respondents of different religious traditions—broken down by the age of the respondent (regardless of the respondent's marital status). Evangelicals who are under the age of 35 have the highest mean level of children under 18 years of age (1.06) when compared to those of a similar age range within the other religious traditions—with the religiously unaffiliated exhibiting the lowest mean score (0.70). For those between the ages of 35 and 50, Catholics outpace evangelical Protestants in terms of the mean number of reported children under 18 years of age (1.41 versus 1.20, respectively, with the religiously unaffiliated once again exhibiting the lowest mean score for the age group).

Though these data must be viewed as being more suggestive than conclusive in nature, the patterns evident in the table are consistent with those found earlier by Roof and McKinney (1987, 158–62). The data suggest, however,

TABLE 3.6
Mean Number of Children under Eighteen
Years of Age by Religious Tradition (controlling for age of respondent)

	Evangelical Protestant	Mainline Protestant	Black Protestant	Roman Catholic	Unaffiliated	Total Population
Ages 18–34	1.06	0.87	1.05	0.98	0.70	0.91
Ages 35–50	1.20	1.17	1.05	1.41	0.99	1.22
Ages 51–65	0.23	0.15	0.32	0.22	0.18	0.22
Ages 66+	0.04	0.02	0.16	0.03	0.09	0.04

Source: Pew Forum Religious Landscape Survey, 2007

that the potential for growth among the evangelical segment of American society is greater than what one might initially conclude based simply on the age distribution of evangelicals. Thus, given these differential birth rates across religious traditions, the natural growth potential of evangelicals is likely to be somewhat greater than those of the other religious faith traditions analyzed.

Regional Location

In addition to the differences already noted, evangelicals differ significantly from those in most other religious traditions in terms of their regional location (see table 3.7). Evangelicals are more heavily concentrated within the South,[15] providing them with a distinctive geographic base.

TABLE 3.7.
Geographical Region and Community Type by Religious Tradition

	Evangelical Protestant (%)	Mainline Protestant (%)	Black Protestant (%)	Roman Catholic (%)	Unaffiliated (%)	Total Population (%)
Region						
Northeast	12	23	20	32	22	22
Midwest	23	29	19	24	23	24
South	49	31	53	22	27	34
West	16	17	8	22	28	21
Community Type						
Urban	25	26	50	35	36	32
Suburban	48	52	37	54	46	49
Rural	27	22	13	11	17	19

Source: Pew Forum Religious Landscape Survey, 2007

It is possible, therefore, that the growth in evangelical Protestantism during the 1960s and 1970s may have partially been a by-product of migration
patterns evident within American society (Hoge 1979). Though conventional
wisdom may hold that regional differences within American society are declining, geographers of American religion generally agree that regionalism
in terms of religion continues to persist in American society (Killen and Silk
2004; Balmer and Silk 2006).[16] In fact, regional differences in religion actually
grew stronger during the twentieth century (Stump 1984a), and the religious
commitments of migrants generally changed in the direction of the level of
religious commitment reflective of the region to which they have moved
(Stump 1984b). Since recent migration patterns have been largely from
Frostbelt to Sunbelt states (more specifically, to the southern states in which
evangelical churches have predominated), such migration patterns may well
have contributed to the growth of evangelicals within American society.

Residential Location

Historically, the strength of American religion has been found in its small
towns and rural areas. And, as can be seen in table 3.7, evangelicals are drawn
disproportionately from rural and small-town America. More than one-quarter of evangelicals reside in rural areas, the highest percentage found among
the major religious traditions examined. While a quarter of evangelicals are
located within urban settings, this level of urban residence constitutes the
lowest percentage across the five traditions examined. Thus, in comparison
to other religious traditions, evangelicals are more likely to reside in rural and
small-town America, locations geographically distant from those centers of
American social life from which many of the symbols and values of modern
American life seemingly originate and are disseminated.

Educational Attainment

Education is an important factor in shaping individual beliefs and personal
lifestyles. There are several reasons why education is attributed to have these
effects. Not only does it expose people to new ideas and alternative explanations, but it provides access to jobs, broadens social networks, and even
fosters "a sense of being part of the social mainstream that is denied to those
with lower levels of education" (Wuthnow 2007a, 82). Yet many evangelicals
exhibit a "conflicted relationship" with institutions of higher education in
that they perceive higher education to be "both friend and foe," with university life viewed as a "spiritual battleground," in which "the public status of
Christianity is at stake" (Bielo 2009, 41).

As is evident in table 3.8, substantial differences do exist between evangelicals and those affiliated with other religious traditions in terms of their educational attainment. The data indicate that evangelicals, as a whole, tend to be less well educated than those within the other major religious traditions. A majority of evangelicals in the latter part of the first decade of the twenty-first century reported that they had only a high school education or less (56 percent), though a majority of Black Protestants (59 percent) and Roman Catholics (53 percent) reported the same. Only within the ranks of mainline Protestants (43 percent) and the religiously unaffiliated (47 percent) does one find less than half reporting a high school diploma as their highest level of educational attainment.

Thus, in comparison to those in other religious traditions, evangelical Protestants continue to rank relatively low in terms of the proportion of its members having completed a college education. Just one-fifth of all evangelicals report having obtained a college degree, with only Black Protestants ranking behind them in terms of educational accomplishments.[17]

TABLE 3.8
Education and Income by Religious Tradition

	Evangelical Protestant (%)	Mainline Protestant (%)	Black Protestant (%)	Roman Catholic (%)	Unaffiliated (%)	Total Population (%)
Education						
Non–High School Graduate	16	9	19	17	13	14
High School Graduate	40	34	40	36	34	36
Some College	24	24	25	21	16	23
College Graduate	13	20	11	16	13	16
Post-College Education	7	14	5	10	19	11
Family Income						
Under $30,000	34	25	47	31	29	31
$30,000–$49,999	24	21	26	20	23	22
$50,000–$74,999	18	18	12	16	16	17
$75,000–$99,999	11	15	7	14	13	13
$100,000 or more	13	21	8	19	19	18

Source: Pew Forum Religious Landscape Survey, 2007

Family Income

Finally, given the historic relationship between education and income levels, evangelicals also ranked relatively low in terms of their level of family income. More than one-half of evangelical Protestants (58 percent) reported family income levels below $50,000, while only a little more than one in ten evangelical Protestants (13 percent) stated that their family income exceeded $100,000. The income level of Black Protestants tended, as a whole, to rank below that of evangelical Protestants. But, in contrast, the reported family income levels of mainline Protestants, Roman Catholics, and the religiously unaffiliated all tended, as a whole, to be higher than that of evangelical Protestants.

The Changing Social Characteristics of Evangelicals

The 2010 Census data revealed that Americans today are older, more Hispanic, less wedded to marriage, are having fewer children, and are more likely to live in the South and West than was true several decades ago. Though the data we have been examining from the Pew Religious Landscape Survey provide some important information related to the social characteristics of evangelical Protestants in the early part of the twenty-first century, examining data from one particular point in time cannot provide any assessment of what changes may have been occurring over time.

As a result, it is unclear just how the social characteristics of evangelical Protestants may have changed, or not changed, over time, and to what extent the broad sociodemographic changes among Americans as a whole are also evident among evangelicals.

For example, despite the lower levels of college-educated adherents within their ranks, have evangelical Protestants today achieved higher levels of educational attainment than evangelicals a generation or two ago? Given the spread of post-secondary education since World War II, it is very likely the case. But, more importantly, have differences in educational attainment actually been narrowing across religious traditions with the passage of time? In other words, is there any evidence of a growing convergence with regard to the social characteristics of evangelical Protestants and the social characteristics of those affiliated with other religious traditions? Here we examine three possible important shifts in the social composition of religious traditions over time: age, marital status, and level of educational attainment.[18] Once again, we will examine patterns found in 1964 and then compare such patterns to those found in 1996 and 2007.

Changing Age Composition

Overall, as shown in table 3.9, those affiliated with the major Christian traditions tended, as a whole, to be somewhat younger in 1964 than their counterparts in 2007. In other words, the religious composition of each of the major religious traditions has aged over the course of the past four decades. In part, this shifting in age composition is a function of an aging population (with the aging of the Baby Boom generation), but it is also partially a function of the greater proportion of youth who report being religiously unaffiliated in 2007 than in 1964.

In 1964, evangelical Protestants, Black Protestants, and Roman Catholics had the highest percentage of young members within their ranks (30 percent or more), whereas mainline Protestants and the religiously unaffiliated

TABLE 3.9
The Changing Age Composition within Religious Traditions over Time

	Year		
	1964 *(%)*	*1966* *(%)*	*2007* *(%)*
Evangelical Protestant			
Under 35 years of age	32	30	26
Over 65 years of age	19	18	17
Mainline Protestant			
Under 35 years of age	23	20	22
Over 65 years of age	22	22	21
Black Protestant			
Under 35 years of age	34	37	32
Over 65 years of age	10	16	14
Roman Catholic			
Under 35 years of age	33	28	28
Over 65 years of age	11	15	15
Unaffiliated			
Under 35 years of age	22	40	43
Over 65 years of age	20	9	7

Sources:

1964: Anti-Semitism in the United States

1996: University of Akron, Second National Survey of Religion and Politics

2007: Pew Forum Religious Landscape Survey

tended to be more middle aged or older. Not only were about one-third of evangelical Protestants, Black Protestants, and Roman Catholics under 35 years of age, but the percentage of those over 65 years of age was substantially less than the percentage of those below 35 years of age within each of these three religious traditions. For example, in 1964, the ratio of young to old among Black Protestants was 3.4 (34 percent divided by 10 percent), 3.0 for Roman Catholics, and 1.68 for evangelical Protestants.

However, by 2007, the percentage of those under 35 years of age within each of the major religious traditions had declined from that evident within their ranks in 1964—the exception being the religiously unaffiliated. For some religious traditions, the decline was only marginal in nature. Among mainline Protestants and Black Protestants, the percentage of members under the age of 35 years declined only slightly between 1964 and 2007 (from 23 percent to 22 percent for mainline Protestants and from 34 percent to 32 percent for Black Protestants). On the other hand, far more substantial declines were evident among evangelical Protestants and Roman Catholics. In 1964, nearly one-third of all evangelicals were under the age of 35 years, but in 2007 only slightly more than one-quarter were. In fact, of all the religious traditions examined, evangelicals exhibited the largest decline of the percentage of young members over the span of the four-decade period of time (from 32 percent to 26 percent)—though Catholics exhibited a nearly identical decline (from 33 percent to 28 percent). As a result, the ratio of young to old among evangelicals declined from 1.68 in 1964 to 1.53 in 2007, while among Roman Catholics it had declined from 3.0 to 1.87 over the same span of time.

The one religious group that grew much younger over the past four decades has been the religiously unaffiliated. Over this period of time, the percentage of those under 35 years of age nearly doubled within its ranks—from 22 percent to 43 percent—while over the same period of time, the percentage of its "membership" over 65 years of age declined substantially.

Changing Marital Status

Given the generally declining percentage of adherents under 35 years of age within each of the major religious traditions, one might anticipate that the proportion of those within those traditions who report being married may well have increased over the past forty years. And, as noted earlier, married people are more likely to attend church and participate in religious life than single people.

On the other hand, we also know that social practices may change over time. And in fact, people are now marrying later in life than was the case several decades ago—so that there are far fewer younger adults who are married today than was true a generation ago. In the 1970s, a majority of those in their twenties were married, but by the turn of the millennium, married couples in their twenties were atypical (Wuthnow 2007a, 23). Moreover, divorce is far more common today than several decades ago,[19] and with greater longevity in life, there is also a greater potential today to have larger proportions of Americans report that they were "previously married, but now widowed." Thus, despite an aging population, it may well be that the proportion of those married within each religious tradition has declined markedly over the course of the past four decades.

Table 3.10 examines the percentage of married respondents within each major religious tradition in the years 1964, 1996, and 2007, as well as the percentage of single respondents across the same three cross-sections in time. Within each religious tradition in 1964, the percentage of affiliates

TABLE 3.10
The Changing Marital Composition within Religious Traditions over Time

	Year		
	1964 (%)	*1966* (%)	*2007* (%)
Evangelical Protestant			
Single	5	16	14
Married	81	66	59
Mainline Protestant			
Single	7	15	15
Married	80	67	57
Black Protestant			
Single	14	36	34
Married	64	43	32
Roman Catholic			
Single	10	20	17
Married	78	63	58
Unaffiliated			
Single	7	29	28
Married	79	52	46

Sources:

1964: Anti-Semitism in the United States

1996: University of Akron, Second National Survey of Religion and Politics

2007: Pew Forum Religious Landscape Survey

who reported that they were single and never married was generally 10 percent or less (the exception being Black Protestants with 14 percent so reporting). Likewise, the percentage of affiliates of each major religious tradition in 1964 who reported that they were married was approximately 80 percent (with Black Protestants once again being the exception at 64 percent).

However, by 2007, major changes had transpired in terms of the marital patterns found within each of the major religious traditions. Over the past several decades, young adults have tended to stay single longer before marrying; as a result, far fewer young adults are married than was true a generation ago. Thus, the percentage of singles within each religious tradition analyzed in table 3.10 has increased dramatically over the past forty years. The percentage of singles basically doubled for mainline Protestants, more than doubled for Black Protestants, tripled for evangelical Protestants, and quadrupled for the religiously unaffiliated between 1964 and 2007. And the percentage of singles among Roman Catholics doubled between 1964 and 1996—but then dropped slightly between 1996 and 2007.

This increase in singles only partially explains the drop in the percentage of married members within each religious tradition. Whereas about 80 percent of adherents within each of the major religious traditions reported that they were married in 1964, slightly less than 60 percent did so in 2007. The exceptions were the religiously unaffiliated (with 46 percent married) and Black Protestants (with 32 percent married). In fact, the percentage of singles among Black Protestants in 2007 actually exceeded the percentage who are married (34 percent versus 32 percent, respectively).

Nevertheless, it appears that evangelical Protestants, mainline Protestants, and Roman Catholics differ more in terms of the timing of marriage than they do in the actual practice of marriage, whereas marriage as a practice for Black Protestants and the religiously unaffiliated appears to be qualitatively different than that for the other three traditions. With regard to the timing of marriage, nearly 70 percent of those within their thirties reported being married—regardless of whether they were evangelical Protestants, mainline Protestants, or Roman Catholics (data not shown). But for those in their twenties, 34 percent of evangelical Protestants indicated that they were married, whereas only 29 percent of Roman Catholics and 24 percent of mainline Protestants did so. With regard to differences in practice, less than 60 percent of the religiously unaffiliated in their thirties reported being married, and only slightly more than 40 percent of Black Protestants did so (data not shown). Consequently, if marriage and child-rearing constitute settling down, then evangelical Protestants typically do so before those affiliated with the other major religious traditions.

Changing Educational Attainment

As was revealed in table 3.8, evangelicals are less likely than mainline Protestants, Roman Catholics, and the religiously unaffiliated to have graduated from college. Do such differences in educational attainment between evangelicals and those of the other religious traditions reflect, therefore, real differences in their commitment to the value of education? Could it be that evangelicals are more distrustful of higher education because they believe that higher education may well undermine the bases of their religious faith? If so, then evangelical Protestants may be simply less prone to seek a college education.

On the other hand, college education is far more common among younger than older Americans. As a result, the proportion of college graduates may have grown among evangelicals over time—though the proportion of college graduates within other religious traditions has likely also increased over the same period of time. Consequently, even though the proportion of college graduates among evangelical Protestants may still not have reached the same level as that within other major religious traditions, the educational gap evident across these traditions may have nevertheless narrowed over the past several decades.

Table 3.11 examines the proportion of those affiliated with the major religious traditions reporting that they have either had some college education or graduated from a college or university across the past four decades. Not surprisingly, much smaller percentages of college graduates were found within each religious tradition in 1964 than in 2007. In 1964, slightly more than one in twenty evangelicals (6 percent) had graduated from college, with only Black Protestants trailing evangelical Protestants at the time in their level of educational attainment. Nearly three times as many mainline Protestants as evangelical Protestants reported being college graduates, and the religiously unaffiliated also had more than twice as many college graduates as evangelical Protestants. Even Roman Catholics, historically a religious "outgroup" in American society, exhibited higher educational attainment than evangelical Protestants in 1964—with 9 percent of their members being college educated.

Over the past forty years, evangelicals have narrowed this education gap in relationship to the other religious traditions. By 2007, the percentage of evangelicals who were college educated more than tripled—as one-fifth of all evangelicals now report they were college educated. In contrast, the percentage of mainline Protestants more than doubled from that evident in 1964. In 1964, the ratio was one college graduate among evangelical Protestants to every 2.5 college graduates among mainline Protestants, but by 2007, that ratio had diminished to 1.7. Nevertheless, though evangelicals closed the education gap in relationship to all other major religious traditions as well, they

TABLE 3.11
The Changing Educational Level within Religious Traditions over Time

	Year		
	1964 (%)	1996 (%)	2007 (%)
Evangelical Protestant			
Some College	11	28	24
College Graduate	6	18	20
Mainline Protestant			
Some College	15	27	24
College Graduate	15	32	34
Black Protestant			
Some College	6	23	25
College Graduate	5	19	16
Roman Catholic			
Some College	10	24	16
College Graduate	9	26	26
Unaffiliated			
Some College	16	25	16
College Graduate	14	21	32

Sources:

1964: Anti-Semitism in the United States

1996: University of Akron, Second National Survey of Religion and Politics

2007: Pew Forum Religious Landscape Survey

continued to trail most other religious traditions in the proportion of college graduates within their ranks—and by rather substantial margins.

However, it may be that the analysis to this point has failed to reveal the real extent to which evangelical Protestants are closing the gap education-ally—given that the analysis thus far has focused on all evangelicals. As a result, the presence of those older evangelicals who were less likely to attend and graduate from college has likely served to "pull down" the proportion of college educated within the ranks of evangelicals as a whole. Consequently, if one were to analyze the level of college education among those of the major religious traditions controlling for generational differences, it may be that the level of college education among the youngest generation of evangelicals mirrors that of their generational counterparts across the other religious traditions.

Table 3.12 presents data analyzing the relationship between being an evangelical and educational attainment while controlling for the particular generation in which the respondent was born. Generally speaking, the data suggest that educational differences evident between evangelicals and non-evangelicals largely reflect generational differences and not differences in commitment to higher education. Though previous generations of evangelicals were less likely to attend and graduate from college than their generational counterparts in other religious traditions, this pattern is no longer evident among the youngest generation (i.e., the millennials) of evangelicals. Millennial evangelicals exhibit rather equivalent levels of college education to that found among millennials within the other religious traditions. Perhaps, then, it is this factor of increased education among young evangelicals that leads some analysts to suggest that a new generation of evangelicals, different from previous generations of evangelicals, is emerging (e.g., Wehner 2007; Pally 2011).

TABLE 3.12
Percentage Having Some College Education within
Religious Traditions (controlling for generational cohort)

	Evangelical Protestant (%)	Mainline Protestant (%)	Black Protestant (%)	Roman Catholic (%)	Unaffiliated (%)	Total Population (%)
Millennials						
Some College	34	35	32	30	32	33
College Graduate	16	17	12	17	14	15
Generation X						
Some College	29	28	33	45	24	27
College Graduate	25	41	20	23	36	31
Baby Boomers						
Some College	28	26	25	26	26	27
College Graduate	22	39	16	29	34	29
Silent						
Some College	18	23	14	20	20	20
College Graduate	11	26	10	16	31	31

Source: Pew Forum Religious Landscape Survey, 2007

Conclusions

Evangelical Protestants constitute a sizable segment of the American people, representing the largest religious tradition within American society. Nevertheless, though they constitute a plurality of Americans religiously, they represent little more than one-quarter of the American people. Their numbers seemingly grew during the 1970s and 1980s, though subsequently their growth has largely leveled off.

Evangelicals continue to exhibit a number of social characteristics that tend to distinguish them from those affiliated with other religious traditions. In relationship to the other major religious traditions, evangelicals have a higher concentration of males. They are more likely to report being married as well as having started family life before they reach the age of 30. And evangelicals are heavily concentrated in southern states and more likely to be found in the rural areas and small towns of American life.

Nevertheless, though evangelicals largely reside in geographical locations away from the major centers of contemporary American social life, younger evangelicals have not necessarily sought to remove themselves from the cultural and intellectual institutions of American society. Not only does there appear to be a growing level of education evident among evangelicals as a whole, but it would appear that younger evangelicals are beginning to enter colleges and universities at a rate that either nearly approaches or already mirrors that evident among those of other major religious traditions.

This relative growth in educational attainment among evangelicals seemingly has several potentially important implications. First, such changes in educational attainment among evangelicals may lead to a growth in confrontation with modernity that could alter important aspects or features of evangelical orthodoxy. With increased education, basic evangelical beliefs may be "softened" as comparisons with other points of view are made. What was once perceived to be the "only way" religiously could simply become perceived to be one of various ways unto salvation, and the religious and social certainties of the past could be replaced by the ambivalence of the present (Hunter 1987). Nevertheless, it is far from clear whether growing levels of education among the coming generation of evangelicals either already has transformed or necessarily will transform evangelical Protestantism.

4

How Firm a Foundation?
The Theological Beliefs and
Religious Behavior of Evangelicals

RELIGIOUS GROUPS, whatever their nature, are defined by their distinctive religious characteristics and not by other factors that may serve also to characterize (but not define) them—for example, their particular social characteristics or political proclivities. Their religious characteristics are their defining qualities, while the latter are characteristics presently associated with those exhibiting such defining religious characteristics.

As defined here, evangelicals are those who are affiliated with certain specified denominations and congregations that are interrelated in some historical and organizational fashion (Kellstedt and Green 1993, 57–58; Smidt, Kellstedt, and Guth 2009, 10). However, given that evangelicals are conceptualized as a social and not a categorical group, it is contended that those so designated tend, as a whole, to exhibit certain distinctive, though not uniform, religious characteristics that justify their classification in this fashion. In other words, evangelicals may not be uniform in their thinking or behavior, but they are nevertheless distinctive in terms of their relative proclivity to exhibit these particular religious characteristics.

The first portion of this chapter examines the religious beliefs and behavior of evangelical Protestants in relationship to those of other traditions of the Christian faith. The second section then analyzes the extent to which evangelicals have exhibited change in their religious beliefs and behavior over time, while the last portion of the chapter examines the extent to which evangelicals are divided religiously in terms of racial, generational, or educational differences.[1]

The Religious Characteristics of Evangelical Protestants

In this section of the chapter we examine the relative importance evangelicals attribute to their religious lives, the content of their religious beliefs, and the nature of their religious behavior. Once again, we examine the extent to which the tendencies of evangelical Protestants either mirror or deviate from those associated with other major religious traditions.

Religious Salience

Religious salience taps the relative importance that one attributes to religion in one's life, and evangelicals generally attest to religion being "very important" to their lives (see table 4.1). When provided with four response options that ranged from "not at all important" to "very important," nearly four-fifths (79 percent) of all evangelicals in the Religious Landscape Survey responded that religion was very important in their lives, with only Black Protestants being more likely to respond similarly (85 percent). In contrast, only a little more than half of mainline Protestants (52 percent) and Catholics (56 percent) did so. Only among the religiously unaffiliated, then, does one find a majority (58 percent) who report that religion is either "not too important" or "not at all important" in their lives (data not shown).

Religious Beliefs

Spiritual Phenomena

Evangelicals, like those who are affiliated with the other major Christian religious traditions, overwhelmingly believe in God. Except for the religiously unaffiliated, it matters little the particular religious tradition with which one is affiliated regarding whether one reports a belief in God, as almost all (97 to 99 percent) do so regardless of their tradition. Even an overwhelming majority of the religiously unaffiliated report a belief in God (70 percent).

Where differences become evident is in terms of their certainty that God exists and the nature of God's being. Among those who believe in God, evangelicals and Black Protestants are far more certain that God exists than are mainline Protestants and Catholics, as a little more than 90 percent of the former two groups and approximately 75 percent of the latter two groups express certainty in the existence of God. Even more than one-half of the unaffiliated indicate that they are absolutely certain God exists (which represents a little more than one-third of all the unaffiliated when those who do not believe in God are included).

TABLE 4.1
Religious Beliefs by Religious Tradition

	Evangelical Protestant (%)	Mainline Protestant (%)	Black Protestant (%)	Roman Catholic (%)	Unaffiliated (%)
Religious Salience					
Religion "very important" in one's life	79	52	85	56	16
Religious Beliefs					
Believe in God	99	97	99	97	70
Absolutely certain of God's existence	91	75	92	74	51
View God as a person, not as a force	80	64	72	61	41
Believe there is a heaven	86	77	91	82	41
Believe there is a hell	82	56	82	60	30
Completely agree miracles still occur	61	42	58	47	25
Completely agree angels and demons active	61	31	60	35	18

Source: Pew Forum Religious Landscape Survey, 2007

Note: Entries show percent agreeing with statement

Differences across the religious traditions are further evident in terms of whether one conceives of God as a person or as an impersonal force. All those affiliated with the major Christian traditions understand God more in terms of a person than as an impersonal force, with approximately two-thirds or more indicating they believe God is a person. However, evangelical Protestants are the most likely to do so (80 percent), while it is the religiously unaffiliated who are most prone to believe in God as an impersonal force, with a majority of the unaffiliated responding to that effect.

Evangelicals, like those affiliated with the other Christian traditions, typically believe in a heaven (86 percent do so), though they, along with Black Protestants, are the most inclined to believe in a hell. Evangelicals are also the most likely to state that they "completely agree"[2] that miracles still occur and that angels and demons remain active in our world. Within every religious tradition examined in table 4.1, there is a greater percentage who report that they believe fully in heaven than they believe fully in hell (or fully in miracles than fully in angels/demons), but the differences in the level of belief between the two are smallest for evangelicals. Thus, for evangelicals, belief in the one is seemingly tied to belief in the other.[3]

Thus, overall, these data suggest that evangelicals believe in a world that transcends the material world. They believe in God, but a God who is a person and not simply an impersonal force. This spiritual world extends beyond simply the presence of a God, as they believe in angels, demons, and the ability of divine healing as well as the occurrence of miracles. And they tend to express a good deal of certainty in their religious beliefs.

Religious Authority

Evangelicals are also more prone to look to religious texts, and particularly the Bible, when seeking religious guidance on matters of daily life and making decisions related to matters of right and wrong. Evangelicals assign absolute authority only to scripture, in that it is seen as God's revelation to human beings; as a result, the "Bible prevails over any other type of instruction in all matters, ranging from the practical to the moral to the spiritual" (Bielo 2009, 53).

When the Religious Landscape Survey asked people what they consulted most for guidance related to questions of right and wrong, respondents were provided with a limited number of responses: religious teachings and beliefs, philosophy and reason, practical experience and common sense, or scientific information. The two most prevalent answers given by the American public were either religious teachings or practical experience (see table 4.2). However, those most likely to look to religious teachings and beliefs were evangelical Protestants, as a majority (54 percent) of evangelicals indicated such. In fact, they were the only tradition in which a majority of the members so responded, as those within the other traditions typically responded that they relied on practical experiences on such matters.

The question of religious authority was posed in a somewhat different manner in the Religious Diversity Survey of 2002–2003. In this case, respondents were provided with just two options: with the Bible posed as one

TABLE 4.2
Views on Religious Authority by Religious Tradition

	Evangelical Protestant (%)	Mainline Protestant (%)	Black Protestant (%)	Roman Catholic (%)	Unaffiliated (%)
Which do you look to most for guidance on questions of right and wrong?[a]					
Religious teachings and beliefs	54	25	44	23	6
Philosophy and reason	4	10	5	10	16
Practical experience/common sense	40	61	48	59	68
Scientific information	2	5	3	7	10
Which of these comes closest to your views concerning your spiritual guidance?[b]					
I mostly trust the Bible	73	49	76	37	18
I mostly trust my personal experiences	23	46	21	55	78
Other	4	6	4	8	4
I believe evolution is best explanation[a]	24	51	38	58	72
Doesn't matter what you believe as long as you are a good person[c]	33	59	39	80	86
Basis for obtaining rewarding life after death[d]					
Right beliefs	52	33	41	21	18
Right behavior	35	54	49	71	65
Both/Neither (volunteered)	13	13	10	9	18

Sources:
[a] Pew Forum Religious Landscape Survey, 2007
[b] Religion and Diversity Survey, 2002–2003
[c] Henry Institute National Survey on Religion and Public Life, 2008
[d] University of Akron, Fifth National Survey of Religion and Politics, 2008

Note: Entries for third and fourth items show percent agreeing with statement source for spiritual guidance and personal experiences the other. Under these conditions, there was a greater tendency for respondents, regardless of their religious tradition, to report that they placed their trust in the Bible than when the option was posed more broadly in terms of "religious teachings and beliefs."[4]

When posed in this manner, roughly three-quarters of both evangelical Protestants and Black Protestants indicated that they trusted the Bible, with Black Protestants slightly exceeding evangelical Protestants in doing so (see table 4.2). Nearly a majority of mainline Protestants (49 percent) cited the Bible as their source for guidance, but approximately an equal percentage (46 percent) stated that they trusted their personal experience. As a religious tradition, Catholics have historically placed less emphasis on the Bible than have Protestants, and, of the Christian traditions examined in table 4.2, they were the least likely to cite the Bible as their source for spiritual guidance, as just a little more than one-third (37 percent) did so. Only the religiously unaffiliated were less likely than the Catholics to respond in such a fashion.

Table 4.2 also analyzes differences in beliefs related to whether "evolution is the best explanation for the origins of human life on earth." This belief is analyzed here under the heading of religious authority because, at least in the eyes of some, evolution is seen as challenging the truth of the biblical account of creation (and thereby the authority of scripture).[5]

Clearly, evangelicals stand largely apart from their fellow Christians in terms of their reported belief in evolution. Only about one-quarter of all evangelicals agree that "evolution is the best explanation for the origins of human life on earth." Even Black Protestants, who have typically approximated evangelicals in the religious beliefs examined in table 4.1, diverge substantially from evangelicals in this matter, as nearly two-fifths (38 percent) of Black Protestants affirm that evolution is the best explanation.

Why, then, do evangelicals seemingly stand relatively alone in their general refusal to express belief in evolution? One cannot say anything with certainty based on this table. However, given the history of evangelicalism in America,[6] it is likely that evangelicals are more prone to view evolution less in terms of a "scientific explanation" and more as symbolic matter concerning whether faith or science serves as the source of truth. In this regard, it is noteworthy that, of all the religious traditions examined in table 4.2, evangelicals were the least likely to indicate that they consulted science for guidance religiously. Thus, for many evangelicals, evolution does not constitute some narrow scientific explanation[7] of how creation unfolded as it represents an alternative explanation of Creation advanced by a competing system of authority to that of the Bible—namely, science. When perceived in this fashion, subscribing to a belief in evolution becomes a test of one's religious faith, as agreeing "evolution is the best explanation" represents a competing explanation to the creation process outlined in the Bible (and not as a developmental process through which the Creator might have acted).

Thus, overall, evangelicals place a heavy emphasis on textual materials, particularly the Bible, as the basis for their religious authority, despite the fact that evangelical Protestantism is commonly viewed as emphasizing religious experiences (e.g., "having had a born-again experience"). Evangelicals assign the principle of absolute authority only to scripture, and consequently, the "Bible prevails over any other type of instruction in all matters" (Bielo 2009, 53). Given this emphasis on religious texts, science is less viewed as an additional, and complementary, basis[8] for religious interpretation and understanding and more as a competing basis of authority with regard to religious understanding.

Bases for Salvation

Religious faiths typically promote certain distinctive religious beliefs as well as precribe particular forms of religious behavior. Though most, if not all, religious faiths emphasize both, the relative emphasis placed on subscribing to the right religious beliefs versus exhibiting the right religious behavior varies from one religion to another.

Even within Christianity itself, different traditions of the Christian faith have come to place greater emphasis on the one rather than the other. This is the case, in part, because the Bible contains certain verses that stand in tension with one another, and different faith traditions within Christianity have chosen to place different emphases on these particular biblical texts. Take, for example, the teachings of Martin Luther (1483–1546), a German priest and professor of theology, who is credited with initiating the Protestant Reformation. Luther drew upon the text of the Apostle Paul penned in the New Testament book of Ephesians (chapter 2, verses 8–9) that reads, "For it is by grace you have been saved, through faith—and this not from yourselves, it is the gift of God—not by works, so that no one can boast" (New International Version), in order to formulate his doctrine of justification contending that salvation or redemption is a gift of God's grace. Thus, for Luther and Protestants historically, there has been a much greater emphasis on the fact that salvation is not earned by good deeds but only as a free gift through faith in Jesus Christ.

Yet, on the other hand, the New Testament book of James (chapter 2, verses 17, 20, and 26) notes that "faith without works" is useless or dead. Consequently, other Christian traditions have placed greater emphasis on works (if not as a basis for salvation, then at least as a mark of redemption). It may be that acts or good deeds do not necessarily provide salvation (in that it is a gift), but that salvation cannot result simply from holding the right beliefs either (in that faith without good works is dead). From these two biblical passages we can see how interpreters of biblical texts may hold both faith and works as reflecting evidence of salvation, yet within different contexts over different points in time, choose to emphasize one or the other, so that members of different Christian traditions may become somewhat more prone to emphasize one over the other—even while seeking to balance the two.

The data presented in the bottom half of table 4.2 reveal that evangelicals place much greater emphasis on the right religious beliefs than do those in most other major religious traditions. When asked whether being a good person was more important than what one believed, evangelical Protestants were the least likely to report agreement with the statement, with only one-third doing so. The same pattern is evident when the question is posed in terms of whether it is right beliefs or right behavior that serves as the basis for obtaining a rewarding life after death, as evangelicals were, once again, the most prone to emphasize the right beliefs (with slightly more than one-half of evangelical respondents choosing that response).

Thus, overall, evangelicals hold that the basis for salvation rests more substantially on subscription to the right religious beliefs rather than on the exhibition of righteous behavior. Though evangelicals would likely note that subscription to these particular beliefs should also be associated with religious deeds, such righteous deeds do not "earn" one's salvation. Rather, evangelicals hold to the biblical admonition to "Believe on the Lord Jesus Christ, and you will be saved" (Acts 16:31, New International Version) as the basis for salvation.

Religious Pluralism

The growing religious diversity of American society may well prompt religious adherents, regardless of their particular faith, to wonder about the credibility of the truth claims of one's own religion in light of the presence of other religious faiths. As noted by Wuthnow (2005, 99), "Among the thorniest questions that religious diversity poses for all the major religious traditions is whether or not they can sustain their historical claims to being uniquely true or at least better than other traditions in relating people to the sacred." How, then, do evangelicals view other, non-Christian, religious faiths and those who adhere to such faiths?

First, like most Americans, evangelical Protestants believe that religious diversity has been good for America.[9] Such a question was posed in the Religious Diversity Survey of 2002–2003 and, as can be seen from table 4.3,

TABLE 4.3
Views on Religious Diversity by Religious Tradition

	Evangelical Protestant (%)	Mainline Protestant (%)	Black Protestant (%)	Roman Catholic (%)	Unaffiliated (%)
Religious diversity has been good for America[a]	81	92	86	89	84
All major religions teach basically same things[a]	64	74	75	83	78
All major religions equally good ways of knowing about God[a]	25	44	35	52	57
Christianity is best way to understand God[a]	79	65	78	53	24
High level of comparative religious knowledge[a]	42	35	29	25	33
Only my own religion leads to eternal life[b]	36	12	34	16	x

Sources:

[a] Religion and Diversity Survey, 2002–2003

[b] Pew Forum Religious Landscape Survey, 2007

Note: Entries show percent agreeing with statement

x – not asked of religiously unaffiliated respondents

more than four-fifths of evangelicals (81 percent) reported agreement with that statement.[10] Yet despite this high level of consensus about the positive benefits of diversity, evangelicals still ranked last in terms of such agreement when compared to the other four religious traditions. Clearly there is a small segment of evangelicals who either are uncertain about the matter or think religious diversity has not been good for American life and society. Nevertheless, even evangelicals stand overwhelmingly in agreement with the general benefits of religious diversity.

But, when thinking about the matter, one may envision this religious diversity more historically in terms of the many Christian (largely Protestant) denominations that arose within the American context or in terms of the more recent religious diversity brought about by the influx of immigrants from non-Christian faith traditions to the United States. Hence, when responding to the question of religious diversity, it is unclear just what may have served as the frame of reference when respondents answered the question.

How, then, do evangelicals view other non-Christian religious faiths? Do they see every major religion (Christianity, Judaism, Islam, Hinduism, Buddhism, etc.) as a means by which to know God? Do they think that all major religions embody truth and largely teach the same things, or are evangelicals rather exclusivistic in terms of which particular faiths may be efficacious in terms of achieving "salvation"?[11]

Again, responses to these questions are likely shaped by the particular frames of reference the respondent employs when trying to answer such questions. When one thinks about the Abrahamic traditions, there are a greater number of commonalities in terms of basic religious understandings (e.g., a creator God, the obligation to help those less fortunate than oneself, similar notions of what is known as the Golden Rule) than when one thinks more in terms of Hinduism or Buddhism. So, once again, how one chooses to respond to this statement will likely be shaped in part by the particular religions one uses as a reference in formulating one's response.

Nevertheless, regardless of the frame of reference that may have been employed, the vast majority of Americans agreed that "all major religions basically teach the same things." Evangelicals were, once again, the least likely to affirm the statement, though nearly two-thirds (64 percent) did so. Consequently, when religious pluralism is viewed from this angle, evangelical Protestants overwhelmingly affirm that all major religions teach many of the same things.

However, despite this recognition, it does not follow that those who so agree necessarily view all religions as being equivalent in nature. Some religions may provide deeper insights, promote different means by which to comprehend the divine, or result in different forms of behavior that, in the end, serve to undermine the perceived equivalency of such faiths in the mind of the beholder. Consequently, table 4.3 also analyzes the extent to which those of different religious traditions are willing to affirm that "all major religions are equally good ways of knowing about God," and the data reveal that evangelicals as a whole are the most reluctant to grant any equivalency to all major religions. Only one-quarter of evangelicals were willing to affirm such a statement, the lowest percentage found among the major religious traditions analyzed in table 4.3. However, most mainline Protestants and Black Protestants were not willing to affirm such a statement either, while only a bare majority of Catholics did so.

Actually, most members of these four Christian traditions maintained that Christianity represented the religious faith that provided the best means by which to understand God. When asked, the overwhelming majority of each of the three Protestant traditions stood in agreement with the statement that Christianity was the best way to know God. Evangelical Protestants and Black Protestants stood most firmly in agreement with the statement, as nearly four of five of both traditions, as well as two-thirds of mainline Protestants, affirmed such a statement. Only a bare majority of Catholics (53 percent), however, responded similarly. Not surprising, the religiously unaffiliated were the most inclined to disagree, as only about one-quarter held that Christianity was necessarily the best way to understand God.

However, even though evangelicals may believe that some religions provide better means to know about God than do other such religions, they nevertheless remain relatively reluctant to claim that only those who adhere to their particular religious faith will necessarily be "saved" or enjoy "eternal life." In response to a question inquiring about the relative efficacy of different faiths, only about one in three evangelical Protestants (36 percent) indicated that "only my religion leads to eternal life." Black Protestants tended to mirror evangelicals in this regard, while only about one in six Catholics and one in nine mainline Protestants made similar claims. Thus, even though evangelical Protestants were the most likely of the various religious traditions to make exclusivistic claims about their religion, they constitute a minority among evangelicals; clearly the overwhelming majority of evangelical Protestants refrained from making such claims.[12]

How does one reconcile, then, the fact that only one-third of evangelicals hold that "only my religion leads to eternal life" with the fact that, as shown in table 3.1, evangelicals also overwhelming claim that "Jesus is the only way to salvation"? We cannot know for sure just how evangelicals who subscribe to both positions come to reconcile these seemingly contradictory positions. But there are several possibilities. First, just what constitutes "other religions" can mean different things to the respondents. Perhaps, when answering this question, evangelicals were more likely to think of other religions in terms of other denominations within the Christian faith rather than other religions outside of Christianity. Such a response, of course, hardly reflects the broader understanding of religious diversity that this set of questions sought to address.

A second possibility is that such evangelicals may hold that "the saving work of Jesus Christ" reflects a "universal reconciliation" that paves the way for all to be saved regardless of the specific faith to which one adheres. A number of recent, and widely sold, books by evangelicals seemingly advance a theology of universal salvation,[13] and some have suggested that the popularity of these books indicate that evangelicals may be shifting their theology (e.g., Beal 2010). Based on such a notion of "universal reconciliation," faithful Muslims would also be saved through the work of Jesus Christ, as would be faithful Jews, and so forth.

A third possibility is simply that evangelicals hold these two beliefs simultaneously without necessarily thinking about their seemingly contradictory nature and, as a result, make no effort to reconcile the two positions. This phenomenon of holding contradictory attitudes and opinions is not uncommon among Americans, having been well documented in many studies of public opinion related to political matters. Thus, given its occurrence in other domains of thought, it could well be that holding seemingly contradictory positions would also be evident in terms of religious thought and opinion.

Religious Traditionalism

As noted in chapter 2, each tradition has traditionalists within its ranks who seek to preserve its long-standing historic interpretations and understanding of sacred texts as well as its particular long-standing liturgical practices. Likewise, each tradition has those who wish to adopt alternative, more recent, theological interpretations, who believe that the church's theological interpretations should stand in greater conformity with contemporary scientific understandings, and/or who desire (or choose) to express their religious faith through alternative practices of liturgy or behavior. And each tradition has its "centrists," those who basically fall somewhere between the two alternative options.

Analytically, this "traditionalist-modernist" divide can be differentiated from other religious variables such as religious salience or religious commitment. Those who are theological "modernists" may well attribute the same levels of the importance of religion in their lives as do those who are "traditionalists" theologically; likewise, they may exhibit the same levels of church attendance or engage in other religious practices with the same devotion and faithfulness as well—despite their differences in theological perspectives and interpretations. Based on this analytical distinction, where do evangelical Protestants fall, and how do they compare on these matters to those in other religious traditions?

In the Religious Landscape Survey, respondents were asked which of the following came closer to their thinking: their church or denomination should (a) preserve its traditional beliefs and practices, (b) adjust its beliefs and practices in light of new circumstances, or (c) adopt modern beliefs and practices. Since this query referenced one's particular church or denomination, only those who were affiliated with a church/denomination were asked the question. And while other means might be adopted to tap this traditionalist-modernist divide,[14] this question certainly does represent an effort to ascertain just where people stand on such matters.

Evangelical Protestants tend to be rather traditionalistic in their views of the historic teaching and practices of their church and denominational life, as nearly two-thirds of all evangelicals (65 percent) responded that their church or denomination should "preserve its traditional practices and beliefs," while one-quarter of evangelicals (27 percent) indicated that their church or denomination should adjust its beliefs and practices in light of new circumstances (data not shown). A somewhat lower percentage of Black Protestants (55 percent), but a majority nonetheless, also affirmed a traditionalist position, while one-third (32 percent) indicated "adjustment." In contrast, less than two-fifths of mainline Protestants and Catholics gave the "preserve" response, while a plurality of each tradition responded that their church or denomination should adjust its beliefs and practices in light of new circumstances. Less than one in six, regardless of religious tradition, indicated that their church or denomination should simply adopt modern religious beliefs and practices, though evangelical Protestants (with 8 percent) were about half as likely to do so as those of the other three Christian traditions.

Religious Behavior

Sociologists of religion have long contended that the importance of religious beliefs in the life of the individual is largely tied to the frequency and character of one's social interaction with others who share a common religious perspective. Without such regular interaction, one's religious practices are likely to diminish in regularity, religious ties are likely to become less salient, and religious beliefs are likely to lose much of their relevance, if not their plausibility (White 1968; Berger 1967).[15] Consequently, though it is important to ascertain the religious beliefs held by evangelicals, it is just as important to understand the nature of their religious practices—particularly in terms of the extent to which they interact with others of their religious faith.

Religious affiliation in the past was largely a reflection of one's ethnic heritage, and neighborhoods and communities a century ago were far more homogeneous religiously. Societies then were more agriculturally based, with transportation and communication structures being much more limited; given these circumstances, one's associates were primarily confined to those within the local community—people who largely shared similar religious beliefs and engaged in similar religious practices. Presumably, therefore, within such contexts, there was far greater day-to-day social interaction with those who shared the same religious faith, with their patterns of social interaction serving to sustain religious beliefs and practices far more easily than in today's society.

However, a number of scholars (e.g., Roof and McKinney 1987; Olson 1993; Hoge, Johnson, and Luidens 1994) have contended that the nature of American religious life has changed substantially over the past decades, as religion has increasingly become detached from its older social moorings. Rising educational levels and increased geographical mobility have, for many, weakened old social relationships that previously existed between being members of particular ethnic groups and religious affiliations, while increased social and cultural assimilation have diminished many religious group differences that were previously linked to custom and heritage. In the wake of these changes, old religious loyalties have weakened, enabling new religious affiliations and identities to emerge in their wake, with religion becoming more fluid and more driven by personal preferences today and less by ties to institutional forms of religious expression.

Still, such increased religious individualism and increased cultural pluralism need not necessarily lead to a decline in religious belief and practices at either the individual or societal level. With subsequent greater urbanization, increased ease of transportation, and expanding modes of communication, one's range of personal contacts has likely grown and one's choices regarding with whom one may wish to associate has likely expanded. And, when given a choice, people tend to interact with people like themselves (McPherson, Smith-Lovin, and Cook 2001), and their personal networks actually become more homogeneous (Fischer 1977).

Thus, the processes of growing urbanization and increased cultural pluralism may not neccessarily lead to more heterogeneous social ties among individuals; rather, the major effect of such changes is simply to increase people's *choice* with regard to whom one associates (Olson 1993, 35). And it is this freedom to choose as one's friends and associates those who largely resemble oneself that leads to the creation of distinctive subcultures, "communities" based more upon sharing common beliefs, values, and practices than sharing a particular geographic location.[16] Certainly the strength of these different subcultures vary, but the more members of a subculture choose to associate with one another, the stronger the subculture.[17]

For religious communities, this gathering together and associating with one another can occur in a variety of ways, but much of it centers around the religious congregation with which one is affiliated, as "the congregation remains the bedrock of the American religious system" (Warner 1994, 54).

Weekly worship certainly provides opportunities for members of a religious community to gather together, as do a host of other potential church activities ranging from Bible study groups, communal prayer meetings, participation in small groups, church socials, and volunteering together for particular church and community endeavors.

Given these potential opportunities for social interaction on a relatively frequent basis, it is not surprising that one's friendship patterns and social networks are also frequently linked to the congregation of which one is a part. People typically choose their congregations based largely on the theological or religious beliefs that they share with other members of the congregation (Putnam and Campbell 2010, 170).[18] And if it is true that people tend, when given a choice, to interact with people like themselves, then congregations become natural sites for friendship formation and the development of social networks. Thus, as noted by Djupe and Gilbert (2009, 3), this "choice of where to attend religious services—what church to call one's own—carries with it significant consequences for the everyday lives of Americans."[19]

Religious Practices

Whether understood in terms of religious behavior or religious practice,[20] evangelical Protestants are somewhat distinctive in the levels to which they engage in certain religious behavior. Table 4.4 examines the frequency with which various religious practices are reported by those affiliated with different religious traditions. Perhaps a beginning point in examining the religious behavior of Americans would be the extent to which they choose to become members of the church, as one may affiliate with a denomination or congregation without becoming a member.[21] As the data reveal, those affiliated with the four Christian traditions exhibit somewhat different patterns of church membership. Approximately three-quarters of evangelical Protestants (74 percent) report church membership, though Black Protestants are somewhat more likely to do so. In contrast, only about two-thirds of mainline Protestants and Roman Catholics report church membership.

However, probably the most commonly used measure of religious behavior is one's level of church or worship service attendance. Research has shown that church attendance exerts a strong influence on individuals, shaping attitudes and behavior within religious, civic, and political life (e.g., Lenski 1963; White 1968; Smidt 2008; Putnam and Campbell 2010, chapter 13). And evangelical Protestants, as a whole, choose to be regularly involved with others in public worship (see table 4.4). Roughly three-fifths of all evangelicals and Black Protestants report that they attend church on a weekly basis, but

TABLE 4.4
Religious Behavior by Religious Tradition

	Evangelical Protestant (%)	Mainline Protestant (%)	Black Protestant (%)	Roman Catholic (%)	Unaffiliated (%)
Member of a Church	74	64	83	67	x
Level of Church Attendance					
Never/Seldom	13	23	12	19	x
Weekly	59	35	59	42	x
Participation in Religious Small Group					
Never	23	45	20	52	x
Weekly	42	17	45	13	x
Participation in Church Social Activities					
Never	14	21	18	33	x
Monthly	51	37	55	25	x
Read the Bible					
Never	9	27	8	36	59
Weekly	60	28	61	22	10
Personal Prayer					
Never	1	3	1	3	32
Daily	79	55	82	59	23

Source: Pew Forum Religious Landscape Survey, 2007

Note: Entries show percent reporting activity levels

x – not asked of religiously unaffiliated respondents

only a little more than two-fifths of Roman Catholics and a little more than one-third of mainline Protestants do so.

However, religious behavior is not limited to one's relative frequency of church attendance. During the time between their weekly worship services, churches frequently offer a variety of educational, social, and religious activities for those who wish to participate. And, during the past several decades, small groups have proliferated within American society (Wuthnow 1994a, 1994b). Of course, the presence of small groups is not limited to religious life, but many of the small groups that are evident in American life are tied to the religious sphere—whether it be Bible study groups, prayer groups, youth groups, singles groups, church sports teams, or church family nights. The dramatic proliferation of small groups over the course of the past several decades is seemingly tied to the changing society in which we live and the desire of people to live in some kind of community with others (Wuthnow 1993). It is in these small groups that members of a congregation can come to feel closer to each other, find friends, share intimate problems, and care for each other. As such, then, participation in small groups helps to foster a greater sense of belonging and a greater commitment to the larger congregation as well (Dougherty and Whitehead 2011).

When one inquires about religious small group activities (e.g., joint Bible studies, weekly prayer meetings, religious educational programs, etc.), two-fifths of evangelicals indicate that they participate in such activities on a weekly basis, and a little more than one-half (51 percent) further indicate that they participate in church social activities on a monthly basis. In these various public activities, evangelicals largely mirror or trail slightly the levels reported by Black Protestants concerning these endeavors—though both evangelical Protestants and Black Protestants substantially outdistance mainline Protestants and Catholics in the frequency with which they engage in these three public religious activities.

Evangelicals also maintain an active devotional life.[22] Roughly four-fifths of all evangelicals (79 percent) report that they pray on a daily basis, and three-fifths (60 percent) state that they read the Bible at least on a weekly basis. Once again, evangelicals largely mirror Black Protestants in the levels to which they report taking part in these activities, and they tend to engage in these acts of religious piety with substantially greater frequency than do mainline Protestants or Catholics.

Overall, therefore, evangelical Protestants and Black Protestants tend to mirror each other in terms of their religious practices, though the percentage of Black Protestants who reported such practices tended to exceed slightly the percentage of evangelical Protestants who did so. On the other hand, mainline Protestants and Catholics not only reported relatively similar levels of frequency with regard to those same religious practices, but they engaged in such activities at a much lower rate than did evangelical and Black Protestants.

However, the greater the perception of similarity in religious beliefs with members of one's congregation, the greater may be the likelihood of one attending worship services, as social similarities, along with shared attitudes and values, foster social connections (McPherson, Smith-Lovin, and Cook 2001, 415). Consequently, table 4.5 examines the relationship between one's level of church attendance and perceptions about the relative extent to which members of one's congregations hold religious beliefs similar to one's own. Clearly, those who perceive a greater level of similarity in religious beliefs to those of other members of their congregation exhibit higher levels of worship attendance.

TABLE 4.5
Frequency of Church Attendance by Number of People
at Church with Same Religious Beliefs (controlling for religious tradition)

	Number of People at Church with Same Religious Beliefs		
Frequency of Church Attendance	*Some/Few (%)*	*Most (%)*	*Nearly All (%)*
All Respondents			
Few Times/Year	38	21	11
Monthly	26	24	18
Weekly	36	55	71
Controlling for Religious Tradition			
Evangelical Protestant			
Few Times/Year	27	16	6
Weekly	41	62	78
Mainline Protestant			
Few Times/Year	46	21	13
Weekly	38	45	64
Black Protestant			
Few Times/Year	22	10	9
Weekly	34	77	76
Roman Catholic			
Few Times/Year	33	22	17
Weekly	50	54	61

Source: University of Akron, Fifth National Survey of Religion and Politics, 2008

But it is also true that the likelihood of reporting that one's church members hold similar religious beliefs as oneself varies by one's religious tradition. In fact, evangelical Protestants are the most likely to report such—with 58 percent reporting that nearly all the people at the church hold the same religious beliefs as oneself (data not shown). Mainline Protestants are least likely to do so (40 percent), with Black Protestants and Roman Catholics falling in between (at 50 percent and 48 percent, respectively).

Given this relationship, the bottom portion of table 4.5 examines how perceptions of greater similarities in religious beliefs among one's fellow parishioners are related to increased levels of church attendance, while controlling for religious tradition. And, as can be seen from the table, this relationship generally holds across each of the religious traditions (though not fully for Black Protestants). Thus, one of the reasons evangelical Protestants exhibit the highest level of weekly church attendance is because they are the most likely to report that "nearly all" who attend their church hold religious beliefs similar to their own; conversely, because mainline Protestants are the least likely to report such, they exhibit the lowest level of weekly church attendance (see table 4.5).

Still, though perceived levels of similarities in religious beliefs shape the frequency of church attendance, it does not fully account for such differences. Even among only those who report that "nearly all" within their congregation hold similar religious beliefs, there are differences in church attendance across religious traditions. Thus, for example, among those who report "nearly all" in their congregation hold similar religious beliefs, evangelical Protestants still report a higher level of weekly church attendance than mainline Protestants (78 percent versus 64 percent, respectively).

But how does an individual come to know whether one's fellow parishioners hold similar religious beliefs? Without additional involvement, fellowship, or discussion outside of the common worship experience, members are relatively free to take whatever they wish from the public worship service and process that information according to their own predisposition (Djupe and Gilbert 2002). Without interacting and talking with others within the congregation, it would be difficult to discern from the worship service alone the extent to which congregational members subscribe to religious beliefs similar to one's own.

Certainly one place in which one can get to know members of the congregation and the nature of their religious beliefs more fully is by participation in religious small groups. Within these smaller groups, participants engage in more personal relationships with other members of the congregation. These interactions may reveal that others hold religious beliefs similar to, or quite different from, what one believes. However, given that people typically are initially drawn to their particular congregations based largely on the theological or religious beliefs that they share with other members of the congregation (Putnam and Campbell 2010, 170), one would anticipate that greater involvement with their fellow church members through participation in religious small groups would likely serve to confirm, rather than disconfirm, such similarities in religious beliefs.

In fact, this is the case. The greater the regularity with which one participates in religious small groups, the greater the likelihood one perceives others within the congregation to hold religious beliefs similar to one's own (data not shown). For example, among those with a religious affiliation but who never participate in religious small groups, only 37 percent of the respondents reported that they believed that nearly all in their congregation held religious beliefs similar to one's own beliefs. However, this percentage monotonically increases as one moves from "never" participates in small groups to participates "weekly" in religious small groups—so that among those who report weekly participation, nearly a full two-thirds (64 percent) claim that nearly all members of their congregation share religious beliefs similar to their own.[23]

Friendship Patterns

Religious congregations constitute the most common form of voluntary associations within American social life both in terms of membership and attendance (Smidt et al. 2008, chapter 3). And, given that people choose houses of worship based on sharing similar religious beliefs, it is not surprising that one's local church may serve as an important site for the formation of friendships. In addition, the fact that one has "trusted friends in the congregation who believe the same way" as oneself serves to reinforce one's sense that "these beliefs are good and true" (Wuthnow 2007a, 117).

People who do not have friends in the house of worship they attend are unlikely to remain associated with the congregation, and should they stay, they are generally not active members of the congregation (Snow, Zurcher, and Eckland-Olson 1980; Olson 1989). Most Americans (56 percent) report that they have at least one close friend who is part of the congregation they attend (Putnam and Campbell 2010, 32), with nearly all congregational members (93 percent) reporting at least one close personal friend in their house of worship (Wuthnow 2004a, 214). Nevertheless, the greater the proportion of friendships drawn from one's congregation, the stronger is the commitment to the congregation and one's religious faith (White 1969; Cornwall 1989; Cavendish et al. 1998; Stroope 2012).

The Pew Religious Landscape Survey did not inquire about the proportion of the respondent's friends who were associated with the house of worship one attends, but the Henry Institute National Survey on Religion and Public Life did so (with those who reported that they never attended church not being asked the question). Friendship patterns vary by religious tradition affiliation, as about one-third of evangelical Protestants and Roman Catholics (30 percent) report that half or more of their friends attend their house of worship, while slightly fewer Black Protestants (28 percent) and far fewer mainline Protestants (21 percent) do so (data not shown).

Why might this be the case? In part, it is likely related to different patterns of church attendance. As can be seen from table 4.6, one's level of church attendance clearly shapes one's friendship patterns. Regardless of religious affiliation, the percentage who report that half or more of their friends are drawn from the church they attend increases as one's frequency of church attendance increases.[24] In other words, as one moves from attending church a few times a year to going to church weekly, the percentage responding that half or more of their friends attend the same house of worship consistently

TABLE 4.6
Proportion of Friends Attending Same House of
Worship by Church Attendance (controlling for religious tradition)

Proportion of Friends Who Attend One's House of Worship	Frequency of Church Attendance		
	Few times a year (%)	Monthly or more (%)	Weekly or more (%)
All Respondents			
None	43	22	16
Less than half	44	51	45
Half or more	14	27	39
Controlling for Religious Tradition			
Evangelical Protestant			
None	30	22	11
Less than half	59	50	44
Half or more	11	29	45
Mainline Protestant			
None	52	15	16
Less than half	44	56	40
Half or more	5	29	44
Black Protestant			
None	73	25	18
Less than half	27	52	51
Half or more	0	22	31
Roman Catholic			
None	30	22	7
Less than half	48	46	36
Half or more	22	33	57

Source: Henry Institute National Survey on Religion and Public Life, 2008

increases. And, generally speaking, about half of weekly church attendees report that one-half or more of their friends attend the same church they do. Thus, the more one attends church, the greater is the likelihood that most of one's friends are part of the same local church.

Nevertheless, though this pattern is consistent, there are differences across the four religious traditions examined. Nearly three-fifths of Catholics (57 percent) who attend Mass weekly indicate that more than half of their friends are drawn from the parish church they attend.[25] In contrast, only about one-third (31 percent) of weekly attending Black Protestants report the same.[26] Mainline and evangelical Protestants exhibit rather similar patterns and fall in the middle of these two extremes.

Even beyond the effects of church attendance on friendship patterns, the more involved an individual is in church life, the greater the likelihood that one's closest friends are drawn from the congregation to which they belong.[27] For example, increased levels of small group participation within the congregation increases the likelihood of reporting a larger proportion of friends drawn from the congregation with which one is affiliated (data not shown). This is even true for those who attend church regularly, as among those who attend church weekly—the more one participates in a small group, the greater the likelihood that a higher proportion of one's friends will be drawn from the congregation one attends (data not shown).[28]

Change over Time

Over the past several decades, there appears to be some growth in the number of those who exhibit a "privatized faith," where individuals may claim a set of religious beliefs (and even engage in certain private religious activities such as personal prayer), but remain disconnected from religious institutions. These "believers but not belongers" (Davie 1994) largely eschew any involvement in an "organized" form of religion, evident, in part, by the fact that those who were religiously unaffiliated nevertheless report a wide variety of different religious beliefs. This same phenomenon of "believing but not belonging" is sometimes captured through the response of some who indicate that they are "spiritual, but not religious."

To what extent, then, have the religious beliefs and behavior of evangelical Protestants changed over time? Is there any evidence of a decline in their level of adherence to certain religious beliefs or their level of church attendance over the past several decades? And are the relative differences in religious beliefs and behavior currently evident between evangelicals and those of other faith traditions actually greater than in the past?

These questions are addressed in table 4.7. It should be noted, however, that the analysis is limited by the particular questions asked in earlier surveys. Here, as in the previous chapter, we employ the Anti-Semitism in the United States survey data gathered in 1964 as the basis for comparison. Consequently, if the 1964 survey did not ask a question related to certain beliefs and behavior, it is impossible to assess the level of change in such beliefs/behavior. In other words, this effort at assessment of change over time was not done by "picking and choosing" which particular results to present; rather, it presents as many comparisons over time as permitted by the data.

Given these particular limitations, one can see from table 4.7 that the patterns of religious change vary by religious tradition. For some traditions,

TABLE 4.7
Changing Religious Beliefs and Behavior of Religious Traditions

	Year		
	1964 (%)	1996 (%)	2007 (%)
Evangelical Protestant			
High religious salience	81	76	79
Believe in God	96	96	99
Jesus is only way to salvation	76	x	88[a]
Believe devil exists/is active	77	88	85[a]
Believe in life after death	89	86	86
Attend church weekly	43	54	58
Mainline Protestant			
High religious salience	72	60	52
Believe in God	90	86	97
Jesus is only way to salvation	47	x	64[a]
Believe devil exists/is active	51	63	66[a]
Believe in life after death	78	80	78
Attend church weekly	34	41	35
Black Protestant			
High religious salience	91	87	85
Believe in God	93	96	99
Jesus is only way to salvation	85	x	89[a]
Believe devil exists/is active	83	81	89[a]
Believe in life after death	82	77	79
Attend church weekly	40	60	59
Roman Catholic			
High religious salience	84	58	56
Believe in God	96	83	97
Jesus is only way to salvation	29	x	65[a]
Believe devil exists/is active	68	x	70[a]
Believe in life after death	82	78	77
Attend church weekly	69	49	42
Unaffiliated			
High religious salience	31	20	16
Believe in God	49	56	70
Jesus is only way to salvation	33	x	34[a]
Believe devil exists/is active	29	x	39[a]
Believe in life after death	33	50	48
Attend church weekly	x	x	x

Sources:
1964: Anti-Semitism in the United States
1996: University of Akron, Second National Survey of Religion and Politics
2007: Pew Forum Religious Landscape Survey

Note: Entries show percent agreeing with statement

x – not asked

[a] Henry Institute National Survey on Religion and Public Life, 2008

there has been a decline in adherence to certain religious beliefs, while in other traditions there has been an increase in the level of adherence to those very same religious beliefs. The same is true with regard to reports of weekly worship attendance.

With regard to evangelical Protestants specifically, the data provide no evidence of any decline over the past forty years in their level of adherence to the religious beliefs analyzed. In fact, if anything, the data suggest that evangelicals are more likely today than in 1964 to hold these religious beliefs. For example, four-fifths of evangelicals expressed high religious salience in 1964, with the same proportion of evangelicals doing so in 2007. Belief in God was virtually universal among all evangelicals in 1964, and the same was true four decades later. Likewise, belief in life after death has remained relatively high, and relatively stable, among evangelical Protestants over the past forty years. But evangelicals today are somewhat more likely to believe that Jesus is the only way to salvation and that the devil exists than they did four decades ago.

Nor do the data provide any evidence of a decline in the reported level of weekly church attendance among evangelical Protestants over the past forty years. If anything, the data suggest that evangelicals are more likely today than in 1964 to attend church weekly. In many ways, this is quite remarkable in that any effects of giving socially desirable responses to the question of one's level of church attendance was likely to be far greater several decades ago than today. Thus, any inflation in reported church attendance due to such "desirability effects" should be much greater in 1964 than in 2007.

However, it is likely that this decline in social desirability effects related to religion is working to suggest a higher level of church attendance among evangelicals today than forty years ago. If there is less social pressure to claim a religious affiliation today than several decades ago, then it is likely that there were far more respondents in the 1960s than today who claimed religious affiliations (including evangelical Protestant affiliations), even though religion was relatively unimportant in their lives. And though they might have claimed a religious affiliation, such individuals may well have not reported that they attended church on a weekly basis, but on a somewhat less regular basis. Obviously, the greater likelihood of the presence of such kinds of religionists within the different religious traditions several decades ago than today would work to depress the level of weekly church attendance within the ranks of evangelical Protestants (or any other religious tradition) in the 1960s compared to that found today.

Like evangelicals, Black Protestants do not exhibit any dramatic shifts in their religious beliefs over the past four decades, as Black Protestants are just as likely today as in 1964 to express belief in God, the devil, life after death, and that Jesus is the only way to salvation. And, like evangelical Protestants, the data suggest that the percentage of those claiming affiliation with some Black Protestant church or denomination report a higher level of weekly church attendance today than those who claimed such affiliations in the mid-1960s.

In contrast, mainline Protestants exhibited stability in some religious beliefs and change in other beliefs; they were more likely to report in 2007 than in 1964 that they believed in God, in the devil, and that Jesus is the only way to salvation. But the proportion of mainline Protestants who reported that religion was highly salient in their lives dropped over the same period of time—from nearly three-quarters of all mainline Protestants in 1964 (72 percent) to only about one-half in 2007 (52 percent).

Catholics and the religiously unaffiliated also exhibit some significant patterns of change. For example, there has also been a substantial decline in the level of salience that Catholics attribute to religion in their daily lives, as the proportion reporting high religious salience dropped between 1964 and 2007 from five-sixths (84 percent) to somewhere between one-half to three-fifths (56 percent). Catholics in the early 1960s were the most likely of all religious traditions to report that they attended church weekly, with more than two-thirds reporting weekly Mass attendance. However, this was prior to the changes in church life made by the Second Vatican Council.[29] Whether directly related to these changes or not, only a little more than two-fifths of Catholics today say they attend Mass weekly, showing a decline of more than 25 percent over the past forty years.

With the growth of the religiously unaffiliated over the past forty years, there has also been a change in the religious nature of those who are religiously unaffiliated. For example, whereas only a minority of the religiously unaffiliated (49 percent) reported a belief in God in 1964, more than two-thirds (70 percent) did so in 2007. Similar increases were also evident within the ranks of the unaffiliated in terms of belief in the devil and belief in life after death, though the percentage reporting high religious salience among the unaffiliated actually dropped in half over the past forty years (from 31 to 16 percent).

Overall, these data suggest that, despite the cultural and social changes that have occurred within American life over the past forty years, evangelical Protestants have not altered the extent to which they adhere to their religious beliefs (at least in terms of those analyzed here) nor in the extent to which they attend church weekly. In fact, the data indicate that the level of weekly church attendance has actually increased, rather than decreased, over that period of time. Thus, to whatever extent the changing cultural values and practices of American life may have challenged their religious beliefs and behavior, evangelicals have been able to survive religiously, if not thrive, over that period of time.

Differences among Evangelicals

Though evangelicals as a whole may not have changed much religiously over the past four decades, important religious differences may exist among evangelicals today. In this section of the chapter, we examine the extent to which racial, generational, or educational differences currently serve to divide evangelicals religiously.

Racial and Ethnic Differences

Each religious tradition is composed of many different denominations. But, in constructing these different categories of religious tradition, we are assuming that what unites these different denominations together supersedes whatever theological or liturgical divisions might divide them.

Most African Americans (though not all) who report a religious affiliation do so with a congregation linked to the Black Protestant tradition (see table 3.4).[30] And most evangelical Protestants are white, even though there also substantial numbers of both African Americans and Hispanics within their ranks. But, given the limited number of respondents within most surveys, many studies have assigned all black Protestants to the Black Protestant tradition category, even when such blacks are affiliated with an evangelical or mainline Protestant category.[31] The net result is that, typically, all evangelical and mainline Protestants are white in terms of their racial characteristics, and all respondents within the Black Protestant tradition are blacks. Racial differences are then conflated with religious differences. Yet, in paraphrasing the words of Greeley and Hout (2006, 70), are not black evangelicals just as much evangelicals as white evangelicals?

In examining religious beliefs thus far, we have found that Black Protestants and evangelicals tend to exhibit relatively similar patterns. Given that Black Protestantism largely originated within evangelical Protestantism, this is not necessarily too surprising. But, as Putnam and Campbell note (2010, 279), "their similarities with evangelicals not withstanding—Black Protestants are not simply evangelical Protestants who happen to be black" in that, though they share a common origin, "the two traditions evolved along very different paths."

Still, one important issue that has not been satisfactorily addressed by scholars is the extent to which black, Hispanic, and white evangelicals "stand together" and exhibit relative unity in their religious beliefs. And to what extent, if at all, do black evangelical Protestants differ in terms of their religious beliefs from their fellow blacks who are affiliated with the Black Protestant tradition? Further, do Hispanic evangelicals differ in terms of religious beliefs from Hispanic Catholics? These are questions we seek to address in this section of the chapter.

Fortunately, given the massive size of the Pew Religious Landscape Survey, there are sufficient numbers of African Americans and Hispanics within the evangelical Protestant category to enable these important comparisons to be made (but something that cannot be done with any confidence in the results when one uses other surveys, given the far more limited number of respondents in them). These various comparisons are presented in table 4.8. Because of the comparatively small numbers of blacks and Hispanics within the mainline Protestant tradition and blacks within the Catholic tradition, data for these categories are not presented in the table. And, given that such comparisons can only be made due to the massive sample size of the Landscape Survey, only religious variables drawn from that survey are analyzed here.

Several important comparisons can be made from the data presented in table 4.8. First, among evangelicals, answers provided to the items tapping different religious beliefs do vary somewhat among white, black, and Hispanic evangelicals. Roughly speaking, there is about a 5- to 10-percentage-point difference in subscribing to such beliefs across the three racial/ethnic categories of evangelicals. On most items, however, black evangelicals were more likely than white or Hispanic evangelicals to report such beliefs. Only on the matter of preserving religious traditions did black evangelicals exhibit the lowest percentage reporting agreement among the three groups of evangelicals. Religious behavior also varies somewhat among white, black, and Latino evangelicals. Roughly speaking, there is about a 10-percentage-point difference in frequency with which the three racial/ethnic categories of evangelicals report engaging in such behavior (with the gap being less than 10 percent for reports of daily prayer and greater for reports of weekly participation in religious small groups). On most items, black and Hispanic evangelicals were relatively similar in their levels of such activity, engaging in the analyzed practices at a somewhat higher level than that reported by white evangelicals.

Table 4.8 also permits a comparison of how the religious beliefs of white, black, and Hispanic evangelicals compare to the religious beliefs of those of the same race/ethnicity found within other religious traditions. First, at least with regard to the particular religious beliefs examined here, white mainline Protestants and white Roman Catholics tend to exhibit relatively similar levels of adherence to these religious beliefs (with differences ranging from 2 to 6 percentage points in nearly all cases), whereas white evangelicals are far more

TABLE 4.8

Religious Beliefs and Behavior by Racial and Ethnic Differences (controlling for religious tradition)

	Evangelical Protestant			Mainline Protestant	Black Protestant	Roman Catholic	
	White (%)	Black (%)	Hispanic (%)	White (%)	Black (%)	White (%)	Hispanic (%)
Religious Salience							
Religion "very important" in life	78	89	84	50	86	52	67
Religious Beliefs							
Believe in God	99	99	98	97	99	98	96
Absolutely certain of God's existence	90	93	83	72	91	74	66
View God as a person, not a force	81	75	74	64	73	66	50
Believe in heaven	86	93	86	78	91	84	77
Believe in hell	82	88	77	56	82	60	60
Completely agree miracles still occur	62	64	69	43	59	46	55
Completely agree spirits active	60	66	71	29	59	30	47
Evolution is best explanation	24	31	40	55	43	58	73
Only my religion leads to eternal life	37	41	43	11	36	11	30
Church should preserve traditional beliefs/practices	66	60	65	38	54	35	47
Religious Behavior							
Weekly church attendance	57	66	68	49	58	42	42
Weekly religious small group participation	39	53	54	33	44	10	19
Monthly church social activities	49	61	56	37	55	24	27
Weekly Bible reading	59	70	69	26	61	17	29
Daily personal prayer	77	83	82	65	82	57	60

Source: Pew Forum Religious Landscape Survey, 2007

Note: Entries show percent agreeing with statement

likely to report subscription to these particular religious beliefs than whites in the other two major Christian traditions.

Second, white evangelical Protestants are more likely than white mainline Protestants to indicate that they engage in the behaviors examined; in turn, white mainline Protestants are more likely to do so than white Roman Catholics. Thus, white evangelicals are far more likely to report engagement in these practices than are whites in the other two major Christian traditions.

Third, a higher percentage of black evangelicals consistently reported adherence to these religious beliefs than did blacks within the Black Protestant tradition. In that sense, there are some important, and consistent, differences between blacks across the two traditions. These differences ranged from 2 to 12 percentage points, depending on the belief and behavior being analyzed (except with regard to daily prayer). But the pattern is uniform regardless of the belief examined: black evangelicals are more "religious" than blacks within the Black Protestant tradition.

Finally, Hispanic evangelicals are far more likely to report adherence to these religious beliefs than are Hispanic Catholics. Differences between Hispanics range from about 10 to 40 percentage points, with Hispanic evangelicals being far more likely than Hispanic Catholics to report subscription to these beliefs and engagement in these various religious practices. Moreover, the differences in adherence to these religious beliefs and in level of religious involvement between white and Hispanic evangelicals are far less substantial than the differences between white and Hispanic Catholics. In other words, there is a far greater level of similarity in the religious behavior of evangelicals across all three racial/ethnic groups than there is between white and Hispanic Catholics on these matters.

Overall, the data presented in table 4.8 suggest that religious tradition does matter and that our category of evangelical Protestants exhibits considerable analytical unity despite certain differences in religious beliefs among evangelicals based on their racial/ethnic composition. Though differences in levels of religious belief exist across different racial/ethnic groups within the evangelical Protestant tradition, such differences tend to be far less pronounced than those between the same racial/ethnic group across the different religious traditions. Differences between black evangelicals and blacks within the Black Protestant tradition, however, are far less substantial than differences among whites and among Hispanics across the same religious traditions. Nevertheless, though differences between black evangelicals and blacks within the Black Protestant tradition are relatively small, a consistent pattern emerges from table 4.8—namely, that black evangelicals are consistently more likely to express adherence to these particular religious beliefs than blacks within the Black Protestant tradition.

Generational and Educational Differences

Table 4.9 compares the religious beliefs of the millennial generation of evangelicals with all older generations of evangelicals combined as well as the religious beliefs of non-college-educated evangelicals with those of college-educated evangelicals. These generational and educational differences among evangelicals are also examined in relationship to those affiliated with other religious traditions in order to ascertain whether the patterns among evangelicals either reflect or diverge from those affiliated with other religious traditions.

In terms of generational differences, there are some variations in reported religious beliefs between those who are part of the millennial generation and those who are not. Millennial evangelicals as well as previous generations of evangelicals exhibit similar levels of high certainty in the existence of God. A small gap does exist between the two generational categories with regard to belief in evolution, with millennial evangelicals being somewhat more likely than non-millennial evangelicals to report belief in evolution (27 percent versus 23 percent, respectively). Where more substantial differences exist, it is typically in the 8- to 10-percentage-point range. Millennial evangelicals are, for example, more likely than previous generations of evangelicals to claim that their religion constitutes the one true faith (45 percent versus 37 percent, respectively). This greater tendency of millennials than non-millennials to claim one's religion as the sole true faith, however, is not unique to evangelicals; it is also evident across all four of the major Christian traditions (though with varying degrees of difference). A gap of 8–10 percent also exists between the two generations of evangelicals in adherence to other religious beliefs examined in table 4.9, with millennial evangelicals being somewhat less likely than older generations of evangelicals to report that religion is highly salient in one's life, to believe that angels and demons are active, and to maintain the need to preserve traditions within the church.

While such generational differences among evangelicals are important, young adults have typically been found to be somewhat less religious than older adults. So perhaps a more important, and revealing, analysis would be to compare evangelicals of the millennial generation with their generational counterparts found within the other religious traditions. For example, to what extent do millennial evangelicals differ from millennial mainline Protestants or millennial Catholics?

Despite the differences that are evident between millennial and non-millennial evangelicals, far greater differences are evident between millennial evangelicals and those millennials affiliated with other religious traditions. For example, in terms of generational differences among evangelicals, there is roughly a 10-percentage-point difference in adherence to the belief that angels and demons are active in the world. But between millennial evangelicals and millennial mainliners and Catholics, there is approximately a 20-percentage-point difference in such belief. Similar differences across religious traditions exist within the same millennial generation with regard to religious salience, belief in evolution, and whether to preserve religious traditions. In other words, affiliation with a particular religious tradition shapes the likelihood of adherence to particular religious beliefs more so than generational differences across those same traditions; millennial evangelicals more closely mirror older generations of evangelicals religiously than they reflect the religious characteristics of millennials within the other religious traditions.

A somewhat similar pattern exists with regard to the educational differences that are present within the ranks of evangelicals. There are some differences in reported religious beliefs between those evangelicals who are college graduates and those who are not. But differences in religious beliefs among evangelicals based on educational differences are not consistently evident— and on some questions there are no differences evident at all. However, where there are differences, evangelicals who are college graduates tend to be more "religious" than their evangelical counterparts who have not graduated from college.[32] Perhaps most surprisingly, evangelicals who are college graduates are more likely to reject evolutionary explanations than evangelicals who have not graduated from college, and evangelicals who are college graduates are also far more likely than other evangelicals to claim that their religion is the one true faith. Only in terms of whether to preserve religious traditions does one find college-educated evangelicals somewhat less religiously conservative than their fellow evangelicals with lower levels of educational attainment.

Once again, however, it is not so much whether one is college educated or not that leads to substantial differences in religious beliefs. Rather, differences in religious beliefs exist primarily across religious traditions—regardless of whether members of those religious traditions are college graduates or not. Thus, among those who have graduated from a college or university, differences in religious beliefs are far greater across religious traditions than are differences within such religious traditions between those who are, and are not, college graduates.

To this point we have simply analyzed generational and educational differences separately. For example, it was shown in table 4.9 that there was a greater tendency for millennials than non-millennials, regardless of religious tradition, to claim one's religion as the sole true faith. But the same table also revealed that evangelicals who are college graduates were more likely than non-college-educated evangelicals to make such a claim. Might college-educated evangelicals who are part of the millennial generation be less inclined to hold this perspective than those college-educated evangelicals

TABLE 4.9
Religious Beliefs by Generational Cohort and
Educational Attainment (controlling for religious tradition)

	Generational		Education	
	Non-Millennial (%)	Millennial (%)	Non-College Graduate (%)	College Graduate (%)
Evangelical Protestant				
High religious salience	80	70	79	81
Absolutely certain of God's existence	91	88	91	92
Completely agree angels and demons active	62	54	61	61
Evolution is best explanation	23	27	25	20
Only my religion leads to eternal life	37	45	36	47
Church should preserve traditional beliefs/practice	66	58	66	60
Mainline Protestant				
High religious salience	53	42	52	52
Absolutely certain of God's existence	76	71	77	71
Completely agree angels and demons active	31	29	35	22
Evolution is best explanation	50	52	45	61
Only my religion leads to eternal life	11	18	14	9
Church should preserve traditional beliefs/practice	38	34	43	28
Black Protestant				
High religious salience	86	81	86	83
Absolutely certain of God's existence	92	90	92	93
Completely agree angels and demons active	58	65	61	55

Evolution is best explanation	36	47	39	35
Only my religion leads to eternal life	34	41	37	27
Church should preserve traditional beliefs/practice	55	56	56	47
Roman Catholic				
High religious salience	58	44	58	53
Absolutely certain of God's existence	76	65	74	74
Completely agree angels and demons active	35	34	38	27
Evolution is best explanation	56	68	56	62
Only my religion leads to eternal life	16	18	19	8
Church should preserve traditional beliefs/practice	38	38	42	29
Unaffiliated				
High religious salience	17	12	19	8
Absolutely certain of God's existence	53	49	56	37
Completely agree angels and demons active	19	17	23	8
Evolution is best explanation	74	73	67	85
Only my religion leads to eternal life	x	x	x	x
Church should preserve traditional beliefs/practice	x	x	x	x

Source: Pew Forum Religious Landscape Survey, 2007

Note: Entries show percent agreeing with statement

x – not asked of religiously unaffiliated respondents

of previous generations? Hence, table 4.10 examines differences in religious beliefs among the millennial generation of respondents in terms of whether or not they had obtained a college degree and compares such differences to similarly educated older generations of respondents according to the religious tradition of which they are a part.

Several important patterns emerge from table 4.10. First, college graduates, regardless of religious tradition, are less likely than non-college graduates to claim that their faith is the one true religion. The only exception to this pattern is found among evangelicals—regardless of the generation from which they are drawn. Millennial evangelicals who are college educated are the most likely of all groups to report that their religion is the one true faith (with 56 percent doing so)—even exceeding by 10 percent such claims made by older, comparably educated evangelicals. In fact, among the millennial generation of respondents, college-educated evangelicals are nearly twice as likely as college-educated Black Protestants to make such a claim and eight times more likely to do so than college-educated Catholics.

Second, it would appear that college education tends to foster a stronger "traditional" religious perspective among millennial evangelicals than it does among college-educated millennials within the other religious traditions. For example, millennial evangelicals who are college graduates are no more likely to report that they believe in evolution than older generations of evangelicals who are college graduates, and such college-educated evangelicals, regardless of the generation of which they are a part, are less likely to report such beliefs than their college-educated counterparts within other religious traditions. Only in terms of "preserving traditions" are college-educated millennial evangelicals somewhat less "traditional" religiously than non-college-educated millennial evangelicals, as the latter are somewhat more likely to respond that their church or denomination should preserve its traditional beliefs and practices. But even in this instance, the marginal difference is only 4 percent—less than the marginal difference found between the same two educational categories within the older generations of evangelicals (7 percent) and less than the marginal difference found between college and non-college-educated Black Protestants of the millennial generation (10 percent). Thus, it would appear, as some other analysts have claimed (e.g., Massengill 2011), that college education functions in a somewhat different fashion for evangelicals than it does for those in other religious traditions in that it does not appear to produce the general liberalizing effects typically assumed to be linked to a college education.

Are there greater generational and educational differences among evangelicals in terms of their religious behavior than in terms of their religious beliefs?[33] Do we see, for example, lower levels of religious practice among the

TABLE 4.10
Religious Beliefs by Educational Attainment
(controlling for generational cohort and religious tradition)

	Millennial Generation		Non-Millennial Generation	
	Non-College Graduate (%)	College Graduate (%)	Non-College Graduate (%)	College Graduate (%)
Evangelical Protestant				
High religious salience	69	75	80	82
Absolutely certain of God's existence	86	93	91	90
Completely agree angels and demons active	54	56	63	61
Evolution is best explanation	28	21	24	21
Only my religion leads to eternal life	44	56	35	47
Church should preserve traditional beliefs/practices	58	54	68	61
Mainline Protestant				
High religious salience	42	41	54	52
Absolutely certain of God's existence	69	73	77	69
Completely agree angels and demons active	31	22	36	22
Evolution is best explanation	50	65	45	61
Only my religion leads to eternal life	18	18	13	9
Church should preserve traditional beliefs/practices	37	18	44	29
Black Protestant				
High religious salience	81	79	87	83
Absolutely certain of God's existence	88	92	92	92
Completely agree angels and demons active	67	54	59	55
Evolution is best explanation	48	42	37	34
Only my religion leads to eternal life	43	32	37	27
Church should preserve traditional beliefs/practices	58	48	56	47
Roman Catholic				
High religious salience	44	41	60	54
Absolutely certain of God's existence	63	64	74	74
Completely agree angels and demons active	35	26	39	27
Evolution is best explanation	69	65	54	62
Only my religion leads to eternal life	21	7	19	8
Church should preserve traditional beliefs/practices	42	22	42	30

Source: Pew Forum Religious Landscape Survey, 2007

Note: Entries show percent agreeing with statement

youngest generation of evangelicals or within its most educated ranks? These
questions are addressed in table 4.11, which examines three different forms of
religious behavior: weekly church attendance, daily prayer, and weekly small
group participation. Once again, members of different religious traditions are
compared in terms of generational and educational differences within their
ranks.

TABLE 4.11
Religious Behavior by Generational Cohort and Educational Attainment
(controlling for religious tradition)

	Generational		Education	
	Non-Millennial (%)	Millennial (%)	Non-College Graduate (%)	College Graduate (%)
Evangelical Protestant				
Weekly church attendance	59	55	56	69
Weekly religious small group participation	42	37	40	48
Daily personal prayer	79	73	77	82
Mainline Protestant				
Weekly church attendance	35	32	33	40
Weekly religious small group participation	16	18	17	17
Daily personal prayer	54	49	54	52
Black Protestant				
Weekly church attendance	59	56	58	64
Weekly religious small group participation	47	36	44	47
Daily personal prayer	83	71	80	82
Roman Catholic				
Weekly church attendance	43	34	41	44
Weekly religious small group participation	13	13	14	10
Daily personal prayer	60	46	59	56
Unaffiliated				
Weekly church attendance	x	x	x	x
Weekly religious small group participation	x	x	x	x
Daily personal prayer	24	18	25	15

Source: Pew Forum Religious Landscape Survey, 2007

x – not asked of religiously unaffiliated respondents

First, in terms of generational differences among evangelical Protestants, one can see that the millennial generation of evangelicals is somewhat less likely than the older generations of evangelicals to engage in these three religious behaviors. Thus, 59 percent of the older generations of evangelicals report that they attend church weekly, whereas 55 percent of millennial evangelicals do so. Basically, for each of the three religious behaviors examined, there is difference of 5 percent in the relative frequency within which such behavior is reported by evangelicals—with older generations being more likely than their millennial counterparts to report engagement in each behavior. Yet, once again, there are greater differences in reported religious behavior within the millennial generation across the religious traditions than there are between the younger generation and older members within each of the religious traditions. In other words, religious tradition affiliation shapes religious behavior far more than generational differences.

Second, greater disparity in religious behavior is found among evangelicals when one examines educational, as opposed to generational, divisions within their ranks. The percentage differences in religious behavior between the two educational categories of evangelicals tend to be nearly double those found in terms of generational differences. However, evangelicals who have graduated from college are far more "religious" than evangelicals who have not, as the former are more likely to report weekly church attendance, daily prayer, and weekly small group participation. Thus, college education seemingly does not have an eroding effect on the frequency with which evangelicals engage in these three activities—rather, college-educated evangelicals are far more faithful religiously than their non-college-educated brethren.

These relationships between religious behavior and educational attainment not only hold among older generations of evangelicals, but they also hold true among the millennial generation of evangelicals. Table 4.12 replicates the analysis of table 4.10—but this time it examines differences in religious behavior among the millennial generation of respondents in terms of differences in educational attainment and compares such differences to similarly educated older generations of respondents according to the religious tradition of which they are a part.

Regardless of religious tradition, college graduates typically attend church more frequently, participate in weekly religious small group activities, and engage in daily prayer overall—and this is true among those of the millennial generation as well as among those born earlier (the exception being among the millennial generation of Catholics). Moreover, it is among the millennial generation of evangelicals that one finds the biggest differences in weekly church attendance and daily prayer according to differences in educational attainment. In other words, among millennials within the other religious

TABLE 4.12
Religious Behavior by Educational Attainment
(controlling for generational cohort and religious tradition)

	Millennial Generation		Non-Millennial Generation	
	Non-College Graduate (%)	College Graduate (%)	Non-College Graduate (%)	College Graduate (%)
Evangelical Protestant				
Weekly church attendance	53	66	57	69
Weekly small group participation	37	39	41	49
Daily prayer	72	80	78	82
Mainline Protestant				
Weekly church attendance	32	33	32	40
Weekly small group participation	18	13	16	17
Daily prayer	48	54	56	52
Black Protestant				
Weekly church attendance	56	60	59	64
Weekly small group participation	34	47	47	46
Daily prayer	70	75	83	83
Roman Catholic				
Weekly church attendance	35	31	42	46
Weekly small group participation	15	7	13	10
Daily prayer	47	44	61	58
Unaffiliated				
Weekly church attendance	x	x	x	x
Weekly small group participation	x	x	x	x
Daily prayer	18	13	28	16

Source: Pew Forum Religious Landscape Survey, 2007

Note: Entries show percent agreeing with statement

x – not asked of religiously unaffiliated respondents

traditions, educational attainment seemingly has a small effect on the religious practices of weekly church attendance and daily prayer (e.g., when arbitrarily using a difference of 5 percent or less), but among evangelicals the level of difference is 13 percent with regard to weekly church attendance and 8 percent with regard to daily prayer. And this "bump" in the frequency of these religious practices among the college educated within the millennial generation occurs despite the fact that the levels of such practices among non-college-educated evangelicals are already relatively high in relationship to non-college-educated mainline Protestants and Catholics—exceeding by 20 percent or more the levels found among non-college-educated mainline Protestants and Catholics.

Conclusions

Generally speaking, evangelicals as a whole tend to be highly religious people. Not only do large proportions of evangelicals report that religion is very important to them, but similarly large segments indicate that they believe in a spiritual world that transcends the material world, that miraculous events still occur, and that there is both a heaven and a hell. They believe in God, but a God who is a person and not simply an impersonal force. And they tend to express a good deal of certainty in their religious beliefs.

Evangelicals also place a great deal of emphasis on textual materials and downplay personal experience as a basis for discerning religious truth. For evangelicals, the Bible serves as the primary basis of religious authority, and historic doctrines of the faith are viewed to embody important religious truths as well—truths that should be preserved rather than modified or dropped in light of new circumstances. While evangelicals do emphasize "a personal relationship with Jesus Christ" and religious experiences, such experiences are always to be assessed for their conformity to the historic standards of the faith. Where the two conflict, the truth of scripture is to prevail over any subjective truth of personal experience.

Evangelicals see religious diversity as a good thing, though to a somewhat lesser extent than do members of other religious traditions. Though they overwhelmingly contend that Jesus is the only way to salvation, only about one-third hold that their religion is the only one that leads to eternal life. Just how these seemingly disparate beliefs are held together at the same time is unclear.

Despite the racial differences that exist within their ranks, evangelicals exhibit a relatively high level of uniformity in their religious beliefs. Certain differences in levels of religious belief are evident among white, black, and Hispanic evangelicals. Nevertheless, differences in religious beliefs are generally far greater for those of the same race across religious traditions than they are in terms of differences in religious beliefs held by different racial groups within the ranks of evangelical Protestants.

Evangelical Protestants are, as a whole, heavily involved in church activities and private devotional life related to their religious faith. They report high levels of weekly church attendance and daily prayer. They are drawn to the social life of their houses of worship, as they frequently attend social activities in their church beyond weekly worship services and prayer meetings. Many, though not all, of their close personal friends are also members of the congregations in which they worship.

Overall, evangelical Protestants today do not differ from Christians in other religious traditions in terms of the religious homogeneity of their personal friendships, as evangelicals do not appear to be any more inclined than others to forge close friendships simply with those drawn from their particular religious community. Whatever distinctive patterns evangelical Protestants may exhibit religiously (or politically) cannot, therefore, be attributed to their being part of a religious community that is rather closed in terms of their friendship patterns. Evangelical Protestants, like other Americans, interact with those outside their religious faith and forge friendships across religious boundaries.

Moreover, based on available evidence, it would appear that there has been virtually no change in the nature of the religious beliefs and behavior of evangelical Protestants over the past forty years. Given the limited number of comparable questions asked, there appears to be no decline in the level to which they report adherence to particular religious beliefs. And, given the data available, it appears that the religious practices of evangelical Protestants have not changed markedly over nearly the last half century. Unfortunately, except for levels of church attendance, there is a lack of comparable data by which to assess change in religious behavior among evangelicals over time. But in terms of reported levels of weekly church attendance, the data would suggest that, if anything, evangelicals are more inclined to report attending church weekly today than in the mid-1960s.

Finally, in terms of factors that may serve to divide evangelicals (and those of other religious traditions), this chapter examined the possible effects of generational and educational differences on the expression of different religious beliefs and reports of religious behavior. Though the millennial generation of evangelicals is somewhat less likely to report adherence to religious beliefs and attendance at weekly church services than are older generations of evangelicals, greater differences emerged between college-educated and non-college-educated evangelicals—with college-educated evangelicals tending to be more "religious" than evangelicals with lower levels of education. Overall, therefore, it appears that college education does little to undermine the religious beliefs and practices of evangelicals; rather, if anything, it appears that advanced education serves to strengthen and solidify the faith of evangelicals.[34]

5

Living for Jesus?
The Social Theology of Evangelicals

KNOWING SOMEONE'S PARTICULAR RELIGIOUS BELIEFS or practices does not necessarily reveal anything about how that person views social and political life. Religion has a vertical dimension as it relates to the divine, but also has a horizontal dimension as it relates to one's fellow human beings. In the previous chapter, we examined evangelical religious beliefs and practices as they related to the vertical axis of religion; in this chapter, we focus on the horizontal dimension as we examine their social theological perspectives.

Social theologies constitute theological perspectives related to the social, cultural, and political problems of the day. These theologies typically assess whether it is important for believers to be concerned about such problems, the appropriate means by which they should address these problems, and the likelihood that such problems can even be resolved. Such assessments of prospects for social reform are usually made in the light of certain assumptions (e.g., assumptions about the nature of human beings, about the nature and purpose of government, and about the direction of human history). Social theologies often identify and prioritize aspects of human life that require attention (e.g., structural conditions, individual morality), and they may even propose a vision for change and suggest general strategies for effecting that change, some of which may involve political activity (Gray 2008, 222).

In this chapter, we examine the social theology of evangelicals and how their perspectives may be similar to, or different from, those held by those affiliated with other religious traditions. Perspectives related to three broad topics are analyzed: views related to the purpose and function of government,[1] views related to the role of religion in public life, and views related to civic norms and values.

The Social Theology of Evangelicals

As we saw in chapter 4, evangelicals typically hold the Bible to be their authoritative text. But, given the purposes for which it was written, the Bible is not a treatise that explicates a specific philosophy related to civic and political matters. Rather, there are various passages that relate to these topics, some directly and others indirectly. Moreover, the particular biblical passages that do address civic and political matters must be assessed to determine whether they represent instructions for a particular historical audience (certain statements, for example, may relate specifically to particular kings or kingdoms in the Old Testament) or represent instructions that transcend time and place.[2]

Christians, as a whole, have long held that government is an institution authorized by God. Though governmental institutions are viewed by most Christians as being legitimate in nature, the authority that is granted to the state is generally viewed as legitimate only insofar as it operates within its "divinely assigned" sphere of authority—as "particular governments or governmental acts may not be [deemed legitimate]" (Chaplin 2009, 214). And, generally speaking, Christians view the primary function of governmental institutions to be that of securing justice and pursuing the common good,[3] with the notion of the common good standing at the heart of the social teaching of the Catholic Church (Longley 2009, 160).

But if Christians believe governments are legitimate institutions that are to pursue justice and seek the common good, then how is it that Christians come to view the role of government differently, as they are far from united on what the government should be doing? (See, for example, table 5.1 below.) This is true for several reasons. First, biblical texts must be interpreted, and one source of differences stems from varying theological interpretations related to the broader biblical themes of creation, fall, and redemption—specifically whether or not governments were occasioned solely because of the fall. For those who view government as arising on the basis of the fall, the political sphere has largely a negative justification: to restrain sin, preserve order, and engage in corrective justice (the "righting of wrongs"). Though such a perspective does not necessarily imply "minimal government," it does diminish expectations related to what governments are able to achieve (Chaplin 2009, 223).

Other theological interpretations provide for a more positive view of the state. These perspectives generally hold that, even in a sinless world, there "would be a need for some kind of authority that held a legitimate right to have its rules followed" (Smidt 2007b, 130).[4] Thus, from this perspective, the function of the state is not simply to hold back sin but to enable "members of society to accomplish more in their life together and fare better than they would simply on their own" (Smidt 2007b, 131). Accordingly, this theological interpretation typically leads to "wider conceptions of the scope of common good and justice, thereby potentially legitimizing more government intervention than would the corrective view" (Chaplin 2009, 224).

Second, in addition to possible different theological perspectives, there are also likely differences among Christians in terms of their analytical understandings regarding principles of justice, the common good, and equality. Even if all Christians were to agree that the state should pursue justice, it is far from clear precisely what that might mean. For example, simply with regard to notions of justice, there are different analytical understandings about whether justice is retributive, distributive, or restorative in nature. Even if one were to restrict the understanding of justice to simply distributive justice, there are still a variety of viewpoints as to what such distributive justice might entail. Thus, even if all Christians believed that governments emerged solely because of human failing and that the primary function of the state is to secure justice, Christians might still, given their different understandings of justice, come to varying conclusions about the nature of governmental power, how governments are best able to secure justice, and the extent to which justice is likely to be fully realized through state action.

Third, assessments about the role of government are also related to other, more empirically based factors: for example, one's interpretation of the powers given by the American Constitution to different levels of government; one's assessments about the present cultural, social, and economic realities within American life; one's judgments related to the root causes of problems currently confronting American society; and one's beliefs related to the likely consequences (both intended and unintended) of governmental actions. Even though these various interpretations, assessments, and judgments do not rest on an individual's theological interpretations or analytical perspectives, they likely shape a person's expectations related to the propriety, need, and wisdom of governmental intervention in particular matters of public life.

Given these differences in theological understandings, analytical perspectives, and empirical assessments, it is likely that affiliation with different religious traditions may color, but not fully shape, one's views about the role and function of government. However, though differences may exist, members of some religious traditions may be more likely than others to espouse particular perspectives on these matters. For example, as was discussed in chapter 1, the social gospel emphasized that the moral and social ills of society were largely the result of social, political, and economic realities over which individuals had little control, and that this view received greater acceptance within what is now known as mainline Protestant denominations than within evangelical denominations. As a result, one might anticipate that mainline Protestants may be more willing to accept structural explanations for social problems than evangelical Protestants, who would, at least historically speaking, be more inclined to advance individualistic explanations.

In fact, evangelicals have generally adhered to an individualistic social philosophy (Hollinger 1983)—a perspective that views structural changes in the institutions of society as not necessarily achieving the greater common good that others anticipate from these changes. Given the inherent sinful nature of humankind, evangelicals are more prone to see efforts to transform the social and political order as being less likely to succeed or to fully accomplish all that may be intended. Moreover, government and institutional structures themselves are tainted by sin, as they are led and administered by fallen human beings. At best, governments may be able to restrain the social manifestations of evil, but they cannot eradicate its root causes, because the root causes of social maladies rest within human nature itself. Thus, evangelicals have generally stressed individual transformation as the key to social change, personal morality over social ethics, and a limited state (Hollinger 1983, 44). Nevertheless, it is hardly likely that all evangelicals hold the same views regarding the role and function of government; as a result, it is probably more accurate to state that this chapter examines the "social theologies" of evangelicals—not their "social theology," as if there were only one such perspective held by evangelicals.

The Role and Function of Government

Surveys do not typically ask respondents what they view the function of government to be. Rather, surveys typically inquire about what the respondent thinks the government should do with regard to certain categories of people (e.g., the poor, illegal immigrants) that may relate to notions of justice or the common good. Helping those less fortunate than oneself is certainly an ethical expectation associated with many different religious faiths, and followers of these different faiths may perceive governmental efforts to address the needs of the poor (or others) as reflecting efforts to secure justice.

What, then, are the views of evangelicals related to the role of government and how, if at all, do their views differ from those expressed by other Americans affiliated with other religious traditions? We begin in table 5.1 with an examination of evangelical attitudes about whether it is the government's responsibility to assist those who can't take care of themselves. When posed in

TABLE 5.1
Views on Role of Government by Religious Tradition

	Evangelical Protestant (%)	Mainline Protestant (%)	Black Protestant (%)	Roman Catholic (%)	Unaffiliated (%)
Government responsible for taking care of those who can't care for themselves[a]	53	62	83	75	73
Government should do more to help needy Americans[b]	57	58	79	63	65
Prefer government with fewer services[b]	48	51	18	39	41

Sources:

[a] Henry Institute National Survey on Religion and Public Life, 2008

[b] Pew Forum Religious Landscape Survey, 2007

Note: Entries show percent agreeing with statement

this manner, a majority of evangelicals (53 percent) expressed agreement with the statement—suggesting that most evangelicals view government as having responsibilities to address the needs of those who are unable to provide for themselves. At the same time, however, evangelicals were the least likely of the religious traditions to respond in such a manner.

Why is it, then, that evangelicals seem to be less concerned with such "matters of justice"? More than likely, it relates to the relative lack of clarity in the question about who should, and who should not, be included in this category of "people who can't take care of themselves." Evangelicals tend to be "accountable freewill individualists," in that they typically view people as beings who "exist independent of structures and institutions, have freewill, and are individually accountable for their own actions" (Emerson and Smith 2000, 76–77). Since evangelicals are prone to view humans as being largely accountable for their actions, it is likely they would respond more cautiously and critically to the phrase "people who can't take care of themselves." It is not that evangelicals deny that there are people who can't take care of themselves (after all, even a majority of evangelicals agreed with the statement). Rather, it is simply that, given the way this item is phrased, evangelicals would likely react with greater caution in agreeing with the statement.[5]

This interpretation is supported, in part, when we compare responses across religious traditions to the statement that "the government should do more to help needy Americans." Once again, of the five religious traditions examined, evangelicals were the least likely to agree. However, it should be noted that evangelicals were more likely to express agreement with this statement than the previous one (57 percent versus 53 percent). Note, secondly, that evangelicals were the only religious tradition to exhibit this pattern; for all other religious traditions, the percentage who agreed with the second statement was consistently less than the percentage who agreed with the first. Thus, when phrased in terms of helping "needy Americans," evangelicals stand in far greater agreement with members of the other religious traditions with the desire that the government do more. Obviously, there continue to be some differences across religious traditions—but these differences are far less (e.g., evangelical Protestants stand in far greater agreement with mainline Protestants and Catholics on this second statement than on the first), and in that sense evangelicals hardly hold a distinctively different position on these matters than most other Americans.

The final item in table 5.1 examines assessments of the role of government somewhat differently—in terms of whether or not one prefers a "government with fewer services" or a "bigger government with more services." Black Protestants are the least likely to favor a smaller government with fewer services, as less than one-fifth within their ranks hold such a position, whereas evangelical and mainline Protestants are the most likely to favor a smaller government with fewer services, with roughly one-half of each tradition doing so. In fact, on this particular matter, Black Protestants tend to stand somewhat apart from members of other religious traditions as they are more likely to look toward government as a means to address those problems that confront them as a community.

However, to a large extent, these differences in views about the role of government examined in table 5.1 reflect racial, rather than religious, differences. Those affiliated with the Black Protestant tradition are largely African Americans, a group whose experiences within American society have left them more economically vulnerable and for whom government has played an important, and liberating, role in their history (e.g., it has freed them from slavery, ensured their voting rights, and expanded their social and economic opportunities).[6] So while evangelicals and Black Protestants tend to stand together in terms of their religious beliefs and behavior, they stand significantly apart when one begins to examine their attitudes about the role and function of government.

Thus, evangelicals are somewhat more prone to articulate an individualistic social philosophy than are members of other religious traditions. And this proclivity is, in part, a reflection of the legacy of the individualism long associated with their religious faith (see chapter 1). Nevertheless, evangelicals are far from united in their assessments of the role and function of governments in contemporary life. In fact, based on the data analyzed here, evangelicals are divided rather evenly in their assessments of whether governments should do more to address certain issues or whether they should provide fewer services.

The Role of Religion in Public Life

The separation of church and state, as reflected in the First Amendment, does not necessarily imply the separation of religion from public life (or, more narrowly, the separation of religion from politics). Religion and public life are intertwined in ways that even the strictest separation of church and state cannot disentangle. For example, in terms of politics, even the highest wall of separation cannot prevent citizens from casting their ballots based on their religious beliefs, their religious identity, or a candidate's religious faith.

Though the role of religion in American democratic life has been, and continues to be, a controversial and contested matter, Americans generally believe that religion has more beneficial, rather than detrimental, effects on American public life (see table 5.2). Thus, when asked whether "religion causes more problems in society than it solves," less than one-third of Americans express agreement (data not shown). Relatively few of those affiliated with each of the major religious traditions tend to espouse such a statement—with about one-fifth of evangelicals, a quarter of Black Protestants, and a third of mainline Protestants and Catholics doing so. Only among the religiously unaffiliated is there a substantial majority who agree that, on balance, religion causes more problems than it solves in terms of its social effects.

It is one thing to believe religion may be beneficial socially; it is quite another to assert that religion serves as a solution to most social problems. On this matter, members of different religious traditions take rather substantially different positions. When asked "if enough people were brought to Christ, social problems would largely take care of themselves," more than two-thirds of evangelicals and nearly three-quarters of Black Protestants expressed agreement with the statement. In contrast, only about one-half of Catholics and mainline Protestants, and one-third of the religiously unaffiliated, did so. Again, these data suggest that evangelicals continue to be largely "individualists" who typically hold (as did revivalists earlier in American history) that social reform is best accomplished through individual regeneration.[7]

Debates today on the public role of religion frequently focus on the presence of religious pluralism within American society. Some contend that, under conditions of religious pluralism, the presence of religion in public life

TABLE 5.2
Views on the Role of Religion in Public Life by Religious Tradition

	Evangelical Protestant (%)	Mainline Protestant (%)	Black Protestant (%)	Roman Catholic (%)	Unaffiliated (%)
Religion causes more problems in society than it solves[a]	21	34	24	33	61
If enough people were brought to Christ, social problems would take care of themselves[b]	68	47	73	52	37
Government should do more to protect morality in society[a]	50	33	48	43	27
Organized religious groups should stand up for their beliefs in politics[b]	81	66	80	65	50
Churches should express their views on day-to-day social and political questions[a]	64	46	69	48	34
Organized religious groups of all kinds should stay out of politics[b]	40	52	36	60	70
It is important to me that a president have strong religious beliefs[b]	84	68	86	66	30

Sources:

[a] Pew Forum Religious Landscape Survey, 2007

[b] University of Akron, Fifth National Survey of Religion and Politics, 2008

Note: Entries show percent agreeing with statement

poses a danger to the body politic because when adherents of a particular faith seek to engage in public life on the basis of their religion they are inclined to impose their particular, singular conceptions of the good onto a pluralistic society. Others would claim that all laws impose someone's conceptions of the good on all members of society, and if pluralism values diversity, then Americans who truly treasure pluralism ought to allow religion and religious faith to be part of the public conversation.

Actually, this debate about the public role of religion in pluralistic societies is part of a much older debate between proponents of two competing visions that have long served as the foundation of American political life: republicanism and constitutional liberalism.[8] Not only are the two perspectives different, they are in many ways quite antithetical. And yet, from the very beginning, American society has reflected and embodied a mixture of the republican and liberal ideals and structures—being a pure type of neither perspective (Bellah and Hammond 1980, 10; Tipton 2007, 37).

The basic issue between these two perspectives is whether the good society and quality of public life in America rests upon the virtue of its people or whether it can emanate from the activities of citizens who are motivated by self-interest alone when such actions are governed through the balancing of conflicting interests (Bellah and Hammond 1980, 8). For republicans, the health of the republic is dependent on virtue (Bellah and Hammond 1980, 10), while many classical liberals have held that "a liberal democracy could be made secure, even in the absence of an especially virtuous citizenry, by creating checks and balances" (Kymlicka and Norman 1995, 291).[9]

Part of the reason that both political philosophies flourish within American political thinking is that many of the Founding Fathers and Framers of our Constitution espoused these conflicting views simultaneously. For example, perhaps the most famous statement of the beneficial effects of using the institutions of government to balance conflicting interests is Federalist No. 10, written by James Madison. Yet Madison also suggested that the Constitution's institutional arrangements of separation of powers and federalism would fail to sustain the republic should "sufficient virtue among men for self-government" be absent. He noted, for example, in Federalist No. 55 that "republican government presupposes the existence of these qualities [virtues] to a higher degree than any other form."

Thus, there is a long tradition in American public life in which religion is seen as a vehicle by which a democratic republic is sustained and where public officials are viewed to have a "custodial responsibility for the spiritual as well as the physical well-being" of members of the body politic (Wacker 1984, 22). For many Americans, including many evangelicals, this tradition draws upon the idea of a covenanted nation that places importance upon America being a "city on a hill." According to this tradition, moral issues are exceedingly practical issues, as moral virtue underpins civic virtue, and republics depend on moral self-restraint in order to thrive. This understanding of the need for virtue in order for democratic government to succeed continues to resonate with the American public—as 90 percent of Americans cite "moral character" as the key defining trait of the good citizen (Wuthnow 1998b, 157).

However, when the issue is examined in terms of whether "government should do more to protect morality in society," most Americans responded (in 2007) that it should not. Of course, when the matter is posed in this manner, such responses do not necessarily mean that respondents believe the government has no responsibility with regard to protecting morality in society—only that the government should not presently do more in relationship to such matters. Nevertheless, members of different religious traditions vary in their thinking on the matter, with evangelicals and Black Protestants being the most likely to hold that the state should be doing more (with approximately one-half of those within their respective ranks responding in the affirmative to the statement), while more than two-fifths of Catholics, one-third of mainline Protestants, and a little more than one-quarter of the religiously unaffiliated did so. Clearly, then, within each religious tradition there are those who see some role for religion in public life (as evident by their claim that the government should do more to protect morality in society), but evangelicals and Black Protestants are the most likely to wish for more governmental involvement in these matters. Still, in this regard, only about half of those affiliated with both traditions express this desire.

What, then, about institutions outside of government? What role should religious institutions and organizations play in public life? To what extent should churches and religious organizations get involved in public matters—particularly political matters?

Table 5.2 also examines these questions, and several important conclusions can be drawn from the responses given. First, not only do most Americans hold that "organized religious groups should stand up for their beliefs in politics," but a majority of members of each religious tradition also agree with the statement—with four-fifths of evangelicals and Black Protestants, two-thirds of mainline Protestants and Catholics, and one-half of the religiously unaffiliated doing so.

Second, when the focus shifts from organized religious groups to churches, Americans, regardless of religious tradition, are less prone to express such support. Within each religious tradition, there is typically a 15- to 20-percentage-point drop in the percentage expressing support when the matter is posed in terms of churches as opposed to organized religious groups. Clearly, Americans are more reluctant to have churches become directly engaged in political activities than to have organized religious groups do so.

Third, substantial segments of members of each of the different religious traditions, including majorities in some faiths, also contend that "organized religious groups . . . should stay out of politics." Two-fifths of evangelicals and more than a third of Black Protestants did so—as did more than one-half of mainline Protestants and three-fifths of Catholics. Note, however, that the first statement ("should stand up") and third statement ("should stay out") are opposed to each other: seemingly, in order to be consistent, one could agree with one statement, but would then need to disagree with the other. In data not shown, analysis revealed that a majority of evangelicals (56 percent) and Black Protestants (54 percent) reported consistent stands reflective of organized religious groups expressing their beliefs in public life, as did nearly half of mainline Protestants (45 percent) and a third of Catholics (32 percent). In contrast, around one-tenth of Black Protestants (9 percent) and evangelicals (14 percent) expressed consistent positions that organized religious groups should "stay out" of politics—as did about one-third of mainline Protestants (30 percent) and Catholics (28 percent). Overall, therefore, a larger percentage in each religious tradition expressed consistent sentiments that churches "should stand up" rather than "should stay out" of political matters—though Catholics were rather closely divided on the matter. The exception, however, were the religiously unaffiliated, with nearly twice as many within their ranks expressing positions consistent with organized religious groups staying out rather than standing up for their positions (43 percent versus 24 percent, respectively).

Finally, another way in which religion might be expressed in public life is through the speeches, actions, and character of public officials—particularly the president. In fact, there is a strong cultural expectation that the president should be religious, as nearly three-quarters of Americans have typically reported that they agree with the statement "It is important that the president should have strong religious beliefs" (Smidt et al. 2010, 32). This general sentiment, however, varies somewhat by religious tradition. Though two-thirds of mainline Protestants and Catholics report it is important to them that the president has strong religious beliefs, evangelicals and Black Protestants are even more prone to do so. Only among the religiously unaffiliated does one find less than a majority reporting the matter to be of importance to them.

Civic Values

Social theologies also embody and promote particular values related to civic and political life. The values we each hold provide us with guidelines about what is, and is not, important to us as well as with standards of reference for making decisions about life within the broader community where we live. Our civic values help to identify what the goals of society and political life should be, and the values we share with others help to define prevailing social and political norms (Dalton 2002, 77).

Table 5.3 analyzes differences across religious traditions in terms of various civic values related to the relative importance of freedom versus order in society, tolerance of minority opinions, equality before the law, and standards of morality. One particularly important conclusion can be drawn from the table—namely, that with regard to these particular matters, evangelical Protestants largely stand alongside their fellow Americans in terms of the extent to which they support these particular values. In other words, evangelicals

TABLE 5.3
Views on Civic Norms and Values by Religious Tradition

	Evangelical Protestant (%)	Mainline Protestant (%)	Black Protestant (%)	Roman Catholic (%)	Unaffiliated (%)
Better to live in an orderly society than allow too much freedom[a]	58	53	55	54	38
Society shouldn't have to put up with those who have political ideas that are extremely different from views of the majority[a]	28	23	25	28	26
No matter what a person's political beliefs, he/she is entitled to same legal rights and protections as anyone else[a]	93	93	96	92	93
There are clear and absolute standards for what is right and wrong[b]	85	77	78	79	67

Sources:

[a] Henry Institute National Survey on Religion and Public Life, 2008

[b] Pew Forum Religious Landscape Survey, 2007

Note: Entries show percent agreeing with statement

are not substantially more likely than those of other religious traditions: (1) to espouse order over freedom, (2) to express intolerance for political ideas that deviate significantly from the views of the majority, or (3) to support differential standings before the law based on the ideas one espouses. Though evangelicals are somewhat more likely than those of other religious traditions to affirm that there are "clear and absolute standards for what is right and wrong," they do not do so in substantially greater percentages than mainline Protestants, Black Protestants, or Roman Catholics. Even the religiously unaffiliated, though somewhat less likely to agree to an absolute standard of morality, overwhelmingly do so.

Overall, therefore, it would appear that evangelical Protestants generally exhibit a rather individualistic social ethic and are somewhat more likely than those in most other religious traditions to favor a more limited state that provides fewer services. Their social theology also seems to align them more fully than others with the republican tradition in American political thought, with evangelicals being somewhat more inclined than those in most other religious traditions to be concerned about public morality and favor the presence of religion in public life. Yet, despite such differences, evangelical Protestants stand together with other Americans in terms of their level of adherence to many civic values—including tolerance for political dissent, equality before the law, and their level of preference for freedom over order. And though evangelicals are somewhat more prone than those of some other religious traditions to hold that there are absolute standards of right and wrong, the extent to which they do so is not substantially greater than that found within other religious traditions.

Change over Time

To what extent, then, has the social theology of evangelical Protestants changed over time? Is there any evidence of a shift in their perspectives related to the role of government or the place of religion in public life? And are the relative differences in social theology currently evident between evangelicals and those of other faith traditions actually greater or smaller today than was true in the past?

These questions are addressed in table 5.4. It should be noted, however, that the analysis is rather restricted in terms of the time span analyzed. The Anti-Semitism in the United States survey of 1964 did not include any questions on social theology that can be used for comparative purposes. Once again, the effort was made to examine as many identical questions on matters related to social theology as possible—but few identical questions are available for analyses over time in which detailed denominational affiliation measures are also available. As a result, our analysis is limited to an examination

TABLE 5.4
Views on Religion in Public Life by Religious Tradition over Time

	Evangelical Protestant (%)	Mainline Protestant (%)	Black Protestant (%)	Roman Catholic (%)	Unaffiliated (%)
1996					
If enough people were brought to Christ, social problems would take care of themselves	73	56	73	x	x
Organized religious groups of all kinds should stay out of politics	38	51	41	51	60
There are absolute standards of right and wrong	87	74	87	73	69
2008					
If enough people were brought to Christ, social problems would take care of themselves	68	47	73	52	37
Organized religious groups of all kinds should stay out of politics	40	52	36	60	70
There are absolute standards of right and wrong	90	78	83	80	63

Sources:

1996: University of Akron, Second Quadrennial Survey of Religion and Politics

2008: University of Akron, Fifth Quadrennial Survey of Religion and Politics

Note: Entries show percent agreeing with statement

x – not asked

of changes in response to three questions asked over a twelve-year span of time (between the years 1996 and 2008); these data are presented in table 5.4.

Based on these limited data, it would appear that some changes have occurred since the mid-1990s in the way different religious groups have responded to these questions. In terms of whether social problems would take care of themselves if enough people were brought to Christ, evangelicals largely continue to believe that individual transformation is likely to have significant social effects, though they appear to be somewhat less convinced of the matter today than previously; the same can be said with regard to mainline Protestants. In contrast, Black Protestants continued to express agreement with the statement at the same high level in 2008 as they did in 1996.

However, when asked whether organized religious groups should stay out of politics, evangelical and mainline Protestants express largely the same opinions today as they did in the mid-1990s. Black Protestants, in contrast, are less likely to hold that organized religious groups should stay out of politics now than previously, but the opposite was true for Catholics and the religiously unaffiliated—as a far greater percentage of each group expressed the desire in 2008 than in 1996 that such religious groups stay out of politics.

Finally, those affiliated with different religious traditions have also shifted in terms of their beliefs concerning the presence of absolute standards of right and wrong. Evangelical Protestants, mainline Protestants, and Catholics were even more inclined in 2008 than in 1996 to hold that such standards exist, whereas Black Protestants and the religiously unaffiliated were less inclined to do so.

Thus, the data presented in table 5.4 suggest that there may have been some changes in perspectives related to social theology among those affiliated with different religious traditions—but that these shifts do not appear to be substantial in nature. In part, this lack of major change may be a function of the limited span of time examined. Nevertheless, dramatic changes in public opinion and attitudes can, and do, occur over a rather short period of time—something not evident with regard to the questions presented in table 5.4. Rather, it would appear that the social theology of evangelicals (as well as those of other religious traditions) remains much the same today as it did in the middle of the last decade of the previous millennium.

Divisions among Evangelicals

Racial and Ethnic Differences

In examining social theology, we have once again found that Black Protestants and evangelicals tend to mirror each other on a number of matters—but exhibit substantially different positions on matters related to the role of government. To what extent, then, do black, Hispanic, and white evangelicals "stand together" in their social theology? To what degree, if at all, do black evangelical Protestants differ in terms of their social theology from their fellow blacks who are affiliated with the Black Protestant tradition? And does religious tradition affiliation make any difference in the social theology of whites or Hispanics?

These matters are addressed in table 5.5. Once again, given the need to engage in subgroup analysis, the questions examined are limited to those contained in the Religious Landscape Survey. Overall, the data presented in table 5.5 suggest (1) the positions of evangelicals on matters of social theology are largely shaped by racial differences, and (2) religious tradition affiliation does shape certain positions on social theology among white respondents, but has less importance in doing so among black and Hispanic respondents.

First, white evangelicals tend to espouse quite different positions on matters of social theology than black evangelicals, particularly with regard to matters related to the role of government (the first three items presented in the table). And though the positions of Hispanic evangelicals on these questions tend to fall closer to (and at times even mirror) those adopted by white evangelicals, white and Hispanic evangelicals also tend to part ways, particularly concerning the role of government.

Second, on most of the questions examined in table 5.5, black evangelicals and blacks in the Black Protestant tradition stand far closer together than do whites and blacks within the same evangelical Protestant tradition. And the same is true in large part for Hispanics—at least when considering the role of government. On this particular matter, the positions of Hispanic evangelicals and Hispanic Catholics are virtually identical—with white and Hispanic evangelicals adopting relatively different positions.

Third, on some matters of social theology, whites tend to adopt relatively similar positions regardless of the particular religious tradition to which they belong, whereas on other matters of social theology, religious tradition shapes the positions whites adopt. For example, relatively small differences exist when one probes about preferences for a smaller government, but substantial differences exist among whites across religious traditions when it comes to the government doing more to protect morality in society or with regard to churches expressing their views on political questions.

Thus, overall, the data suggest that both race and religious tradition serve to shape perspectives related to social theology. On matters related to the role of government, blacks and Hispanics, regardless of their religious tradition, tend to stand together—adopting far different positions as a group than whites on such matters. Yet, on other aspects of social theology, whites and Hispanics divide more on the basis of religious, rather than racial, differences—with

TABLE 5.5

Social Theology by Racial and Ethnic Differences (controlling for religious tradition)

	Evangelical Protestant			Mainline Protestant	Black Protestant	Roman Catholic	
	White (%)	Black (%)	Hispanic (%)	White (%)	Black (%)	White (%)	Hispanic (%)
Government should do more to help needy Americans	54	81	65	57	80	60	67
Prefer government with fewer services	53	21	22	53	18	50	18
Government should do more to protect morality in society	49	50	59	33	48	39	53
There are clear standards for right and wrong	86	79	84	77	78	79	78
Churches should express their views on social and political questions	62	71	60	45	69	31	53

Source: Pew Forum Religious Landscape Survey, 2007

Note: Entries show percent agreeing with statement

white evangelicals adopting different positions on such matters than white mainline Protestants or Catholics or with Hispanic evangelicals adopting positions much closer to those of white evangelicals than Hispanic Catholics. Consequently, though the ranks of evangelicals are not substantially divided along racial lines when it comes to religious beliefs and behavior (see table 4.8), evangelicals are far more substantially divided along racial lines when one examines differences in their social theology.

Generational and Educational Differences

Previously, it was found that the religious beliefs and behavior of evangelicals differed relatively little in terms of generational or educational differences within the ranks. Differences among evangelicals, however, came to the fore when examining their social theology along racial lines. Is the same true, then, with regard to generational and educational differences among evangelicals? Are there also greater generational and educational differences among evangelicals in terms of their social theology than what was previously found with regard to their religious beliefs and behavior?

In fact, it is with regard to social theology that we see the beginnings of a possible basis for recent claims that a new generation of evangelicals is emerging (e.g., Wehner 2007; Fitzgerald 2008; Pally 2011). Though generational differences are not evident between millennial evangelicals and older evangelicals across every measure of social theology, there are some substantial generational differences among evangelicals related to certain matters of social theology (see table 5.6).

These generational differences suggest that millennial evangelicals are more likely than older evangelicals to favor a more activist government and that, in so doing, they more closely mirror other millennials than they do their older evangelical brethren. Several pieces of evidence tend to substantiate this contention. First, older evangelicals are far more likely than millennial evangelicals to prefer a government with fewer services. Whereas half of older evangelicals (52 percent) report that they prefer a smaller government, only about one-quarter of millennial evangelicals (28 percent) do so. In fact, in each instance, the millennial generation within each religious tradition is substantially less willing to report a preference for a government with fewer services than the older coreligionists. As a result, millennial evangelicals more closely mirror the preferences expressed by other millennials, regardless of their religious tradition, than they do the preferences expressed by older evangelicals.

Second, millennial evangelicals are more likely than older evangelicals to agree that government needs to do more to help the needy. Once again, millennials within each religious tradition are more likely than their older brethren to favor the government doing more to help the needy (the exception being millennials in the Black Protestant tradition). And when one compares the positions of millennials across all five religious traditions, such differences are much less in magnitude than when comparing the positions of the older cohorts across those same traditions.[10]

Third, within each of the five religious traditions examined, a higher percentage of millennials than non-millennials favor government doing more to protect morality in society. Once again, the overall expectation among millennials is that the government should take a more active role in addressing social problems—though in this instance in terms of protecting morality. Moreover, when one excludes the religiously unaffiliated, differences among millennials on this matter are also far less than that among the older cohorts of members across the same religious traditions.

Non-college-educated and college-educated evangelicals also express somewhat different social theologies. Non-college-educated evangelicals are far more likely than their college-educated co-religionists to favor an activist government. Thus, within each religious tradition, the college graduates are far more likely than those with lower levels of education to be more likely to prefer a government that provides fewer services, less likely to want government to do more to help the needy (though the difference between Black Protestants on this matter is rather small in magnitude), and less likely to desire government to do more to protect morality (though the difference between evangelicals on this matter is rather small in magnitude).

Moreover, having a college education tends to magnify differences in social theology across religious traditions. In other words, when examining a particular issue (e.g., whether the government should do more to help the needy), the spread between the highest and lowest percentages across religious traditions is always greater when comparing college graduates than when comparing non-college graduates. In other words, having had a college education magnifies differences in social theology across the religious traditions.

Finally, differing levels of educational attainment among evangelicals have mixed effects—with college education magnifying some differences in social theology among evangelicals while hardly having any effect on other matters. For example, differences in preference for a government with fewer services between evangelicals on the basis of educational attainment is 20 percent—the largest difference for any of the five religious traditions. Likewise, college-educated evangelicals are less likely than their less educated brethren to agree that government should do more to help the needy, and this level of difference between the two categories of evangelicals (16 percent) is once again the largest across each of the five religious traditions. On the other hand, educational attainment exhibits little effect on the position of evangelicals related

TABLE 5.6
Social Theology by Generational Cohort and
Educational Attainment (controlling for religious tradition)

	Generational		Education	
	Non-Millennial (%)	Millennial (%)	Non-College Graduate (%)	College Graduate (%)
Evangelical Protestant				
Government should do more to help needy	56	65	60	44
Government do more to protect morality	49	55	50	48
Prefer government with fewer services	52	28	44	64
Churches should express social/political views	63	73	63	69
Religion causes more problems than it solves	21	24	22	18
There are clear and absolute standards	85	84	84	86
Mainline Protestant				
Government should do more to help needy	57	63	61	53
Government do more to protect morality	32	45	38	25
Prefer government with fewer services	54	30	47	58
Churches should express social/political views	46	50	46	46
Religion causes more problems than it solves	33	41	34	35
There are clear and absolute standards	76	78	80	70
Black Protestant				
Government should do more to help needy	80	76	79	76
Government do more to protect morality	47	54	50	38
Prefer government with fewer services	19	14	17	28

Churches should express social/political views	67	77	70	65
Religion causes more problems than it solves	24	27	25	23
There are clear and absolute standards	76	78	80	70
Roman Catholic				
Government should do more to help needy	61	69	65	56
Government do more to protect morality	42	49	46	34
Prefer government with fewer services	43	22	35	52
Churches should express social/political views	47	57	47	49
Religion causes more problems than it solves	33	38	34	32
There are clear and absolute standards	79	78	80	74
Unaffiliated				
Government should do more to help needy	64	70	67	62
Government do more to protect morality	25	33	32	14
Prefer government with fewer services	45	29	39	46
Churches should express social/political views	33	39	36	35
Religion causes more problems than it solves	62	59	58	70
There are clear and absolute standards	67	67	72	54

Source: Pew Forum Religious Landscape Survey, 2007

Note: Entries show percent agreeing with statement

to whether the government should do more to protect morality or whether absolute standards exist—with differences between the two categories of evangelicals exhibiting the smallest magnitude of difference across the five religious traditions. Thus, depending on the particular matter of social theology being examined, college education can make a considerable, or hardly any, difference in the positions adopted by evangelicals.

Religious Differences

A number of social theorists (e.g., Wuthnow 1988; Hunter 1991) have contended that important differences often exist between traditionalist and more modernist members of the major religious traditions, as religious traditions have been increasingly polarized by theological, social, and cultural conflicts into a "conservative," "orthodox," or "traditionalist" faction on one side, and a "liberal," "progressive," or "modernist" one on the other. Although scholarly analyses of these divisions have often focused on the political manifestations of this division (Williams 1997; Fiorina, Abrams, and Pope 2005; Nivoli and Brady 2006), the bases of its original formulations were rooted in theological developments, with the competing camps within the same tradition being characterized by alternative belief systems, different religious practices, and adherence to rival religious movements.[11] Previous research (e.g., Green 2007; Smidt et al. 2010) has revealed that important political differences exist between traditionalist and more modernist members of the major religious traditions, though little effort has yet been expended to examine the effects of traditionalism on social theology.

For the analysis presented in this volume, members of each religious tradition are classified into traditionalist and non-traditionalist categories based on the answer the respondents provided to the question of whether they thought that their "church or denomination should preserve its traditional beliefs and practices," "adjust [them] in light of new circumstances," or "adopt modern beliefs and practices."[12] Those who offered the first answer ("should preserve") were classified as "traditionalists," whereas those who provided one of the other two answers ("adjust" or "adopt") were classified as "non-traditionalists."[13]

Clearly, important differences in social theology are evident within each religious tradition based on whether or not the respondent can be classified as a religious "traditionalist" (see table 5.7). Several important patterns are evident. First, when comparing traditionalists and non-traditionalists on specific questions, the difference in positions always moves in the same direction within each of the four traditions (with one exception—the preference for a government with fewer services among Black Protestants). For example,

TABLE 5.7
Social Theology by Religious Traditionalism (controlling for religious tradition)

	Non-Traditionalist (%)	Traditionalist (%)
Evangelical Protestant		
Government should do more to help needy	64	54
Government should do more to protect morality	44	54
Prefer government with fewer services	44	52
Churches should express social/political views	59	68
Religion causes more problems than it solves	27	17
There are clear and absolute standards	82	87
Mainline Protestant		
Government should do more to help needy	61	53
Government should do more to protect morality	29	43
Prefer government with fewer services	50	55
Churches should express social/political views	44	51
Religion causes more problems than it solves	39	25
There are clear and absolute standards	74	84
Black Protestant		
Government should do more to help needy	81	80
Government should do more to protect morality	45	51
Prefer government with fewer services	22	17
Churches should express social/political views	66	72
Religion causes more problems than it solves	28	22
There are clear and absolute standards	78	80
Roman Catholic		
Government should do more to help needy	65	60
Government should do more to protect morality	38	51
Prefer government with fewer services	39	43
Churches should express social/political views	44	56
Religion causes more problems than it solves	38	27
There are clear and absolute standards	77	83

Source: Pew Forum Religious Landscape Survey, 2007

Note: Entries show percent agreeing with statement

traditionalist evangelicals are less likely than non-traditionalist evangelicals to agree that the government should do more to help the needy; this same pattern is evident among mainline Protestants, Black Protestants, and Roman Catholics. Thus, traditionalism basically works in similar ways on matters of social theology across all four religious traditions.

Second, religious traditionalism tends to be broader in its scope of influence in shaping social theology than either generational or educational differences. Six different matters related to social theology are examined in table 5.7. And if one uses the arbitrary figure of a 5-percentage-point difference in positions on each matter of social theology, then this magnitude of difference is attained within each tradition more consistently on the basis of religious differences within their ranks than on the basis of generational or educational differences. For example, among evangelical Protestants, there is a difference of 5 percent or more between traditionalists and non-traditionalists for each of the six items examined. In comparison, this level of difference on matters of social theology is attained only four times when generational differences are examined among evangelicals and only three times when educational differences are examined. Based on similar comparisons, religious differences among mainline Protestants, Black Protestants, and Catholics are also broader in the scope of their effects than are generational or educational differences within their ranks. Only among Black Protestants is there an exception to this pattern—as both educational and religious differences attained the 5-percent level of difference in four of the six cases.

However, the effects of generational and educational differences can be greater in their magnitude of differences than those of religious differences. For example, in terms of stated preferences for a smaller government, a difference of 24 percent was evident between millennial and non-millennial evangelicals, a difference of 20 percent between non-college-educated and college-educated evangelicals, and a difference of 8 percent between traditionalist and non-traditionalist evangelicals. Consequently, though differences in religious traditionalism may affect a wider scope of matters related to social theology than do either generational or educational differences, generational and educational differences can nevertheless have substantially greater effects on particular matters of social theology than differences in traditionalism.

Controlling for Multiple Variables Simultaneously

Having established that differences related to race/ethnicity, generational cohort, educational attainment, and religious traditionalism all serve to shape evangelical responses to matters related to social theology, the question becomes: Which of these factors most strongly shapes such responses? To control for the relative effects of each of these four factors, a multiple classification analysis (MCA) was performed. MCA accommodates the use of categorical variables in multivariate analysis and avoids the necessity of using dummy variables.[14] Thus, the distinct advantage of using MCA is that it can provide a single *beta* value for a categorical variable as a whole, rather than a number of scores for each of the categories of that particular variable, with the magnitude of the *beta* value revealing the relative strength of the relationship once the effects of the other variables in the analysis have been taken into account. The *beta* values for each of the independent variables are presented in table 5.8.

However, before examining the results, three particular points should be noted. First, analysis is limited to evangelicals only. In other words, the analysis seeks to determine which of these four factors is the most important in shaping the responses of evangelicals; it does not reveal whether these factors are necessarily of similar import among those affiliated with other religious traditions. Second, because the analysis includes racial/ethnic differences, only questions related to social theology found in the Pew Religious Landscape Survey are analyzed. Finally, this analysis employs the dichotomous coding of generational cohort, educational attainment, and religious traditionalism found in the previous tables, with the three-fold classification of white, black, and Hispanic used for race/ethnicity. In other words, it does not employ a potentially fuller range of variation related to each of the independent variables (e.g., the education variable in the analysis was based on college versus non-college educated rather than some education variable that could run from less than an eighth grade education through attaining some post-graduate degree).[15]

Six different dependent variables related to social theology are examined in the table. Educational differences (*beta*=.15) are the most important factor shaping evangelical responses to whether the government should do more to help the needy—with racial/ethnic differences trailing closely behind

TABLE 5.8
Assessing Divisions among Evangelical Protestants on Social Theology: A Multivariate Analysis

	Government should help needy	Government should protect morality	Smaller government preferred	Churches should express views	Religion causes problems in society	Absolute standards for right and wrong
Race/ethnicity	.13	.06	.22	.05	.01	.03
Generational	.04	.04	.16	.09	.04	.01
Educational	.15	.02	.13	.05	.04	.00
Religious traditionalism	.09	.11	.08	.11	.11	.09
R^2	.05	.02	.11	.02	.02	.01

Source: Pew Forum Religious Landscape Survey, 2007

(*beta*=.13). However, educational differences among evangelicals hardly matter when examining the remaining five questions related to social theology; only with regard to whether religion causes more problems in society than it solves do educational differences rank as high as second in relative importance—and even in that case it was tied with generational differences in relative importance (*beta*=.04).

Racial and ethnic differences among evangelicals best explain preferences related to governmental size, but these same racial and ethnic differences hardly mattered when most other matters of social theology are considered (except, as noted above, with regard to helping the needy). Overall, generational differences also exhibited relatively little importance in accounting for differences among evangelicals in terms of social theology, though generational differences ranked second in relative importance with regard to preferences related to governmental size and whether churches should stay out of political matters.

Rather, the most important factor to explain differences among evangelicals on matters of social theology was religious traditionalism. On four of the six items examined in table 5.8, it exhibited the largest *beta* value. In other words, differences in religious traditionalism were generally far more important than differences in racial/ethnic composition, generational cohort, or differences in educational attainment in accounting for differences among evangelicals on matters related to social theology.

Conclusions

Evangelical Protestants generally exhibit an individualistic social ethic. As a result, they are more prone, when compared to those affiliated with other religious traditions, to favor a more limited state that provides fewer services. They are also somewhat more inclined than those in other religious traditions to be concerned about public morality and favor the presence of religion in public life.

Nevertheless, despite these differences, evangelical Protestants largely stand together with other Americans in terms of their level of adherence to other civic values—including tolerance for political dissent, equality before the law, and their level of preference for freedom over order. And though evangelicals are somewhat more inclined than those of some other religious traditions to contend that absolute standards of right and wrong exist, the extent to which they do so is not substantially greater than what is evident within the other religious traditions.

Where comparisons are possible, it appears the positions that evangelicals have adopted on matters of social theology have hardly shifted over the course of the past decade or so. This was also true with regard to the social theology expressed by those affiliated with the other religious traditions as well.

Finally, differences in social theology are evident among evangelicals in terms of racial/ethnic divisions, generational cohort, educational attainment, and religious traditionalism. But when the effects of these four different variables are examined in a simultaneous fashion, it appears that the major fault line dividing evangelicals in matters of social theology primarily relates to differences in religious traditionalism found within their ranks.

6

They Will Know We Are Christians by Our Love? The Civic Life of Evangelicals

THE STUDY OF CIVIL SOCIETY and its contribution to democratic life has exploded over the past two decades (Cohen 1999, 263). Though many commentators and analysts often equate public life with politics, involvement in public life is actually far broader and more encompassing than engagement in politics (Cochran 1990, 51). Political life is aimed at "influencing the selection of governmental personnel and/or the actions they take," whereas civic life reflects publicly spirited action, generally nonremunerative in nature, that is *not* guided "by some desire to shape public policy" (Campbell 2004, 7). Thus, the political engagement of citizens, a topic that will be addressed in the next chapter, is but a component of their larger public or "civic" endeavors.

Engagement in civic life exhibits the common thread of working to sustain and build one's community, as civic engagement denotes "people's connection with the life of their communities" (Putnam 1995, 665). Participation in public life can be exhibited in various ways, for example, through joining associations and organizations, volunteering, or making charitable contributions. It can also encompass a range of activities, such as working as a volunteer in a soup kitchen, participating in a book club, leading a boys' or girls' club, or organizing some charitable event.

Engagement in public life is essential to human flourishing. When one participates in, shares responsibilities for, and develops affective ties to some social entity outside oneself—whether it be a voluntary association, a church, a neighborhood, or a workplace—it adds a dimension to human experience beyond that present in the private realm. Moreover, this participation in civic life not only serves to balance the limitations of private life, but it also serves to moderate some of its negative tendencies.[1] Generally speaking, a citizenry that actively participates in civic life is lauded and met with approval by analysts and practitioners alike.

This chapter examines the civic life of evangelicals. It examines how evangelicals view other members of society in terms of interpersonal trust and their perceptions about whether their values are under attack. It analyzes the extent to which evangelicals choose to volunteer in service to others, donate to charitable causes, join voluntary associations, and exhibit tolerance toward others within society. Once again, we will compare evangelicals to those affiliated with other major religious traditions, track changes over time where possible, and then examine the civic life of evangelicals along the four potential fault lines that may serve to divide evangelicals today—namely, the racial, generational, educational, and theological divisions within their ranks.

The Civic Life of Evangelicals

In his book on evangelicals, Christian Smith (1998) has argued that evangelical Protestants have flourished, in part, because evangelicals have socially constructed distinctions that serve to differentiate them from various relevant "outgroups." On the one hand, evangelicals see themselves as different from others in that "the evangelical tradition's entire history . . . presupposes and reflects strong cultural boundaries with nonevangelicals" (Smith 1998, 121). Moreover, evangelicals are more likely to see themselves as "embattled," with their values under attack and their social status as one of "second-class" citizens (Smith 1998, 131–42). Yet, rather than withdrawing from civic life, they have chosen to engage the pluralism of contemporary American society. Thus, evangelicals are prone neither to a rigid sectarianism that fully separates them from public life nor to some religious or cultural accommodationalism in which evangelicals embrace prevailing cultural values and practices. In the words of the title of Smith's book, evangelicals are embattled and thriving, but the fact that they are thriving supposedly derives, in large part, from the fact that they are not only engaged but also embattled.

Here we will examine the extent to which evangelicals are engaged, yet perceive themselves as embattled. We begin our analysis of the civic life of evangelicals with an examination of the extent to which evangelicals maintain a certain "social distance" from other Americans. We then shift to examine the extent to which they may get involved in civic life through organizational involvement, acts of generosity, and then expressions of tolerance toward those with whom they may disagree.

Expectations of Others

A generalized trust in others (i.e., "social trust") involves expectations related to whether other people are reliable, predictable, competent, or caring. Though social scientists have long engaged in the study of social trust, its nature and consequences are matters of some dispute (e.g., Jackman and Miller 1998; Levi and Stoker 2000).

One area of dispute has been the source of trust itself. Some scholars have suggested that interpersonal trust is positively related to participation in the voluntary associations of civil society, including religion (Putnam 2000), while others have concluded interpersonal trust results from a citizen's confidence in government, particularly government's stability and power to enforce agreements between citizens (Brehm and Rahn 1997; Levi and Stoker 2000, 493–95). A related question concerns the scope of interpersonal trust. Though participation in religious life may generate trust among one's co-religionists, it may not necessarily lead them to develop high levels of trust in those outside their own religious group.[2] Indeed, some scholars have suggested that the evidence for the emergence of a generalized trust is weak even when citizens belong to heterogeneous groups, despite their exposure to a wide range of people and ideas (Theiss-Morse and Hibbing 2005).

Given Christian Smith's arguments discussed above, as well as certain theological considerations,[3] one might anticipate that evangelicals would be less trusting and more suspicious of others than those affiliated with other religious traditions. Consequently, the upper portion of table 6.1 examines the extent to which Americans of different religious traditions report people can be generally trusted—as well as whether they think that people generally look out for themselves and whether they try to take advantage of others (based on responses to the General Social Survey of 2010).

The first thing to note in table 6.1 is that most Americans are reluctant to report that other people can be trusted. Within none of the five religious traditions examined did even a majority of members indicate that they thought people as a whole could be trusted. Mainline Protestants tend to be the most trusting of others, Black Protestants the least trusting. Evangelicals were far less trusting of others than mainline Protestants, but evangelicals largely mirror the patterns found among Catholics and the religiously unaffiliated. Thus, overall, the level of generalized trust exhibited by evangelicals does not appear to be dramatically different from those affiliated with most other religious traditions.

The bottom portion of table 6.1 examines the extent to which those affiliated with different religious traditions report certain tensions or threats from living in contemporary American life. Here the questions are drawn from the Pew Religious Landscape Survey and reflect the totality of all such questions

TABLE 6.1
Expectations of Others and Perceptions of Cultural Tension by Religious Tradition

	Evangelical Protestant (%)	Mainline Protestant (%)	Black Protestant (%)	Roman Catholic (%)	Unaffiliated (%)
People can be trusted[a]	32	49	15	33	38
People should look out for themselves[a]	46	30	60	44	46
People take advantage of others[a]	42	23	62	38	41
There is a natural conflict between being a religious person and living in modern society[b]	52	34	51	36	x
My values are threatened by Hollywood[b]	54	42	36	44	29

Sources:

[a] General Social Survey, 2010

[b] Pew Forum Religious Landscape Survey, 2007

Note: Entries show percent agreeing with statement

x – not asked of religiously unaffiliated respondents

posed in the survey. Based on these responses, it would appear that evangelicals are more inclined to see themselves as being embattled than those of other religious traditions. A majority of evangelical Protestants (as well as a majority of Black Protestants) see a natural conflict between being a religious person and living within modern society; in comparison, only a little more than one-third of those affiliated with the other religious traditions do so. Just what serves as the basis of this perceived conflict is unclear—whether it is science itself, contemporary media, institutions of higher education, or social and religious change. But, regardless of the reason, evangelicals are somewhat more likely than those in most other religious traditions to report that there is a conflict between being a religious person and living in modern society.

This perception of being embattled is further evident in terms of whether one believes that one's values are under attack by Hollywood. On this matter, evangelical Protestants and Black Protestants part company, as evangelicals are far more likely than those of other religious traditions to express perceptions of their values being under attack by the entertainment industry.[4]

Thus, overall, evangelicals are somewhat less trusting of others than are mainline Protestants, but their overall levels of social trust mirror those expressed by Roman Catholics and the religiously unaffiliated as a whole, and exceed substantially the levels of trust expressed by Black Protestants. Yet, despite hardly being distinctive in terms of their relative distrust of others, evangelicals do report higher levels of tension and conflict from living in contemporary American society. On the basis of the evidence here, we cannot say whether this perception of being embattled contributes to the relative religious vitality of evangelical Protestantism, but evangelicals are the most likely of the religious traditions examined to report such tension and conflict with the broader culture of which they are a part.

Organizational Involvement

The United States is known as a nation of joiners, as Americans have long exhibited a propensity to join with others for various collective purposes. Already in the early 1800s, Alexis de Tocqueville (1969, 199) wrote that "the power of association has reached its uttermost development in America."[5] This proclivity to form and join associations might represent nothing more than a cultural curiosity were it not for the importance that social theorists have attributed to participation in civic associations. In fact, many social theorists have insisted that democracy requires civic associations that are not specifically political in nature but that function as sources of meaning and social engagement for its members. For Tocqueville and his followers, democracy cannot survive unless its citizens continue to participate actively, joining with others of similar mind and interest to address matters of common concern.

Of course, associations can take various forms, and discussions of associational involvement do not always differentiate between and among those forms. For example, participation in organizations such as parent-teacher associations (PTA) or Kiwanis clubs reflects involvement in voluntary associations, but friendship groups and social networks are also forms of association. Nevertheless, much of the theoretical focus related to voluntary associations has been in terms of "a formally organized named group, most of whose members—whether persons or organizations—are not financially recompensed for their participation" (Knoke 1986, 2), with social interaction within voluntary organizations being "distinguished by virtue of being organized, purposeful, voluntary, and non-remunerative" (Miller 2003, 8).

Typically, when seeking to ascertain membership in voluntary associations, surveys have employed a battery of questions in which respondents are asked whether they belong to any club or organization that fits into some broad category (e.g., "literary, art, discussion, or study group"; "farm organizations"; "professional association"). And different survey organizations choose to capture these memberships using either a wider or a narrower array of different kinds of associations.[6] The more encompassing the list provided, the higher the proportion of respondents who report membership in some voluntary association (Ulzurrun 2002, 501). Interestingly, though there are good theoretical reasons to view church membership as a form of membership in a voluntary association, it is not customarily treated as such—despite the fact that church membership reflects the most common form of affiliation with a voluntary association within American life.[7]

Previous analyses have revealed that those affiliated with certain religious traditions are more prone than those in other traditions to join such organizations (e.g., Wuthnow 1999), and table 6.2 confirms previous findings that mainline Protestants are generally the most likely to report such associational memberships (with approximately three-quarters doing so), while the religiously unaffiliated are the least likely to do so (with approximately one-half

TABLE 6.2
Associational Membership by Religious Tradition

	Evangelical Protestant (%)	Mainline Protestant (%)	Black Protestant (%)	Roman Catholic (%)	Unaffiliated (%)
Member of a voluntary association[a]	70	76	61	57	53
Adding congregational membership[b]					
Member of neither	7	7	9	16	29
Member of voluntary association only	18	31	16	22	71
Member of congregation only	13	6	8	9	0
Member of both	62	56	68	53	0

Sources:

[a] General Social Survey, 2010

[b] Saguaro Social Capital Benchmark National Survey, 2000

Note: Entries show percent stating affiliation

doing so). Evangelical Protestants trail mainline Protestants in the extent to which they report membership in voluntary associations (70 percent versus 76 percent, respectively), but their membership levels still exceed those of Black Protestants and Roman Catholics (61 percent and 57 percent, respectively).[8]

Thus, despite whatever their tensions may be with the broader culture, evangelicals tend to be relatively active in civic life. They join civic organizations (beyond congregational membership) at a relatively high rate—trailing only mainline Protestants in their proclivity to join such associations. Moreover, their level of civic engagement exceeds that evident for both Black Protestants and Catholics, and substantially exceeds that evident among the religiously unaffiliated. Evangelicals may perceive themselves to be embattled, but they are nevertheless actively engaged in civic life.

Generosity

Despite the social distance that (some) evangelicals may feel toward other Americans, do they choose to be generous toward others as measured in terms of "gifts of time and money" (something that Putnam and Campbell [2010, 444] have labeled "acts of generosity")? Acts of volunteering and charitable giving tend to go together, as those who do the one are more likely to do the other as well (Hodgkinson, Weitzman, and Kirsch 1990, 102ff; Putnam 2000, 118).

On the one hand, volunteering constitutes any activity that is freely given to benefit another person, group, or organization (Wilson 2000, 215). Previous research has shown that members of religious congregations volunteer their time more frequently (and volunteer more hours) than those who are not (e.g., Hodgkinson, Weitzman, and Kirsch 1990, 102), and studies of religion and volunteering further reveal that higher levels of worship attendance are related to greater levels of volunteering (e.g., Hodgkinson et al. 1996; Wuthnow 1999; Brooks 2003; Campbell and Yonish 2003; Wuthnow 2004b). Of course, it is not surprising that religious people engage in religious volunteering. But regular churchgoers are not only more likely to volunteer for religious causes, they are far more likely to volunteer for secular causes as well, as "religious volunteering does not crowd out secular volunteering" (Putnam and Campbell 2010, 445).

Likewise, one of the most consistently reported findings regarding religion and giving is that persons who are religious are more likely to donate money to charitable organizations and, among those who do make charitable contributions, to give more money than those who are less religious. This pattern holds true whether one considers financial gifts to all charitable organizations, only to religious organizations, or only to secular organizations (e.g.,

Hodgkinson, Weitzman, and Kirsch 1990, 103, 107; Regnerus, Smith, and
Sikkink 1998; Nemeth and Luidens 2003). Thus, "heavy religious giving does
not crowd out giving to secular causes, but instead accompanies it, so that religious people give more to both religious and nonreligious causes" (Putnam
and Campbell 2010, 449).

However, given that this study examines evangelicals, the question becomes whether evangelicals differ from members of other religious traditions
in the extent to which they may exhibit such generosity. Does this generosity,
then, vary across affiliation with different religious traditions?

Table 6.3 addresses this matter. The first thing to note from the table is that
different survey organizations have chosen to pose their volunteering question in different ways. Some have asked, for example, whether the respondent
has volunteered sometime over the past year, others have asked in terms of
volunteering over the past month, and still other surveys have asked questions about volunteering within the particular church with which they are
affiliated. Obviously, different results are obtained depending on the way in
which the question is posed.

Nevertheless, overall, evangelicals appear to volunteer at levels similar to, if
not somewhat greater than, those of other religious traditions. When one examines volunteering in terms of having done so during the past month, evangelicals trail slightly those within the other Christian traditions (particularly,
mainline Protestants) in doing so. But when examined in terms of having
volunteered over the course of a longer span of time, evangelical Protestants
seemingly lead the way, as 62 percent of evangelical Protestants reported that
they had volunteered at some point over the past year.

Of course, much of this reported volunteering may have been done within a
religious context. And when asked whether some, if not all, of the volunteering
done was religious in nature, approximately three-fifths of evangelical, mainline, and Black Protestants reported that they volunteered for some religious
group in the past year, though less than half of Catholics (46 percent) did so.

Still, religious volunteering does not generally diminish the level of volunteering done for more secular causes. In fact, as is evident in the upper
portion of table 6.3, evangelical Protestants were just as likely to report that
they had volunteered for some nonreligious group in the past year as they had
for a religious group (with three-fifths of evangelicals reporting that they had
volunteered in each capacity). On the other hand, both mainline Protestants
and Catholics were more likely to report that they had volunteered for nonreligious than religious groups. Actually, Black Protestants constituted the only
Christian tradition in which members were somewhat more likely to have
volunteered for a religious than a nonreligious group—though the difference
in doing so was not very substantial. But even this distinction between reli-

TABLE 6.3
Volunteering and Charitable Contributions by Religious Tradition

	Evangelical Protestant (%)	Mainline Protestant (%)	Black Protestant (%)	Roman Catholic (%)	Unaffiliated (%)
Volunteer Activity					
Volunteered past month[a]	29	38	32	31	26
Volunteered past year[b]	62	57	56	58	57
Volunteered for religious group in past year[c]	60	58	63	46	x
Volunteered for nonreligious group past year[c]	60	73	58	70	77
Volunteered in church to do community work[d]	72	66	70	57	x
Charitable Contributions					
No charitable contributions in past year[c]	20	16	22	28	41
Donated more than $25[a]	85	86	73	78	66

Sources:

[a] General Social Survey, 2010

[b] Henry Institute National Survey on Religion and Politics, 2008

[c] Faith Matters Survey, 2005

[d] Pew Forum Religious Landscape Survey, 2007

Note: Entries show percent reporting activity/contributions

x – not asked of religiously unaffiliated respondents

gious and secular volunteering may underestimate the level of volunteering done to aid those outside one's religious group as, when asked whether they had volunteered "to do community work through their place of worship," the majority of those affiliated with each of the four Christian traditions reported they had done so, with evangelical Protestants being slightly more likely than those within the other religious traditions to report having done so.[9]

Much the same can be said in relationship to charitable giving. Evangelicals are just as likely as, if not more likely than, those of other religious traditions to report giving money and/or goods to charitable causes in the past year. The greatest differences are evident between those who are religiously affiliated and those who are not, as those who are religiously unaffiliated tend to be far less generous in terms of charitable contributions—at least when examined in terms of having donated as little as $25 or more toward charitable causes. Moreover, as was evident in chapter 3, there are important differences in family income levels across the five religious traditions, with income levels among evangelical and Black Protestants as a whole being lower than that found among those within the remaining three traditions. Consequently, should charitable giving be examined in terms of the proportion of total family income given to causes outside the family, differences in charitable giving across religious traditions might well be far more substantial than what may be evident here, with evangelical and Black Protestants giving a greater proportion of their income to charitable causes than those of other religious traditions.[10]

Political Tolerance

The conventional approach to assessing political tolerance has been to focus on responses to questions that test the limits of a citizen's forbearance of specified groups. This approach to the study of tolerance among Americans has been employed for more than a half century; as a result, a certain conventional wisdom has emerged related to what kinds of groups are more likely or unlikely to exhibit tolerance. Probably the one variable most centrally tied to expressions of tolerance is education. For example, Nunn et al. (1978, 169) state that education is the "single most powerful predictor of tolerance," and Nie et al. (1996, 148–49) conclude that "the more educated . . . the more likely citizens are to support freedom of expression for many different types of groups under a range of circumstances."

A number of studies have linked religion and religious variables to political tolerance (e.g., Stouffer 1955; Glock and Stark 1966; Smidt and Penning 1982; Beatty and Walter 1984; Wilcox and Jelen 1990; Reimer and Park 2001). And conventional scholarly wisdom holds that religiosity and political tolerance are inversely related—the more religious one is, the less tolerant politically one is likely to be (Woodberry and Smith 1998). In fact, in their recent study, Putnam and Campbell (2010, 444) note that although "religious Americans are, in fact, more generous neighbors and more conscientious citizens than their secular counterparts," they are nonetheless "also less tolerant of dissent than secular Americans."

Some scholars (e.g., Gibson 2006), however, are beginning to question both the adequacy of the conceptualization and the validity of standard measures of tolerance, and thereby the conventional wisdom that has emerged based on their use. Certainly, considerable concern has been expressed related to how one should conceptualize tolerance (e.g., Conyers 2001; Griffiths and Elshtain 2002; Stetson and Conti 2005). To be sure, there are some clear qualities and non-controversial features of tolerance that most definitions capture. For example, tolerance certainly does not mean that one either stands in *agreement* or *endorses* the position(s) held or the action(s) conducted by others. On the contrary, tolerance entails "a willingness to permit the expression of ideas or interests one opposes" (Sullivan, Pierson, and Marcus 1982, 2). Nor does tolerance imply *indifference* to those ideas or interests, since by definition the tolerant person stands in opposition to what he or she tolerates—and often vigorously so.[11]

In order to assess levels of tolerance, the General Social Survey (GSS) has periodically employed a battery of questions that many scholars have used to assess patterns of political tolerance. With these questions, respondents are asked about certain categories of people (e.g., atheists, communists, homosexuals, militarists, and racists) and then are polled as to (1) whether they should be allowed to speak in the community, (2) whether books promoting their viewpoints should be permitted to be placed within a public library, and (3) whether such individuals should be permitted to teach in a college or university. Opposition to such actions is then viewed as an expression of "intolerance."

Table 6.4 examines the relationship between religious tradition affiliation and expressions of tolerance as conventionally measured. Previous research has shown that the extent to which such tolerance is granted depends in part on the type of groups under consideration—and on the nature of the activity examined, as regardless of the group under consideration, respondents typically provide greater latitude in permitting such groups to speak, a constitutionally protected freedom (e.g., Smidt et al. 2008, 195–97). Consequently, rather than examining all such relationships, the data presented in the table are restricted to an examination of four groups (namely, atheists, racists, militarists, and homosexuals) and two modes of activity (namely, engaging in public speaking and allowing them to teach in a college or university).

Clearly, given this approach, there are some marked differences across religious traditions in response to these matters. For each of the five religious traditions, the lowest percentages are found when examining tolerance related to those who claim that blacks are inferior and the largest percentages are found when examining actions related to homosexuals; likewise, for each tradition examined, a larger percentage states that people from such a group be allowed to speak than allowed to teach.

Nevertheless, given the eight comparisons made in table 6.4, mainline Protestants and the religiously unaffiliated are consistently the "most

TABLE 6.4
Conventional Political Tolerance by Religious Tradition

	Evangelical Protestant (%)	Mainline Protestant (%)	Black Protestant (%)	Roman Catholic (%)	Unaffiliated (%)
Allow someone to speak who:					
Is a homosexual	80	93	79	90	92
Is against all churches and religion	73	86	65	73	88
Advocates military to run country	66	78	55	69	79
Claims blacks are inferior	57	70	54	55	73
Allow someone to teach in a college or university who:					
Is a homosexual	78	90	76	87	90
Is against all churches and religion	60	70	50	55	79
Advocates military to run country	55	60	51	56	70
Claims blacks are inferior	51	56	41	46	59

Source: General Social Survey, 2010

Note: Entries show percent agreeing with statement

tolerant," as both groups exhibit relatively similar levels of willingness to permit the particular activities for the groups under consideration. In contrast, the lowest percentages are typically found among evangelical and Black Protestants, though Black Protestants sometimes exhibit similar levels to, and sometimes lower levels than, evangelicals. Interestingly, those affiliated with each of the major Christian traditions are more "tolerant" of those who stand "against all churches and religion" than they are toward those who might be labeled as "racists."

But if tolerance is neither indifference nor the acceptance of people whose ideas and practices one already approves, then tolerance should really be examined only among those who stand in opposition to such ideas or actions, as tolerance is hardly evident among those who do not oppose such matters in the first place. Consequently, table 6.5 first presents the percentage of each religious tradition that holds that sexual relations between two adults of the same sex is "always wrong," and then it examines expressions of tolerance for homosexuals to teach *only among* those within each tradition who held this particular viewpoint. This examination is limited to homosexuals because comparable objections related to the practices of "atheists," "racists," and "militarists" are not available in the survey.

Clearly, as shown in table 6.5, evangelical and Black Protestants are the most likely to respond that such sexual relations are always wrong, being nearly twice as likely as mainline Protestants and Catholics to hold such a position, and more than three times as likely as the religiously unaffiliated. However, when the willingness to allow homosexuals to teach in a college setting is examined only among those who hold such behavior as being "always wrong," differences across religious traditions in terms of tolerance diminish—though they do not totally disappear. When viewed from this perspective, mainline Protestants continue to be the most tolerant, with evangelicals

TABLE 6.5
"True" Political Tolerance by Religious Tradition

	Evangelical Protestant (%)	Mainline Protestant (%)	Black Protestant (%)	Roman Catholic (%)	Unaffiliated (%)
Believe sexual relations between two adults of same sex is always wrong	74	43	71	40	22
Among only respondents who believe sexual relations between two adults of same sex is always wrong: *Allow homosexuals to teach in college*	72	79	69	72	66
Among only respondents who believe homosexuality is something people cannot change: *Allow homosexuals to teach in college*	93	93	82	91	93

Source: General Social Survey, 2010

Note: Entries show percent agreeing with statement

and Catholics trailing slightly behind, followed closely by Black Protestants, and then it is the religiously unaffiliated who exhibit the lowest level of tolerance on the matter.

According to data from the 2010 General Social Survey, evangelicals are the most prone of all religious traditions to believe that homosexuality is something that people choose (data not shown). Only 30 percent of evangelicals reported that they believe that homosexuality is something that people cannot change, whereas approximately 70 percent of mainline Protestants, Catholics, and the religiously unaffiliated do so. Black Protestants (43 percent) fall between evangelical Protestants and the other three religious traditions.

It is this propensity to believe that homosexuality is a choice that contributes to evangelicals being somewhat more intolerant of allowing homosexuals to teach in college. As can be seen in the lower part of table 6.5, when one limits the analysis only to those who believe that homosexuality is something people cannot change, there are virtually no differences across religious traditions in their willingness to allow gays to teach in such centers of learning. More than 90 percent, regardless of religious tradition, would allow such a practice (though Black Protestants trail somewhat behind at 82 percent).

Thus, evangelicals as a whole do not appear to be highly intolerant of other groups in society (at least in terms of the groups conventionally examined through the General Social Surveys). First, a majority of evangelicals, regardless of the group examined, were willing to allow members of such groups to teach in college and universities (the form of action that typically generates the lowest level of support, regardless of the group analyzed). Nor were evangelicals substantially more politically intolerant than those affiliated with the other Christian traditions—generally trailing mainline Protestants, the most politically tolerant religious tradition, by 5 to 10 percentage points—depending on the particular comparison made. Moreover, the rank ordering of "intolerance" toward the groups examined (i.e., in terms of racists, militarists, atheists, and homosexuals) were the same for evangelicals as they were for the remaining four traditions. And, finally, when one restricts the analysis of political tolerance to those who truly object to the behavior of the group under consideration, evangelicals are hardly more intolerant than those within other religious traditions.

Change over Time

American society has changed considerably over the past four decades, and analysts have also noted some important changes within American civic life as well. For example, social trust appears to have declined and, according to some analysts (e.g., Putnam 2000), so has the propensity of Americans to join civic associations. American society has grown more culturally diverse, and questions emerge as to whether Americans may have grown more, or less, tolerant of such cultural differences.

To what extent, then, have evangelical Protestants changed over time in terms of their relationship with other Americans? Is there any evidence of a decline in social trust among evangelical Protestants or that they have become less likely to join civic organizations over the past three or four decades? Have they become more, or less, tolerant of cultural differences over that same period of time? And are the differences currently evident between evangelicals and those of other faith traditions actually greater or smaller today than in the past?

In tracing change over time, this chapter will employ data from the General Social Surveys, rather than data from the Pew Religious Landscape Survey of 2007 and the Anti-Semitism in the United States study of 1964. This shift occurs only in this chapter, and it is done for the following reasons. First, not only did the Landscape Survey ask very few questions related to civic life, but the questions they did ask were unique to their study; as a result, no direct comparisons to earlier points in time are possible. Second, most of this chapter has focused on data gathered in the General Social Survey of 2010; thus, table 6.6 compares data from the 2010 General Social Survey with data from the 1974, 1987, and 1998 General Social Surveys. These particular GSS surveys were chosen because they had identical questions to the ones previously examined in the 2010 survey and because they fall approximately a decade apart from each other.

As seen in table 6.6, evangelicals have changed over time—as have those affiliated with other religious traditions. Evangelicals, like those of other religious traditions (except Black Protestants), have become less trusting of others over the past two decades.

Nevertheless, despite this decline in trust in others, the percentage of evangelicals reporting associational memberships in 2010 (70 percent) largely mirrored the percentage of evangelicals who reported such in 1974 (73 percent). Though this represents a slight decline in the level of such memberships, evangelicals actually exhibited the smallest decline in such memberships among the five religious traditions over the time span examined. Like most other religious traditions, evangelical Protestants exhibited a decline in reported memberships between 1974 and 1987, but then exhibited the greatest jump in associational memberships between 1987 and 2010 (6 percent). As a result, evangelical Protestants ranked only behind mainline Protestants in their level of memberships in voluntary associations in 2010.

TABLE 6.6
Civic Life by Religious Tradition over Time

	1974 (%)	1987 (%)	1998 (%)	2010 (%)
Evangelical Protestant				
Most people can be trusted	x	41	37	32
Member of voluntary association	73	64	x	70
Allow atheist to speak	45	62	65	73
Allow homosexual to speak	33	44	63	78
Mainline Protestant				
Most people can be trusted	x	57	50	49
Member of voluntary association	80	74	x	76
Allow atheist to speak	65	65	80	86
Allow homosexual to speak	51	59	83	90
Black Protestant				
Most people can be trusted	x	15	17	15
Member of voluntary association	74	57	x	61
Allow atheist to speak	48	61	58	65
Allow homosexual to speak	57	52	76	76
Roman Catholic				
Most people can be trusted	x	47	37	33
Member of voluntary association	70	68	x	57
Allow atheist to speak	69	75	76	73
Allow homosexual to speak	62	68	83	87
Unaffiliated				
Most people can be trusted	x	46	31	38
Member of voluntary association	59	62	x	53
Allow atheist to speak	82	88	94	88
Allow homosexual to speak	72	88	86	90

Sources: General Social Survey, 1974, 1987, 1998, 2010

Note: Entries show percent agreeing with statement

x – not asked

But it is in terms of conventional measures of political tolerance that evangelicals have exhibited the greatest change. In 1974, evangelicals were the least likely of those affiliated with the five religious traditions to indicate that they would be willing to allow someone who is against all churches and religion to speak and they also were the least likely to state that homosexuals should be allowed to teach in college. However, with regard to both matters, the percentage of evangelicals who expressed a willingness to permit either consistently increased across each point in time. Consequently, though evangelicals today still trail members of some of the other religious traditions in their willingness to permit such "atheists" to speak and gays to teach in college, they have narrowed such differences considerably over that period of time. For example, in 1974, evangelicals trailed Catholics by 24 percent in their willingness to allow atheists to speak, but the two religious groups were equally willing to do so in 2010. In 1974, evangelicals trailed Catholics by 29 percent in their willingness to allow homosexuals to teach in colleges and universities, but now trail Catholics by only 9 percent.

Divisions among Evangelicals

Having seen the changes among evangelicals over time, we now turn our attention to the extent to which differences exist among evangelicals today. These differences are examined in terms of racial and ethnic differences as well as in terms of generational, educational, and religious differences.

Racial and Ethnic Differences

As noted previously, in most surveys, analyses of racial and ethnic differences among evangelicals are hampered by the small number of respondents that fall within the black and Hispanic evangelical Protestant categories. This problem has been bypassed through the use of the Pew Religious Landscape Survey, with its massive sample size. However, this also means that analyses of racial and ethnic differences among evangelicals must be limited to the data gathered through the Landscape Survey.

Table 6.7 examines all the questions for the Pew Religious Landscape Survey that have been previously analyzed in this chapter—namely, whether one has volunteered "to do community work through their place of worship," whether they believe there is a natural conflict between being a religious person and living in modern society, and whether they agree that their values are under attack by Hollywood (and the entertainment industry). Responses to these items are then examined in terms of whether the respondent is a white, black, or Hispanic evangelical, a white mainline Protestant, a black within the Black Protestant tradition, or a white or Hispanic Catholic. Consequently, this analysis permits a comparison of the extent to which racial or ethnic differences may outweigh differences in religious traditions in shaping perspectives and activities in relationship to civic life.

On some matters related to civic life, racial and ethnic differences among evangelicals matter little. The levels of community volunteering within one's

TABLE 6.7
Civic Life by Racial and Ethnic Differences (controlling for religious tradition)

	Evangelical Protestant			Mainline Protestant	Black Protestant	Roman Catholic	
	White (%)	Black (%)	Hispanic (%)	White (%)	Black (%)	White (%)	Hispanic (%)
Volunteer in church	71	75	74	66	69	57	54
Natural conflict between being religious and living in modern society	53	54	52	33	51	33	41
My values threatened by Hollywood	57	34	50	42	34	45	45

Source: Pew Forum Religious Landscape Survey, 2007

Note: Entries show percent agreeing with statement

church are virtually the same for white, black, and Hispanic evangelicals. Moreover, not only do white evangelicals volunteer at higher levels than white mainline Protestants and white Catholics, but black evangelicals also volunteer at higher levels than blacks within the Black Protestant tradition, as do Hispanic evangelicals in comparison with Hispanic Catholics. Thus, in terms of such forms of volunteering, religious tradition appears to outweigh racial/ethnic differences in terms of shaping individual responses.

Similarly, the responses of black and Hispanic evangelicals reflect the responses of white evangelicals on the matter of whether there is a natural conflict between being religious and living in modern society. A little more than half of each ethnic/racial group among evangelicals holds such a position, with white evangelicals being far more likely to express such a position than white mainline Protestants and white Catholics. The same is true for Hispanic evangelicals in comparison to Hispanic Catholics. However, though black evangelicals mirror other evangelicals in the frequency with which they express the presence of such a conflict, blacks in the Black Protestant tradition exhibit a pattern reflective of evangelicals. Thus, it is hard to discern in this instance whether black evangelicals are standing together with other evangelicals or with other blacks in the Black Protestant tradition.

However, racial/ethnic differences tend to outweigh religious traditions in shaping responses on whether one's values are threatened by Hollywood. Though a majority of both white and Hispanic evangelicals agree on the matter, differences between white and Hispanic evangelicals are slightly greater than the differences between Hispanic evangelicals and Hispanic Catholics. Moreover, the responses of black evangelicals far more closely mirror those of their racial group in the Black Protestant tradition than they do the responses of other evangelicals.

Thus, overall, the results of table 6.7 reveal that both religious tradition and racial/ethnic differences shape responses to the three questions, though affiliation with a religious tradition seemingly has somewhat greater power than racial or ethnic differences. Certainly, rather substantial differences exist among whites across religious traditions, and the patterns among Hispanic evangelicals generally mirror those of white evangelicals more closely than they do those of other Hispanics in the Catholic tradition. And though black evangelicals do not deviate far from blacks in the Black Protestant tradition on these matters, they exhibit relatively similar patterns to white evangelicals on two of the three items. Only on the item related to whether or not their values are threatened by Hollywood do the responses of black evangelicals more closely reflect other blacks in the Black Protestant tradition than they do the responses of white evangelicals.

Generational and Educational Differences

Because we are not examining racial differences in this portion of the chapter, the analysis of generational and educational differences among evangelicals will include items from both the Pew Religious Landscape Survey and the 2010 General Social Survey. Thus, in addition to examining responses to the three items examined in the previous table, we examine generational and educational differences among evangelicals in relationship to matters of social trust, membership in voluntary associations, and the willingness to allow homosexuals to teach.

Do generational divisions emerge among evangelicals in terms of their engagement in public life? And are any generational differences greater or smaller than divisions among evangelicals in terms of the presence or absence of a college education?

Table 6.8 addresses these questions. Overall, these data reveal that there are some important generational differences among evangelicals and that many of these differences reflect differences that are also found within other religious traditions. Perhaps the greatest, and most consistent, difference between millennials and older co-religionists within each of the five religious traditions relates to social trust. Millennials, regardless of religious tradition, exhibit far less social trust than non-millennials. Likewise, millennials across all religious traditions are consistently less likely to perceive that their values

TABLE 6.8
Civic Life by Generational Cohort and Educational Attainment (controlling for religious tradition)

	Generational		Education	
	Non-Millennial (%)	Millennial (%)	Non-College Graduate (%)	College Graduate (%)
Evangelical Protestant				
Volunteered through church[a]	71	74	70	79
Natural conflict with modern society[a]	53	46	54	47
My values threatened by Hollywood[a]	56	41	53	61
Most people can be trusted[b]	35	10	27	49
Member of voluntary association[b]	73	70	69	74
Allow homosexual to teach[b]	77	88	75	89
Mainline Protestant				
Volunteered through church[a]	66	69	63	72
Natural conflict with modern society[a]	34	40	38	26
My values threatened by Hollywood[a]	43	34	42	41
Most people can be trusted[b]	50	36	36	66
Member of voluntary association[b]	75	76	68	88
Allow homosexual to teach[b]	89	100	86	97
Black Protestant				
Volunteered through church[a]	70	69	69	74
Natural conflict with modern society[a]	51	50	52	44
My values threatened by Hollywood[a]	37	27	35	38
Most people can be trusted[b]	18	5	12	33
Member of voluntary association[b]	67	*	55	*
Allow homosexual to teach[b]	76	80	72	97
Roman Catholic				
Volunteered through church[a]	56	64	54	63
Natural conflict with modern society[a]	36	38	38	31
My values threatened by Hollywood[a]	46	35	44	44
Most people can be trusted[b]	36	21	25	56
Member of voluntary association[b]	59	40	48	70
Allow homosexual to teach[b]	85	94	83	97
Unaffiliated				
Volunteered through church[a]	x	x	x	x
Natural conflict with modern society[a]	x	x	x	x
My values threatened by Hollywood[a]	29	27	31	23
Most people can be trusted[b]	42	26	28	57
Member of voluntary association[b]	57	57	41	68
Allow homosexual to teach[b]	88	94	85	98

Sources:

[a] Pew Forum Religious Landscape Survey, 2007

[b] General Social Survey, 2010

Note: Entries show percent agreeing with statement

x – not asked of religiously unaffiliated respondents

* – too few respondents for percentage to be meaningful

are being threatened by Hollywood and are consistently more likely to state that they would allow homosexuals to teach. Still, on some other matters, differences between millennials and older members of the various religious traditions are quite modest in scope. This is true, for example, with regard to having volunteered for community service through one's house of worship and with regard to being a member of a voluntary association (though millennial Catholics are far less likely to report membership in a voluntary association than non-millennial Catholics).

Nevertheless, generational differences tend to be greatest within the evangelical Protestant tradition. This is evident with regard to social trust, whether one perceives one's values being threatened by Hollywood, whether one holds that there is a natural conflict between religion and living in modern society, and whether one is willing to allow homosexuals to teach (although the percentage difference among evangelicals on this matter is the same as that among mainline Protestants and is only slightly larger than that found among Black Protestants). Overall, then, these patterns of greater differences between millennial and non-millennial evangelicals than between the two generational categories within the other religious traditions provide some additional evidence to bolster the contention that a "new generation" of evangelicals may be emerging.

Still, despite these substantial generational differences, religious tradition affiliation also continues to shape responses to matters related to public life. Among non-millennials, evangelicals exhibit the highest percentage of respondents who perceive their values being threatened by Hollywood. And despite the presence of substantial generational differences among evangelicals on this matter, millennial evangelicals are also the most likely of all millennials to hold these perceptions. Similarly, among non-millennials, evangelicals rank only ahead of Black Protestants in terms of their levels of social trust and their willingness to allow homosexuals to teach, and this same pattern also holds true within the millennial generation. Thus, though the data provide some evidence that a "new generation" of evangelicals may be emerging in relationship to matters of public life, important differences across religious traditions continue to remain even within the millennial generation.

Differences in educational attainment also shape matters related to engagement in public life. For example, college graduates, regardless of religious tradition, are far more likely than non-college graduates to state that people can be generally trusted, be a member of a voluntary association,[12] volunteer, and express a willingness to allow homosexuals to teach, while they are less likely to state there is a natural conflict between being religious and living in modern society.

The data in table 6.8 also reveal that, regardless of religious tradition, differences in civic values and behavior are generally greater in relationship to whether or not one has graduated from college than in terms of generational differences. Thus, for example, there is an 11-percentage-point difference between millennial evangelicals and non-millennial evangelicals as to whether homosexuals should be allowed to teach, but a 14-percentage-point spread between evangelicals based on differences in educational attainment. In fact, for each of the items examined in table 6.8, generational differences rarely exceed educational differences within each religious tradition; only with regard to perceptions that one's values are being threatened by Hollywood are generational differences generally greater than educational differences.

However, evangelicals are the exception to this general pattern. Among evangelicals, generational differences exceed educational differences on two items: perceptions that one's values are threatened by Hollywood, and beliefs that most people can be trusted. And, on a third item (namely, whether there is a natural conflict between being religious and living in modern society), the spread between millennial and non-millennial evangelicals is equivalent to the gap found between college-educated and non-college-educated evangelicals.

Therefore, greater differences in civic values and behavior are evident in relationship to generational, than educational, differences among evangelicals than within other religious traditions. These findings then lend additional support to two observations. First, as noted in previous chapters, college education tends to operate somewhat differently among evangelicals than among those of other religious traditions. Second, these data provide additional supporting (though far from conclusive) evidence for the notion that a new generation of evangelicals may be emerging in which younger evangelicals may be exhibiting substantially different positions than their older co-religionists.

Religious Differences

As noted in the previous chapter, a number of scholars have contended that there has been a restructuring of American religion over the past several decades. This restructuring has not only led to a deepening cleavage between the more traditionalist and more modernist members of each major religious tradition, but it has resulted in traditionalists within one religious tradition exhibiting attitudes and behavior closer to traditionalists in other religious traditions than to modernists within their own religious tradition. Are these religious divisions within religious traditions then more important than the generational and educational divisions we have just examined? Do religious traditionalists within each religious tradition exhibit substantially different patterns of civic values and behavior than those who are non-traditionalists within that tradition?

As can be seen from the data presented in table 6.9, traditionalists and non-traditionalists do differ in terms of their patterns of engagement in civic

TABLE 6.9
Civic Life by Religious Traditionalism (controlling for religious tradition)

	Non-Traditionalist (%)	Traditionalist (%)
Evangelical Protestant		
Volunteered through church[a]	69	74
Conflict between being religious and living in modern society[a]	45	57
My values threatened by Hollywood[a]	47	59
Most people can be trusted[b]	31	29
Member of voluntary association[b]	54	84
Allow homosexual to teach[b]	84	74
Mainline Protestant		
Volunteered through church[a]	67	69
Conflict between being religious and living in modern society[a]	31	40
My values threatened by Hollywood[a]	38	49
Most people can be trusted[b]	56	37
Member of voluntary association[b]	75	83
Allow homosexual to teach[b]	93	90
Black Protestant		
Volunteered through church[a]	69	72
Conflict between being religious and living in modern society[a]	50	52
My values threatened by Hollywood[a]	35	37
Most people can be trusted[b]	20	11
Member of voluntary association[b]	55	70
Allow homosexual to teach[b]	92	76
Roman Catholic		
Volunteered through church[a]	56	61
Conflict between being religious and living in modern society[a]	34	40
My values threatened by Hollywood[a]	39	53
Most people can be trusted[b]	32	34
Member of voluntary association[b]	57	55
Allow homosexual to teach[b]	91	71

Sources:

[a] Pew Forum Religious Landscape Survey, 2007

[b] General Social Survey, 2010

Note: Entries show percent agreeing with statement

life. Traditionalists, regardless of religious tradition, are more likely than non-traditionalists to report that they are a member of some voluntary association (except among Catholics),[13] to have volunteered for community service through their house of worship, to see a natural conflict between religion and living in modern society, and to view their values as being threatened by Hollywood. Finally, when compared to the non-traditionalists within their tradition, traditionalists are less likely to believe that most people can be trusted (except for Catholics) and less willing to allow homosexuals to teach in college.

But are these religious differences substantially greater than the generational and educational differences evident within each tradition? Overall, it would appear that, on the basis of the matters examined here, the differences between traditionalists and non-traditionalists within each religious tradition tend to be smaller in magnitude than those based on educational differences within that tradition. For example, differences among Black Protestants based on educational differences exceed the differences found between traditionalists and non-traditionalists within their ranks for each of the six variables related to civic life; differences between traditionalists and non-traditionalists exceed differences based on education among mainline Protestants only once (with regard to perceptions related to whether one's values were threatened by Hollywood), and only twice among Catholics (with regard to perceptions related to whether one's values were threatened by Hollywood and with regard to one's willingness to allow homosexuals to teach).

However, among evangelical Protestants, differences based on religious traditionalism exceed differences based on educational attainment for three of the variables related to civic life. Once again, being a college graduate does not shape attitudes and behavior to the same extent among evangelicals as it does among those affiliated with the other religious traditions. Rather, differences based on a traditionalist/non-traditional divide seem to have the greatest power shaping responses among evangelicals—at least in terms of these matters related to civic life. Thus, even though responses to matters of civic life by religious traditionalism typically move in the same direction across each of the four religious traditions examined, it would appear that the relative importance of religious traditionalism in shaping civic attitudes and behavior tends to be greatest among evangelicals.

Controlling for Multiple Variables Simultaneously

Having shown that one's race and ethnicity, generational cohort, educational attainment, and religious traditionalism can all shape the nature of evangelical perceptions of, and involvement in, civic life, we now seek to determine which of these factors most strongly shapes evangelicals' perceptions and involvement. Once again, to control for the relative effects of each of these four factors, a multiple classification analysis (MCA)[14] was performed using the Pew Religious Landscape Survey,[15] with the *beta* values[16] for each of the independent variables presented in table 6.10. Once again, as was the case for the MCA conducted in the previous chapter, the analysis is limited to evangelicals, with the analysis based on the employment of the coding of the variables used in the previous tables.

Three different dependent variables related to civic life are examined in the table. Educational differences (*beta*=.10) among evangelicals represent the most important factor shaping volunteering practices among evangelicals' responses, though educational differences are far less important in coloring evangelicals' perceptions about whether their values are threatened by Hollywood or whether there is natural conflict between being a religious person and living in contemporary society.

Differences among evangelicals related to race/ethnicity and religious traditionalism most fully account for different perceptions related to the extent to which the entertainment industry poses a threat to one's values—with whites and religious traditionalists being most likely to indicate that Hollywood poses a threat. However, with regard to volunteering or perceptions of conflict related to a religious person living in modern society, racial/ethnic differences among evangelicals matter little. Likewise, once the other three independent variables are taken into account, generational differences among evangelicals hardly have any effects on differences in civic engagement among evangelicals—except with regard to whether one's values are threatened by Hollywood, as millennial evangelicals are far less likely than older evangelicals to perceive such threats.

Rather, once again, it is differences in religious traditionalism among evangelicals that most fully account for differences in their civic life. Of the

TABLE 6.10
Assessing Divisions among Evangelical Protestants
on Civic Life: A Multivariate Analysis

	Volunteer	My values threatened by Hollywood	Conflict between religion and modern society
Race/ethnicity	.02	.12	.02
Generational	.02	.08	.04
Educational	.10	.06	.04
Religious traditionalism	.06	.12	.11
R^2	.01	.04	.02

Source: Pew Forum Religious Landscape Survey, 2007

four independent variables examined in table 6.10, the religious traditional-ism variable exhibits the largest *beta* value with regard to two of the three dependent variables (namely, whether one's values are threatened by Holly-wood and whether there is natural conflict between being religiously devout and living in modern society), while it ranked second in importance behind education in relationship to volunteering.

Conclusions

Though evangelicals do not exhibit greater levels of distrust of others, they nevertheless report higher levels of tension and conflict with American soci-ety than those affiliated with other religious traditions. Still, despite these ten-sions and conflicts with the broader culture, evangelicals tend to be relatively active with regard to engagement in civic life. They join civic organizations at a relatively high rate; they volunteer at levels similar to, if not somewhat greater than, those of other religious traditions; and they are just as likely as, if not more likely than, those of other religious traditions to report giving money and/or goods to charitable causes in the past year.

Moreover, despite perceptions to the contrary, evangelicals do not appear to be highly intolerant of others. They are only marginally more intolerant than mainline Protestants—the most politically tolerant religious tradition. Moreover, over the past several decades, evangelicals have actually become much more tolerant socially and politically—exhibiting the greatest level of change among the religious traditions analyzed.

In accounting for variation in civic engagement among evangelicals, both differences in educational attainment and differences in level of religious traditionalism served as the best explanatory variable—depending on the specific dependent variable examined. Differences in educational attainment best explained whether evangelicals were more or less likely to volunteer, with college-educated evangelicals volunteering more frequently than non-college-educated evangelicals. But differences in religious traditionalism best explained whether evangelicals perceived threats from the environ-ment within which they lived—whether it was in terms of one's values being threatened by Hollywood or in terms of being a religious person living within modern society.

7

We're Marching to Zion?
The Politics of Evangelicals

THOUGH A POLITICAL SYSTEM may constitutionally mandate an institutional separation of church and state, not even the highest wall of separation between the two can prevent individuals from deciding to cast their ballots based on personal religious convictions or religious group affiliations. And since political life in democratic societies involves people choosing the particular goals, values, and policies they wish to have promoted, it is almost inevitable that religion and politics will intersect.

Nevertheless, the relationship between religious faith and politics varies over time. Politics always transpires within particular domestic and international contexts. With the passage of time, these contextual circumstances can change rather quickly and considerably, and with these developments can come changes in the extent to which, as well as the ways in which, religion and politics become intertwined.

Given the major changes that have occurred within international and domestic politics since 1900, it is not surprising that, over this period of time, evangelical Protestants have exhibited somewhat different patterns related to their engagement in American political life. In fact, over the course of these years, evangelicals have experimented with three different forms of political engagement: a movement politics that challenged existing political institutions; a quiescent politics that remained largely removed from, or only marginally engaged in, political life; and a regularized politics in which evangelicals actively engaged within the political process through participation in interest groups and political parties (Green 2005, 15).

As a result, evangelicals have exhibited various waves of political engagement (Hunter 1987, 117–30; Wilcox 1992). Following the Scopes Monkey Trial in the 1920s, evangelicals became largely invisible within American public life, as they largely exhibited a quiescent politics.[1] But a half century later, the election of "born-again" President Jimmy Carter in 1976, along with the subsequent rise a few years later of Jerry Falwell's Moral Majority, marked the beginning of a new evangelical engagement with politics, and they have remained relatively involved politically in the decades ever since (Smidt 2008, 10–13). With these alterations, the political prominence of evangelicals has ebbed and flowed over time.

Nevertheless, despite their long-standing presence within American society, there continues to be considerable debate about the place of evangelicals in public life. Many analysts, public leaders, and ordinary American citizens are perplexed by, and at times even concerned about, the goals and significance of the latest evangelical foray into the political sphere. While some see evangelical involvement as representing an effort to build a theocratic "Christian America" that would legally impose their moral standards on all other Americans (e.g., D'Antonio 1989; Diamond 1989), others contend that the voting priorities and internal divisions among evangelical Protestants are "both widely and wildly misunderstood" (Greeley and Hout 2006, 39).

At the same time, evangelicals themselves are divided over the goals and extent of their political involvement, as there is an ongoing debate within their ranks as to how, and the level to which, they should be engaged in political life (e.g., Sider and Knippers 2005; Wallis 2005, 2008; Zimmerman 2007; Black 2008; Bretherton 2010; Ryden 2010). Some evangelical leaders contend that evangelicals should not be directly involved in political life as "the tensions between the Christian faith and democratic liberalism are so fundamental that the church can only be described as a resident alien living in the midst of the worldly kingdom" (Ahearn 2003, 198). From this perspective, the church is viewed as "a beachhead, an outpost, an island of one culture in the middle of another" (Hauerwas and Willimon 1989, 12), with the political order being totally "outside the perfection of Christ." Others argue that evangelicals should be engaged with others in the public square in order to bring about those changes in society that foster the broader public good. From this perspective, then, the role of Christians in democratic societies is not to be that of "a resident alien, but that of a responsible, yet critical, citizen" (Ahearn 2003, 202).

Given that the most recent wave of their political engagement began in the late 1970s, some analysts have wondered whether we might now be witnessing the beginning of a new evangelical withdrawal from politics. In fact, some evangelical leaders (e.g., Thomas and Dobson 1999) have argued that the effort to transform American culture through the acquisition of political power has failed; as a result, evangelicals should withdraw from political life. In this regard, it is noteworthy that those organizations that earlier brought evangelicals to the polls on Election Day are now either disbanded (e.g., the Moral Majority) or in significant organizational disarray (e.g., the Christian Coalition).[2]

To what extent, then, is there evidence that evangelicals are once again withdrawing from political life—reflecting their long-standing pattern of cyclical engagement in the public sphere? And are evangelicals less divided politically than those affiliated with other religious traditions? This chapter addresses these matters by analyzing the political discontent, issue positions, ideological perspectives, partisanship, and voting behavior of American evangelicals today and by comparing them to members of the other major religious traditions. In addition, the chapter examines what changes have occurred politically among evangelicals over the past forty years. And, finally, the chapter analyzes evangelicals in terms of the four potential fault lines that may serve to divide their ranks politically—namely, in terms of possible racial/ethnic, generational, educational, and theological divisions within the group.

The Political Life of Evangelicals

When thinking about the political characteristics of evangelical Protestants, it is necessary that one avoid treating them as a monolithic group (Smith 2000, 13). All too often, when talking about different social groups, analysts begin to treat certain distinctive characteristics manifested by some members as if they were uniformly present among all members. In other words, the political inclinations evident among some members are all too easily ascribed to all who belong to the group. Consequently, when examining the political characteristics of evangelicals, it is important to note not only the extent to which evangelicals may be divided politically, but the extent to which the political patterns found among evangelicals may be similar to, or only marginally different from, the patterns found among those affiliated with the other major religious traditions.

General Orientations toward Politics

Perhaps a good place to begin our analysis is to examine the extent to which evangelicals are politically discontented. Discontent can be important politically in that social and political movements originate, in part, on the basis of the presence of grievances among movement members.[3]

Based on the questions posed in the Landscape Survey, evangelicals exhibit a relatively high level of political discontent. As shown in table 7.1, less than one-third of evangelicals expressed satisfaction with "the way things are going in the country today" or with "the way the political system is working." When asked a year later (2008) whether "elected officials in Washington lose touch with people pretty quickly," evangelicals overwhelmingly agreed with the statement (82 percent).

However, the data also reveal that evangelicals are hardly distinctive in their level of political dissatisfaction—as they do not exhibit greater dissatisfaction than those within other religious traditions. Most Americans in 2007 were hardly satisfied with "the way things are going in the country today" or with "the way the political system is working," as less than one-third, regardless of religious tradition, agreed with either statement. Likewise, evangelicals were hardly distinctive in terms of their views of whether elected officials quickly lose touch with the people who elected them, as three-quarters or more of those within each of the other religious traditions affirmed that perspective as well.

Nor is the level of political attention among evangelicals necessarily any greater or less than that found among affiliates of other religious traditions. When asked the extent to which they follow what is going on in government and public affairs, slightly more than one-half of all evangelicals responded that they did so "most of the time" (the response option capturing the highest level of attention). Though evangelicals ranked second behind mainline Protestants in their expressed levels of attention, evangelicals were only marginally more attentive than those within the other religious traditions. Of course, one may follow politics more out of "necessity" than out of pure personal interest, but most Americans are only marginally interested in politics. Except for mainline Protestants, a higher percentage within each religious tradition indicated that they were only slightly or not at all interested in politics than reported that they were very interested in politics. Once again, the patterns among evangelicals basically mirror those affiliated with the other major religious traditions.

In fact, evangelicals stand out as being somewhat distinct politically only with regard to the influence of religion in shaping their political thinking. When asked what factor most influences their thinking about government and public affairs, nearly one-third of all evangelicals (29 percent) reported that it was their religious views. In contrast, less than one-fifth of Black Protestants and less than one-tenth of mainline Protestants, Catholics, and the religiously unaffiliated did so. Clearly, evangelicals are more prone than those of other religious traditions to contend that their religious views are important when it comes to their political thinking.

TABLE 7.1
General Orientation toward Politics by Religious Tradition

	Evangelical Protestant (%)	Mainline Protestant (%)	Black Protestant (%)	Roman Catholic (%)	Unaffiliated (%)
Satisfied with way things are going in the country today[a]	31	29	18	32	32
Satisfied with way political system is working[a]	31	28	22	31	23
Elected officials in Washington lose touch with people quickly[b]	82	84	82	77	75
Follow what's going on in government and public affairs most of time[a]	52	58	47	50	50
Interested in politics and national affairs[c]					
Not at all/only slightly	36	24	46	38	35
Somewhat interested	38	41	35	36	32
Very interested	26	36	19	26	34
When thinking about government and public affairs, which factor most influences your thinking?[a]					
Personal experience	31	39	29	36	41
Views of family and friends	6	7	7	8	6
What is seen or read in media	17	20	24	24	20
Religious views	29	8	18	9	3
Education	8	16	10	14	17
Something else	9	10	12	9	13

Sources:

[a] Pew Forum Religious Landscape Survey, 2007

[b] Henry Institute National Survey on Religion and Public Life, 2008

[c] Faith Matters Survey, 2006

Note: First four entries show percent agreeing with statement

Nevertheless, even here one must be careful about portraying the way evangelicals engage in political decision making. First, it is important to remember that less than one-third of evangelicals reported that it is their religious views that most shape their political thinking, and it would be a gross distortion to think that all, or even most, evangelicals approach politics in such a fashion. Second, most respondents, regardless of their religious tradition, typically indicate that it is their personal experiences that most shape their political thinking—and this is also true of evangelicals.

Stands on Political Issues

Just where do evangelicals, then, stand on matters of public policy? To what extent do they differ in their policy positions from those of other religious traditions? And if they do diverge in such matters, do evangelicals hold distinctively different political positions across the whole spectrum of economic, social, and foreign policy positions, or primarily only in relationship to a few, highly visible, issues?

Table 7.2 analyzes the issue positions of evangelicals, and it compares their responses to the responses of those affiliated with the other major religious traditions. The initial two questions in the table focus on economic issues, the next two questions on foreign policy, and the final three questions on social policy.

As is evident from the table, there are important differences in the issue positions expressed by members of the five religious traditions. Note that for five of the seven political issues examined, the difference between the highest and lowest percentage across the five groups exceeds 15 percent. And in one of the two exceptions (clergy endorsing candidates), differences still exceeded 10 percent. Thus, religious tradition affiliation appears to shape political positions across a wide range of political issues.

Economic Issues

Despite the fact that there is considerable variation across the major religious traditions in the policy positions expressed by those affiliated with each tradition, evangelical Protestants do not adopt policy positions on economic matters that differ markedly from those of the other religious traditions (at least as reflected in the issue positions examined here). For example, evangelicals overwhelmingly favor the government doing more to help the needy, with nearly three-fifths of all evangelicals (57 percent) responding in such a manner (see table 5.1). This level of support basically mirrors that found about mainline Protestants, but it trails slightly that expressed by Catholics

TABLE 7.2
Issue Positions by Religious Tradition

	Evangelical Protestant (%)	Mainline Protestant (%)	Black Protestant (%)	Roman Catholic (%)	Unaffiliated (%)
Stricter environmental laws cost too many jobs and hurt economy[a]	38	29	41	34	25
Free trade good for economy even if means loss of some U.S. jobs[b]	31	31	24	30	33
Best way to ensure peace is through military strength[a]	40	30	21	26	22
Best for future of country to be active in world affairs[a]	37	40	23	37	34
Abortion should be illegal in most or all cases[a]	65	34	49	48	25
Homosexuality is way of life that should be accepted by society[a]	28	58	43	62	74
Clergy should be permitted to endorse candidates during religious services[b]	30	28	35	24	27

Sources:

[a] Pew Forum Religious Landscape Survey, 2007

[b] Henry Institute National Survey on Religion and Public Life, 2008

Note: Entries show percent agreeing with statement

and the religiously unaffiliated. On the other hand, Black Protestants largely stand alone in their extensive support for the government doing more, as nearly four-fifths within their ranks (79 percent) favored such a position.

Likewise, the positions of evangelicals differ only marginally, rather than substantially, from the other religious traditions in response to stricter environmental laws. On this matter, evangelicals stand closer to Black Protestants, as approximately two-fifths of each tradition opposed more stringent laws based on economic concerns, while about one-quarter to one-third of mainline Protestants, Catholics, and the unaffiliated reported such a position. And differences across religious traditions are even smaller with regard to policy positions related to favoring free trade, with patterns among evangelicals mirroring those found among mainline Protestants, Catholics, and the religiously unaffiliated.

Thus, on these various economic matters, the policy positions of evangelical Protestants differed more marginally than substantially from those adopted by others. If anything, the policy positions of Black Protestants stand more distinctly apart from those of the remaining other religious traditions. Quite likely, the more distinctive economic positions of Black Protestants are a reflection of their greater economic vulnerability overall.[4]

Foreign Policy Issues

On foreign policy matters, the evidence is more mixed as to whether evangelicals express positions that are only marginally, or more substantially, different from those of the other religious traditions. When asked whether it would better for the United States to "pay less attention to problems overseas and concentrate on problems here at home" or whether it would be better "for the future of our country to be active in world affairs," the positions reported by evangelical Protestants were largely similar to those of mainline Protestants, Catholics, and the religiously unaffiliated, as more than one-third within each group responded it would be best to remain active in world affairs. Only the stance of Black Protestants differed more substantially from the others.

On the other hand, evangelicals stood more apart from the other religious traditions in holding that "the best way to ensure peace is through military strength." Two-fifths of all evangelicals adopted such a stance, but not even one-third of mainline Protestants or Catholics did so—and only about one-fifth of Black Protestants and the religiously unaffiliated expressed such a viewpoint. Clearly, in terms of reliance on military strength, evangelicals stand somewhat apart from those within the other religious traditions. Yet, even here, this stance was adopted by less than a majority of evangelicals.

Consequently, though evangelicals may be somewhat more inclined than others to hold that peace is best achieved through military strength, they do not as a whole necessarily advance such a position.

Social Issues

It is primarily with regard to various social issues that one finds evangelicals standing more apart from other Americans in the policy positions they adopt. Probably the two most prominent social issues within American politics over the course of the past several decades relate to abortion and gay rights. And on these matters of public policy, evangelicals tend to stand much further apart from those affiliated with the other major religious traditions than they do on matters related to economic or foreign policy issues.

As shown in table 7.2, nearly two-thirds of evangelicals (65 percent) contend that abortion should be illegal in most or all cases. In contrast, roughly half (though less than a majority) of Black Protestants and Catholics held such a position, and only one-third of mainline Protestants and a quarter of the religiously unaffiliated did so. And when asked whether "homosexuality is a way of life that should be accepted by society," only a little more than one-quarter of evangelicals (28 percent) responded in the affirmative, whereas more than two-fifths of Black Protestants (43 percent) did so, and a substantial majority of mainline Protestants (58 percent) and Catholics (62 percent), as well as an overwhelming majority of the religiously unaffiliated (74 percent), did so.

The analysis of issue positions found in table 7.2 has thus far been limited to those questions found in the Religious Landscape Survey. The only two social issues examined in the Landscape Survey related to abortion and homosexuality, and, if the analysis of social issues were restricted to these two issues alone, one might naturally assume that evangelicals generally stand apart from other Americans across a whole range of matters that might be deemed social issues. This is not necessarily the case. Though other examples could be marshaled, table 7.2 includes one additional social issue to reveal that the extent to which evangelicals part company from other Americans on social issues depends on the particular issue examined. For example, as can be seen at the bottom of table 7.2, evangelicals are no more accepting of clergy endorsing candidates during religious services than those affiliated with other religious traditions. When asked whether ministers should be permitted to endorse candidates during worship services, less than one-third of evangelicals (30 percent) responded affirmatively, a lower percentage than found among Black Protestants (35 percent) and approximately the same percentage as among mainline Protestants (28 percent) and the religiously unaffiliated (27 percent). Thus, with regard to clergy endorsing candidates during religious services, the positions of evangelicals are not distinctly different from those expressed by members of most other major religious traditions.

Conclusions

Several conclusions can be drawn from this brief analysis of the issue positions expressed by members of different religious traditions. First, differences in policy positions do not always pit those who are "religious" against those who are "secular" in religious orientation. Only on three of the issues examined (i.e., the environment, abortion, and homosexuality) does one find that the religiously unaffiliated are located at one end of the spectrum (exhibiting either the highest or the lowest percentage expressing such a position) with one of the four religious traditions located at the other end. Thus, for most of the issues examined, the maximum percentage differences across these religious traditions would not change were the religiously unaffiliated simply dropped from the analysis.

Second, on most issues, evangelicals do not express policy positions that place them at some extreme end of the political spectrum. Actually, this is not too surprising in that the political attitudes and opinions of most Americans are neither consistently liberal nor conservative in the positions they adopt over a wide range of issues (Flanigan and Zingale 1983, 110). Though evangelicals may express conservative positions on some political issues, most evangelicals (as well as most of those of other religious traditions) do not do so across all political issues. Only in terms of three specific policies examined (specifically, relying on a strong military, discouraging homosexuality, and making most abortions illegal) did evangelicals more typically fall at one end of the political spectrum in which their positions exhibited a 10-percentage-point gap from the positions expressed by those of another religious tradition. Thus, though evangelicals hold distinctive policy positions on a limited number of policy matters, they typically hold positions on most political issues that are largely reflective of those expressed by other Americans.

Ideological Orientations and Partisanship

Most Americans typically express only a modest interest in politics; as a result, they typically do not invest a great deal of time in becoming informed politically. Consequently, the positions that Americans adopt on policy issues do not reveal the level of coherence and consistency one would expect were their positions arrived at "through the applications of a common underlying set of political ideals" (Flanigan and Zingale 1998, 131).

Given this situation, scholars have found it helpful to distinguish between one's "operational" ideology (reflecting one's typical positions on issues along a left–right continuum) and one's "symbolic" ideology (reflecting one's ideological self-classification). When asked, most Americans are quite willing to classify themselves in terms of ideological labels such as "liberals," "moderates," or "conservatives." For many citizens, the ideological self-classifications they report and the particular positions they adopt on specific issues do not fully coincide.[5]

When asked their ideological orientation, a plurality in every religious tradition, except evangelicals, responded that they were political "moderates," with approximately two-fifths of each religious tradition reporting such. Even among evangelicals, roughly one-third indicated that they were moderates ideologically (see table 7.3).

Moreover, Americans are more prone to classify themselves as political conservatives than as political liberals. Excepting the religiously unaffiliated, a larger percentage of adherents within each religious tradition responded that they were conservative rather than liberal. Even among Black Protestants, a higher percent chose to classify themselves as either "very conservative" or "conservative" (38 percent) than as "very liberal" or "liberal" (23 percent). Of all the groups, evangelicals were the most prone to adopt the conservative label, as more than one-half (56 percent) identified themselves as either "very conservative" or "conservative," and only a little more than one-tenth as political "liberals."

However, people may use different bases for classifying themselves ideologically. For example, a person could chose to label oneself as a political conservative on the basis of one's economic positions (being a fiscal conservative) or on one's stands on social issues such as abortion or gay rights (being a social conservative). Given the general lack of coherence and consistency across issue positions that is typical for most Americans, the fact that one chooses a conservative label does not mean, therefore, that such a person necessarily adopts conservative positions on many current political issues. Moreover, the conservative label can also be claimed simply as a relative assessment of one's political positions in relationship to those exhibited by others. For example, evangelical college students in the late 1990s were far more prone than their evangelical counterparts two decades earlier to classify themselves as political conservatives—even though their specific stands on political issues were more liberal than the positions adopted by evangelical college students nearly twenty years earlier (Penning and Smidt 2002, chapter 6). Thus, a far higher percentage of evangelicals can claim to be political conservatives than the percentage who actually adopt conservative positions on particular political issues.

TABLE 7.3
Ideological Orientations and Partisanship by Religious Tradition

	Evangelical Protestant (%)	Mainline Protestant (%)	Black Protestant (%)	Roman Catholic (%)	Unaffiliated (%)
Political Ideology[a]					
Very conservative	13	5	9	6	3
Conservative	43	33	29	34	18
Moderate	32	43	39	41	42
Liberal	9	15	16	16	25
Very liberal	3	4	7	4	11
Close to Christian Right[b]					
Very close	14	5	19	3	1
Close	29	12	22	14	10
Neutral	32	28	25	32	16
Far	10	17	16	18	18
Very far	14	39	18	33	55
Partisan Identification[a]					
Democrat	24	29	66	33	31
Independent— lean Democrat	10	14	12	19	24
Independent	16	16	12	19	23
Independent— lean Republican	12	10	3	10	10
Republican	38	31	7	24	13
2008 Presidential Vote Choice[c]					
Obama	24	54	94	56	76
McCain	76	46	6	44	24

Sources:

[a] Pew Forum Religious Landscape Survey, 2007

[b] University of Akron, Fifth National Survey of Religion and Politics, 2008

[c] Henry Institute National Survey on Religion and Public Life, 2008

When we examine partisan self-identifications, far fewer evangelicals label themselves as Republicans than claim to be conservative in terms of political ideology (see table 7.3). Or, stated differently, evangelicals are more likely to classify themselves as Democrats than label themselves as political liberals. Slightly more than one-third of evangelicals (38 percent) claim to be Republicans, with nearly one-quarter of evangelicals (24 percent) classifying themselves as Democrats. The percentage of evangelicals who identify themselves as independents (when including "leaners") is equivalent to the percentage who adopt the Republican label (38 percent), with the percentage of independents leaning toward the Republican Party only slightly exceeding the percentage leaning toward the Democratic Party (12 versus 10 percent, respectively).

Nevertheless, of the five religious traditions examined in table 7.3, evangelical Protestants are the most closely aligned with the Republican Party. No other religious tradition, except for mainline Protestants, exhibits a higher percentage of Republican party identifiers than Democratic party identifiers—though only a slightly higher percentage of mainline Protestants identify with the Republican Party than with the Democratic Party. Black Protestants are the most closely aligned with the Democratic Party, followed by the religiously unaffiliated, and then by Catholics, who are somewhat more likely to identify as Democrats (33 percent) than Republicans (24 percent).

However, when confronted with the decision to cast their ballot for a Democratic or Republican candidate for president, evangelicals have chosen overwhelmingly in recent years to vote for the Republican nominee. As can be seen in table 7.3, slightly more than three-quarters of evangelicals (76 percent) reported voting for John McCain in the 2008 presidential election, whereas a majority of members of all the other religious traditions reported choosing Barack Obama. And despite Mitt Romney's Mormon faith, evangelical voters continued to strongly vote Republican in the 2012 president election as well (Pew Forum on Religion & Public Life 2012). Thus, it is primarily in terms of their ideological self-classifications, their partisan identifications, and their votes for presidential nominees that evangelicals largely stand apart from those affiliated with the other religious traditions.

The Christian Right and Tea Party Movements

Movements tend to be broader than the specific organizations associated with them. For example, not all who would consider themselves supporters of the environmental movement are formal members of an organization working to protect the environment. Evangelicals have long been linked to the Christian Right movement, and it is true that the core of its support has historically come from them (Wilcox 1992; Wilcox and Larson 2006).

Nevertheless, though the largest component of the Christian Right constituency may be drawn from the ranks of evangelicals, it does not follow that most evangelicals necessarily align themselves with the goals advanced by the Christian Right. And, in fact, far fewer evangelicals claim that they feel close to the Christian Right than identify as political conservatives (see table 7.3),[6] and twice as many evangelicals report being far from the Christian Right than claim to be a political liberal. Actually, a higher percentage of Black Protestants than evangelical Protestants report feeling "very close" to the Christian Right.[7]

Whereas the present manifestation of the Christian Right emerged prior to the 1980 presidential election, the more recent Tea Party movement began in the months following the 2008 presidential election. In the congressional elections of 2010 that movement clearly helped the Republican Party gain control of the House of Representatives and make additional gains in the Senate. To what extent, then, do evangelicals[8] stand behind the Tea Party movement?

Despite its emergence less than two years earlier, most Americans already reported by early August 2010 that they had heard or read about the Tea Party movement (see table 7.4), with the religiously unaffiliated exhibiting the lowest level of recognition of the movement (at 75 percent recognition).[9] Though some viewed the Tea Party to be merely an extension of the Republican Party, most

TABLE 7.4
Perspective on Tea Party Movement by Religious Tradition

	Evangelical Protestant (%)	Mainline Protestant (%)	Black Protestant (%)	Roman Catholic (%)	Unaffiliated (%)
Heard or read about Tea Party movement[a]	81	83	78	81	75
Tea Party part of Republican Party[b]	32	32	50	31	42
Favorable view of Tea Party[c]	54	36	23	41	28
Agree with Tea Party[c]	34	22	5	20	14
Supporter of Tea Party[d]	28	19	6	23	21
Agree with Christian Right and Tea Party[a]	20	9	5	8	2

Sources:

[a] Pew Religion and Public Life Survey, July 21–August 5, 2010

[b] Pew Research Center Survey, March 30–April 3, 2011

[c] Pew Research Center Survey, August 17–21, 2011

[d] Gallup News Service Poll, November 28–December 1, 2011

Note: Entries show percent agreeing with statement

Americans, regardless of their particular religious tradition, viewed it as an independent movement outside the domain of the Republican Party. However, Black Protestants and the religiously unaffiliated, the two religious traditions most heavily Democratic in their partisan identifications, were the most likely to view the Tea Party as part of the GOP (at 50 percent and 42 percent, respectively).

Since Tea Party supporters "are more conservative on economic issues and the size of government than . . . Republicans in general" (Clement and Green 2011, 1), and given that evangelicals tend to prefer a smaller government with fewer services (see table 5.1), one might anticipate that evangelicals would be more likely than those affiliated with the other major religious traditions to back the Tea Party movement. This expectation is borne out in table 7.4, as evangelical Protestants, when compared to those of other religious traditions, were the most likely to express a favorable view of, or stand in agreement with, the Tea Party.

Nevertheless, it is also clear that the level of support that evangelicals extend to the Tea Party movement is dependent on the way in which the question is asked. For example, in the August 2011 survey of the Pew Research Center, a majority of evangelicals (54 percent) indicated that they held a favorable view of the Tea Party, but when asked in the same survey whether "From what you know, do you agree or disagree with the Tea Party movement?" only a little more than one-third of evangelicals (34 percent) reported agreement with the movement.

This pattern of lower levels of expressed Tea Party support when asked in terms of "agreement with" as opposed to "favorable views of" the movement is evident within each of the five traditions. Clearly the way the question is posed affects the level of support expressed for the movement. Further, when the Gallup survey organization asked respondents a few months later whether or not they were a "supporter" of the Tea Party, the percentages within each of the religious traditions tended to mirror the patterns found when respondents were asked about their "agreement with" as opposed to "favorable views of" the Tea Party movement.

There is, of course, some overlap between support for the Tea Party movement and support for the Christian Right movement. Overall, about half of those who claim to be part of the Tea Party movement also consider themselves part of the Christian Right (Public Religion Research Institute 2012). The same is true when examined in terms of expressions of agreement with the two movements, as half of those who stand in agreement with the Tea Party also report standing in agreement with the Christian Right (data not shown).[10] However, when analyzed in terms of the percentage of members within each tradition who agree with both movements, only one-fifth of all evangelicals can be so classified. Though this level of support was slightly more than double that found among mainline Protestants and Roman Catholics, only a small fraction of all evangelicals actually report support for both endeavors.[11]

Change over Time

Of course, patterns that exist today may be different from what persisted decades ago. For example, it was suggested earlier in the chapter that evangelicals have exhibited a cyclical pattern of political engagement and that its current wave of engagement began in the 1970s. Likewise, previous research has shown that the partisan identification of evangelicals was far more Democratic several decades ago (Kellstedt et al. 2007; Smidt 2008). Are these changes, or any other political changes, evident among evangelicals when we examine their political characteristics over time?

Table 7.5 addresses this question by examining four different political variables by religious tradition over time: partisan identification, affection for the Christian Right, voting turnout in presidential elections, and the political party of the candidate for whom the respondent voted in the past presidential election. In 1964, nearly half of all evangelicals (45 percent) were Democratic in their partisan identifications, while only about one-third (34 percent) reported being Republicans. Clearly evangelicals are now more Republican and less Democratic in their partisan identifications than they were more than four decades ago in 1964. This change largely transpired between 1964 and 1996, as the march toward the Republican Party among evangelicals has not continued following the 1996 election. In fact, the percentage of Democratic partisan identifiers among evangelicals is somewhat larger today than in 1996.

Over the same period of time, changes have also occurred in the partisan identifications of those affiliated with the other four religious traditions. The pattern of partisan change among Catholics mirrors that of evangelicals—though Catholics were, and continue to be, far more Democratic in their partisan identifications than evangelicals. The percentage of Democratic identifiers among Catholics has diminished dramatically over the past four decades, and though Republican identification grew within their ranks between 1964 and 1996, it has not grown subsequently. As a result, the percentage of Democratic identifiers among Catholics today still exceeds the percentage of Republican identifiers.

The pattern of partisan change is somewhat different among mainline Protestants. Mainline Protestants have long constituted the historic base of the Republican Party coalition, and they continued in their relatively high level of Republican partisan identifications between 1964 and 1996. However,

TABLE 7.5
Political Characteristics by Religious Tradition over Time

	1964 (%)	1996 (%)	2007 (%)
Evangelical Protestant			
Partisan Identification: Democrat	45	23	27
Partisan Identification: Republican	34	44	43
Close to Christian Right	x	55	43*
Voted in last presidential election	61	77	75
Voted for Republican presidential candidate	55	65	76
Mainline Protestant			
Partisan Identification: Democrat	37	29	32
Partisan Identification: Republican	42	42	34
Close to Christian Right	x	30	17*
Voted in last presidential election	82	84	80
Voted for Republican presidential candidate	57	51	61
Black Protestant			
Partisan Identification: Democrat	81	66	72
Partisan Identification: Republican	9	9	8
Close to Christian Right	x	56	41*
Voted in last presidential election	56	80	72
Voted for Republican presidential candidate	12	10	17
Roman Catholic			
Partisan Identification: Democrat	62	36	38
Partisan Identification: Republican	15	30	27
Close to Christian Right	x	30	17*
Voted in last presidential election	77	79	76
Voted for Republican presidential candidate	16	44	56
Unaffiliated			
Partisan Identification: Democrat	45	32	35
Partisan Identification: Republican	18	24	15
Close to Christian Right	x	14	11*
Voted in last presidential election	59	68	63
Voted for Republican presidential candidate	36	34	35

Sources:

1964: Anti-Semitism in the United States

1996: University of Akron, Second National Survey of Religion and Politics

2007: Pew Forum Religious Landscape Survey

x – not asked

* – University of Akron, Fifth National Survey of Religion and Politics, 2008

between 1996 and 2007, the percentage of Republicans declined dramatically, while the percentage of Democratic identifiers among mainline Protestants inched slightly upward.

Black Protestants were overwhelmingly Democratic in their partisan iden-tifications in 1964, and the same is true today—though the overall percentage of Democrats within their ranks has declined slightly, shifting more toward political independence than toward identification with the Republican Party. The same can also be said for the religiously unaffiliated. Though the reli-giously unaffiliated are less Democratic in their partisan identifications today than they were in 1964, they are currently no more Republican than previ-ously—as the percentage of Democratic identifiers continue to be more than twice that of Republican identifiers within their ranks.

Though evangelicals have remained Republican in their partisan identifica-tions since 1996, the percentage who report they feel close to the Christian Right has actually declined since then. In 1996, more than half of evangelical Protestants indicated that they felt some level of closeness to the Christian Right, but that level of closeness had dropped considerably only a decade later—from 55 to 43 percent. In this regard, evangelicals are again much like those in the other religious traditions, as all Americans, regardless of their religious tradition, expressed far lower levels of affection for the Christian Right in 2007 than in 1996 (the exception being the religiously unaffiliated, who already expressed exceedingly low levels of closeness in 1996). Neverthe-less, though the level of support for the Christian Right among evangelicals today is far lower than it was previously, they continue to remain the religious tradition most likely to express feelings of closeness (though only a little more than two-fifths of all evangelicals express such sentiments).

The Anti-Semitism Survey was fielded in 1964, but the survey occurred prior to the presidential election of that year. Hence, both the reported turn-out variable and the reported partisan vote for president variable in the 1964 survey relate to the 1960 presidential election between John F. Kennedy and Richard M. Nixon. Given the historic anti-Catholicism among many Protes-tants at the time (including evangelical Protestants), it is likely that higher lev-els of voter turnout were evident among both Protestants and Catholics in the 1960 election than in the previous or subsequent elections. This may result in the initial levels of voting turnout data found in table 7.4 being somewhat elevated for that particular period of time.

It should also be noted that the level of turnout reported by survey re-spondents typically exceeds the actual level of turnout in an election.[12] This is not necessarily a problem in that the analysis here compares "apples with apples"—namely, verbal reports of turnout and the pattern of change in such verbal reported levels over time.[13]

Nevertheless, the data in table 7.5 still reveal the surge to the polls that has occurred among evangelicals over the past four decades. Today, evangelical Protestants exhibit a higher level of voter turnout than in the 1960 election, when many may well have gone to the polls in an effort to prevent a Catholic from being elected president. Slightly more than three-fifths of all evangelicals (61 percent) reported having cast a ballot in the 1960 presidential election, but three-quarters (75 percent) reported doing so in the 2004 presidential election.

Like evangelicals, Black Protestants reveal a pattern of increased voter turnout over time. Of course, the 1960 presidential election occurred prior to the Civil Rights Voting Act of 1963 that sought to ensure the rights of African Americans to cast ballots on Election Day. Certainly, the level of reported voter turnout among Black Protestants jumped dramatically between the 1960 election and the 1996 election, with the reported turnout for the 2004 election dropping below the level reported in 1996—only to jump again in 2008 when Barack Obama became the first African American to be the standard bearer of a major party as its nominee for president (Smidt et al. 2010, 182–84).

On the other hand, the level of voter turnout among mainline Protestants and Catholics has remained relatively stable over the same period of time. The reported turnout among mainline Protestants slightly exceeds that among Catholics for each of the time periods examined. However, the data may be somewhat misleading for Catholics, who surged to the polls in 1960 to elect the first Catholic to the Oval Office; it is possible that voting rates among Catholics in 1960 conceal what otherwise may have been a pattern of increased reported voter turnout between the late 1950s to the mid-1990s.

As noted earlier, the data for the presidential vote reported in 1964 relate to the level of voting for Nixon in the 1960 presidential election. Even though most evangelicals were Democratic in their partisan identifications at the time, a majority nevertheless cast their ballots for Nixon in 1960. Yet despite this inflated Republican voting in 1960 (given the anti-Catholic ballots that may have been cast in that election), evangelicals have moved progressively in even greater numbers in voting for Republican presidential candidates, as over the past four decades, there has been a steady increase in the percentage voting Republican.

However, mainline Protestants have been somewhat more variable in their level of voting for the Republican nominee for president. In each cross-section of time, a majority of mainline Protestants have reported voting for the GOP candidate. Nearly three-fifths of all mainline Protestants (57 percent) reported that they had voted for Nixon in 1960, though a bare majority of mainliners (51 percent) voted Republican in 1996, only to shift in a more GOP direction in 2004.[14]

Over the past forty years, Black Protestants have exhibited a very low, though somewhat variable, level of voting for the Republican presidential candidate; regardless of the year examined in table 7.5, less than one-fifth of Black Protestants reported having voted in the last election for the Republican presidential candidate. Over the same period of time, Catholics have, however, moved rather dramatically in a more Republican direction in terms of presidential voting. As a result, there was a dramatic increase in reported votes for the Republican candidate between the 1960 election (16 percent) and the 1996 election (44 percent).[15] And even though John Kerry was only the second Catholic to be a major party nominee for president, Catholics did not flock to Kerry in 2004—as a majority of Catholics (56 percent) in 2007 reported casting their ballot for George W. Bush. Finally, the religiously unaffiliated have exhibited a relatively steady, but low, level of voting for Republican presidential candidates over the four decades examined—as only about one-third of the unaffiliated reported voting for the GOP nominee in each of the elections examined.

Divisions among Evangelicals

Having seen the changes among evangelicals over time and how they relate to those found among affiliates of the other major religious traditions, we can now turn our attention to the extent to which differences exist among evangelicals today. These differences are examined, as in previous chapters, in terms of racial and ethnic, generational, educational, and religious factors.

Racial and Ethnic Differences

Our analysis of racial and ethnic differences among evangelicals has, thus far, suggested that religious tradition generally appears to have somewhat greater power in shaping responses on matters of religious beliefs, religious behavior, social theology, and civic engagement than do racial and ethnic differences within their ranks. In other words, the responses of black evangelicals overall have more closely reflected the patterns evident among other evangelicals than they have the responses of blacks within the Black Protestant tradition. And the same has been true with regard to Hispanics, with Hispanic evangelicals more closely reflecting patterns found among other evangelicals than they do those found among Catholic Hispanics. Consequently, though racial and ethnic differences among evangelicals may exist, these differences are generally smaller than that found among members of the same racial or ethnic group across religious traditions.

Though "the relationship among race, religion, and politics is not fully understood" (Wald and Brown 2007, 294), there are reasons to expect that these previous patterns of relative cohesion of evangelicals may not continue to hold when discussing the political characteristics of white, black, and Hispanic evangelicals. Previous research has found, for example, that "African American Christians vote differently than those whites whose religious beliefs mirror their own" (Cooper and Smidt 2012, 186), with religion mediating the relationship between African Americans and presidential candidates (Harris-Lacewell 2008, 208) and race mediating the relationship between black and white Christians who otherwise hold relatively similar religious beliefs (Cooper and Smidt 2012).

Table 7.6 examines the political characteristics of white, black, and Hispanic evangelicals and compares them to the same racial and ethnic groups found in different religious traditions.

Several patterns emerge from the table. First, religious tradition affiliation shapes and colors the political views and behavior of white Christians. For the most part, white evangelicals stand apart from white mainline Protestants and white Catholics in terms of their political attitudes and behavior. On occasion, the views of white mainline Protestants and white Catholics deviate from each other (e.g., attitudes on abortion), but generally the political attitudes and behavior of white evangelicals stand apart from the political positions and actions exhibited by both white mainline Protestants and white Catholics, who typically resemble each other politically.

Second, the political opinions and attitudes of black evangelicals sometimes more closely reflect the political opinions and attitudes of other evangelicals than those of other blacks within the Black Protestant tradition. For example, the percentage of black evangelicals who report that religious beliefs shape their political thinking more closely mirrors the responses found among other evangelicals than resembling other blacks in the Black Protestant tradition. The same is true on the question of whether homosexuality as a way of life should be accepted, or discouraged, by society. But black evangelicals fall between other evangelicals and blacks in the Black Protestant tradition when we examine their views on abortion. Yet, in terms of other political attitudes, partisan identification, and presidential vote, black evangelicals far more closely reflect the positions adopted by other blacks in the Black Protestant tradition than they do their evangelical co-religionists of a different race or ethnic origin. So, on these matters, there is far more political cohesion among African Americans, regardless of their religious tradition, than among evangelicals regardless of their racial or ethnic differences.

On the other hand, Hispanic evangelicals stand more in agreement politically with their white co-religionists than with their fellow Hispanics in the

TABLE 7.6
Political Characteristics by Racial and
Ethnic Differences (controlling for religious tradition)

	Evangelical Protestant			Mainline Protestant	Black Protestant	Roman Catholic	
	White (%)	Black (%)	Hispanic (%)	White (%)	Black (%)	White (%)	Hispanic (%)
Religious beliefs shape my political thinking	30	28	30	8	18	9	9
Abortion should be illegal in most or all cases	66	57	70	33	48	46	55
Homosexuality is way of life that should be accepted by society	27	33	32	59	44	61	64
Stricter environmental laws cost too many jobs and hurt economy	40	39	41	30	41	31	43
Best way to ensure peace is through military strength	50	22	30	35	22	33	17
Best for future of country to be active in world affairs	41	24	43	44	24	41	37
Ideology: conservative	59	40	46	38	37	40	37
Party identification: Republican	47	8	34	36	7	32	15
Presidential vote in 2004: Bush	80	20	70	62	14	59	42

Source: Pew Forum Religious Landscape Survey, 2007

Note: Entries show percent agreeing with statement

Catholic tradition. When one examines the percentage differences between white and Hispanic evangelicals across the various political variables found in table 7.6, such differences are almost always far smaller than those found between Hispanic evangelicals and Hispanic Catholics. Of course, ethnicity still plays some role in these matters, as there are also some differences evident between white and Hispanic evangelicals. Nevertheless, the relative political cohesion among white and Hispanic evangelicals is far greater than that evident among Hispanics across the two religious traditions.

Thus, both religious tradition and race shape the political cohesion of Americans, but the patterns tend to vary for different racial and ethnic groups. Overall, white and Hispanic evangelicals exhibit far more political cohesion as a religious group than either whites or Hispanics as racial or ethnic groups; black evangelicals, however, frequently join other blacks from the Black Protestant tradition in their political proclivities.

Generational and Educational Differences

Does there appear to be an emerging new generation of evangelicals who diverge politically from their older co-religionists? And are the generational and educational differences among evangelicals in terms of their political attitudes and behavior any greater than that found among those affiliated with the other major religious traditions? These questions are addressed in table 7.7, which examines political attitudes, ideological orientations, and partisan identifications of affiliates of the five religious traditions broken down by generational and educational differences within their ranks.

Millennial evangelicals are politically much like their peers within the other religious traditions in that millennials within each religious tradition are more likely than their older co-religionists to state that homosexuality as a way of life should be accepted by society as well as to hold that most/all abortions should be illegal. Likewise, regardless of religious tradition, millennials are less likely than their older co-religionists to hold that peace is best obtained through military strength, to classify oneself as a political conservative, or to identify oneself as a Republican.[16] All of this suggests that a new generation of evangelicals may be emerging politically, one that exhibits distinctively different political proclivities than older evangelicals.

At the same time, it is also true that there continues to exist a substantial gap politically between evangelical millennials and millennials in the other religious traditions. For example, whereas 41 percent of millennial evangelicals expressed the position that homosexuality as a way of life should be accepted by society,[17] 70 percent of millennial mainliners and 79 percent of millennial Catholics did so. Even a majority of Black Protestants (57 percent) agreed with the statement. Though such extensive differences among millennials across the various religious traditions are not evident with regard to the other political characteristics examined in table 7.7, differences among millennials across the religious traditions generally exceed differences found between

TABLE 7.7

Political Characteristics by Generational Cohort and Educational Attainment (controlling for religious tradition)

	Generational		Education	
	Non-Millennial (%)	Millennial (%)	Non-College Graduate (%)	College Graduate (%)
Evangelical Protestant				
Abortion should be illegal in most/all cases	64	68	65	66
Homosexuality should be accepted by society	26	41	28	28
Stricter environmental laws too costly	41	33	40	36
Peace best ensured through military strength	47	38	45	47
Ideology: Conservative	58	46	55	62
Party identification: Republican	43	41	40	53
Mainline Protestant				
Abortion should be illegal in most/all cases	33	42	39	25
Homosexuality should be accepted by society	57	70	53	69
Stricter environmental laws too costly	30	29	34	23
Peace best ensured through military strength	35	26	35	31
Ideology: Conservative	39	31	42	31
Party identification: Republican	35	32	33	36
Black Protestant				
Abortion should be illegal in most/all cases	49	52	52	36
Homosexuality should be accepted by society	40	57	42	48
Stricter environmental laws too costly	41	42	45	27
Peace best ensured through military strength	23	24	24	16

Ideology: Conservative	38	36	41	25
Party identification: Republican	8	8	8	6
Roman Catholic				
Abortion should be illegal in most/all cases	47	51	50	43
Homosexuality should be accepted by society	60	79	59	69
Stricter environmental laws too costly	34	37	38	26
Peace best ensured through military strength	29	22	28	30
Ideology: Conservative	41	31	41	34
Party identification: Republican	28	24	25	33
Unaffiliated				
Abortion should be illegal in most/all cases	23	33	31	13
Homosexuality should be accepted by society	73	81	69	87
Stricter environmental laws too costly	25	27	30	15
Peace best ensured through military strength	25	21	26	18
Ideology: Conservative	23	17	24	15
Party identification: Republican	16	12	16	12

Source: Pew Forum Religious Landscape Survey, 2007

Note: First four entries within each religious tradition show percent agreeing with statement younger and older generations of evangelicals. Thus, in the end, the evidence that suggests that a new generation of evangelicals is emerging is somewhat mixed. Younger evangelicals do differ in many ways politically from their older co-religionists. Nevertheless, political differences within the millennial generation across religious traditions are frequently more substantial than differences between younger and older evangelicals.

Nor does college education appear to significantly divide the ranks of evangelicals politically (see table 7.7). Generally speaking, on the four major issues examined, the political attitudes of college-educated evangelicals reflect those of evangelicals who have not graduated from college. Only in terms of ideological orientations and partisan identifications do the political characteristics of college-educated evangelicals deviate from those with less education, as college-educated evangelicals are more likely than those not so educated to label themselves as political conservatives and to identify with the Republican Party.

Thus, once again, we see that college education among evangelicals has different effects than it does within other traditions. Evangelicals who are college educated are more likely than those who are not college educated to classify themselves as conservatives ideologically, whereas the reverse pattern is evident across each of the other religious traditions. Likewise, those evangelicals who have graduated from college and those who have not are equally likely to state abortion should be illegal in all or most instances and that homosexuality as a way of life should not be accepted by society, whereas in each of the other religious traditions, college graduates are typically far less likely than those with less education to express these positions.

Religious Differences

As discussed in chapter 5, religious differences among members of each religious tradition have been examined to determine whether they can be classified as religious traditionalists.[18] And, clearly, important political differences are evident within each religious tradition based on whether or not the respondent can be classified as a religious "traditionalist" (see table 7.8).

Several important patterns emerge from the table. First, traditionalists, regardless of the religious groups with which they are affiliated, are more likely to contend that abortion should be illegal in most or all instances, that homosexuality should not be accepted by society, that stricter environmental laws are too costly economically, and that peace is best accomplished through military strength; they also are more likely than non-traditionalists to classify themselves as ideological conservatives and to label themselves as Republicans, though some differences between traditionalist and non-traditionalist Black Protestants are rather small in magnitude.[19]

TABLE 7.8

Political Characteristics by Religious Traditionalism (controlling for religious tradition)

	Non-Traditionalist (%)	Traditionalist (%)
Evangelical Protestant		
Abortion should be illegal in most/all cases	50	73
Homosexuality should be accepted by society	45	19
Stricter environmental laws too costly	32	43
Peace best ensured through military strength	36	51
Ideology: Conservative	41	65
Party identification: Republican	34	48
Mainline Protestant		
Abortion should be illegal in most/all cases	26	49
Homosexuality should be accepted by society	70	40
Stricter environmental laws too costly	25	39
Peace best ensured through military strength	28	44
Ideology: Conservative	29	54
Party identification: Republican	30	44
Black Protestant		
Abortion should be illegal in most/all cases	42	54
Homosexuality should be accepted by society	55	36
Stricter environmental laws too costly	40	43
Peace best ensured through military strength	22	23
Ideology: Conservative	31	43
Party identification: Republican	6	10
Roman Catholic		
Abortion should be illegal in most/all cases	38	64
Homosexuality should be accepted by society	72	47
Stricter environmental laws too costly	29	43
Peace best ensured through military strength	24	35
Ideology: Conservative	31	52
Party identification: Republican	24	33

Source: Pew Forum Religious Landscape Survey, 2007

Note: First four entries under each religious tradition show percent agreeing with statement

Second, for evangelical Protestants, mainline Protestants, and Roman Catholics, religious traditionalism is far more important than generational or educational differences in shaping political responses. In other words, for each of these three traditions, the percentage differences evident between traditionalists and non-traditionalists exceeds those evident when each item is examined in terms of generational or educational differences. On the other hand, among Black Protestants, the relative importance of having a college education tends to outweigh religious traditionalism in their political effects, as in four out of six comparisons percentage differences were greater for Black Protestants when examined in terms of whether one had graduated from college as opposed to whether one was a religious traditionalist.

Controlling for Multiple Variables Simultaneously

Having shown that one's race and ethnicity, generational cohort, educational attainment, and religious traditionalism can all shape evangelical stands on political issues, turnout on Election Day, presidential vote choice, and partisan as well as ideological self-identification, we now seek to determine which of these factors most strongly shapes these political responses. Once again, we control for the relative effects of each of these four factors by means of multiple classification analysis (MCA),[20] using the Pew Religious Landscape Survey,[21] with the *beta* values[22] for each of the independent variables presented in table 7.9. The analysis is again limited to evangelicals, and it is based on using the coding of the variables employed in the previous tables.

Six different dependent variables related to politics are examined in the table: two social issues related to abortion and gay rights, two election-related variables of turnout and presidential vote choice, and two self-identification variables related to ideological and partisan identification. Of the four independent variables examined in the analysis, the MCA reveals that race and ethnicity best accounts for differences in presidential vote choice and partisan identifications among evangelicals, as black and Hispanic evangelicals are much more likely than white evangelicals to vote Democratic (*beta*=.32) and less likely to classify themselves as Republicans in terms of their partisan identifications (*beta*=.27). Race and ethnic differences also account for some differences in ideological self-classifications (*beta*=.09), though it ranks a distant second in relative importance for explaining variation in ideological orientations among evangelicals.

Generational and educational differences best explain differences in voting turnout among evangelicals, with millennial evangelicals being far less likely to report that they voted in the 2004 presidential election than their older co-religionists (*beta*=.30). Educational differences also help to explain turnout, as college-educated evangelicals are more likely than their less educated co-religionists to report to the polls on Election Day (*beta*=.19).

However, it is religious traditionalism that best accounts for most political differences among evangelicals. First, religious traditionalism ranks first in the magnitude of its *beta* coefficient for three of the six dependent

TABLE 7.9

Assessing Divisions among Evangelical Protestants on Politics: A Multivariate Analysis

	Abortion illegal	Homosexuality accepted	Voted last election	2004 presidential vote	Ideology	Party ID
Race/Ethnicity	.05	.03	.06	.32	.09	.27
Generational	.05	.08	.30	.02	.05	.03
Educational	.03	.00	.19	.06	.07	.13
Religious traditionalism	.23	.26	.04	.18	.22	.14
R^2	.06	.08	.14	.14	.07	.11

Source: Pew Forum Religious Landscape Survey, 2007

variables examined: differences in issue positions on abortion, differences in positions on homosexuality, and differences in ideological self-classification. In these matters, traditionalist evangelicals are more likely than their non-traditionalist brethren to adopt more restrictive views on abortion, to hold that homosexuality should be discouraged by society, and to classify oneself as a conservative ideologically.

In addition, religious traditionalism ranked second to race and ethnicity in its relative importance in accounting for differences in partisanship both in terms of partisan self-identifications and presidential vote choice. Only with regard to voting turnout does religious traditionalism not seem to play much of a factor in shaping evangelical decisions to go to the polls. Though race and ethnicity are the most important factors in shaping the partisanship of evangelicals, religious traditionalism among evangelicals plays a more important role than race and ethnicity overall in terms of its range of influence politically. Thus, these findings are largely consistent with earlier findings that, among white evangelicals, "moral standards traditionalism is a particularly important explanation of conservatism on a wide range of issues" (Brint and Abrutyn 2010, 328).

Conclusions

Evangelicals are distinctive neither in their level of political dissatisfaction—as they do not exhibit greater dissatisfaction than those within other religious traditions—nor in their level of political distrust—as they are no more likely than others to think that elected officials easily lose touch with the people who elected them. Where evangelicals are distinct politically concerns the extent to which they claim religion influences their political thinking.

With regard to public policy, evangelicals largely stand in agreement with most other Americans in the positions they adopt. The economic policy positions of evangelical Protestants differ only marginally from those adopted by others, with the policy positions of Black Protestants standing more apart from those of the remaining other religious traditions. In terms of foreign policy, evangelicals stand somewhat apart from those of the other religious traditions in holding that "the best way to ensure peace is through military strength." But it is primarily with regard to the issues of abortion and homosexuality where one finds evangelicals adopting policy positions that place them farther apart from other Americans. On most issues, evangelicals do not express policy positions that place them at some extreme end of the political spectrum. Thus, even though evangelicals do hold some distinctive policy positions on a limited number of policy matters, they typically hold positions on most political issues that reflect those expressed by other Americans.

Far fewer evangelicals label themselves as Republicans than claim to be conservative in terms of political ideology, but most evangelicals have voted Republican over the course of the past several elections. Evangelical Protestants are somewhat more likely to express a favorable view of, or stand in agreement with, the Christian Right and the Tea Party than most other Americans, though it is also clear that the level of support that evangelicals extend to these movements is dependent on the way in which the question is asked. Nevertheless, only about one-fifth of all evangelicals view both the Christian Right and the Tea Party in a favorable light.

Evangelicals are now more Republican and less Democratic in their partisan identifications than they were in 1964. Most of this shift in partisan identifications among evangelicals occurred between 1964 and 1996. And despite the fact that evangelicals have remained over the past two decades largely Republican in their partisan identifications, the percentage of evangelicals who report they feel close to the Christian Right has actually declined over the same period of time.

Overall, race and ethnic differences among evangelicals best account for differences in the partisanship of evangelicals, but differences in religious traditionalism most fully shape political differences among evangelicals. Those evangelicals who are religious traditionalists are far more conservative in their positions on social issues and in their ideological self-identifications than are non-traditionalist evangelicals, and they are also more prone to be Republican in their partisan identifications and presidential vote choice than non-traditionalists (though religious traditionalism ranked second to racial/ethnic differences among evangelicals in explaining these partisan preferences).

8

In the Sweet By and By?
Evangelicals and the Future

SCHOLARS HAVE TYPICALLY APPROACHED the study of evangelicals, as well as other social groups, in terms of analyzing either those who are considered to be the leaders or "elites" of the group or those who fall within the rank-and-file members of the group. The first approach is typically far easier, less costly, and more subjective, as analyses of the spoken and written words of selected group leaders are far simpler, more readily available, and less costly than conducting one's own national survey.[1] The greater subjectivity of the elite approach is largely evident in the selection of just who is to be analyzed and the particular comments selected to be reported and discussed.[2] But, far more important, problems arise when analysts suggest, either implicitly or explicitly, that the views of these "elites" basically reflect and embody the views of their supposed constituencies.

In this study, evangelical Protestants have been defined, based upon their affiliation with a particular set of religious bodies, as members of a distinctive religious tradition. As members of a religious tradition, evangelicals exhibit a characteristic way of interpreting and responding to the world. As such, their defining qualities relate to religious, and not political, life.

Evangelicals are a social, and not a categorical, group in that their cohesion is established through religious affiliations and the extended networks of social interaction that are generated through those religious ties. So defined, evangelicals belong to a religious tradition long evident within American religious life and are not a religious movement spread across different religious traditions, given that their social location is established by, and limited to, their particular denominational or congregational affiliations. And they are evangelicals simply because of these particular affiliations—not because they choose to label themselves as such.

If one desires to know what evangelicals truly believe or the actual kinds of behavior in which they engage, then it is necessary to examine what ordinary evangelicals say and do—and not what those designated as representatives of the group (whether as elites or as spokespersons) say or do. Thus, this study has focused its attention on how ordinary evangelicals think and behave. Because evangelicals are a social group, they exhibit certain social and political tendencies that distinguish them from other religious groups, but these distinguishing marks reflect tendencies—not uniformities. These distinguishing tendencies, however, are more prevalent within their particular tradition than within other religious traditions; as a result, they display an overall pattern religiously that differentiates them from other traditions. Overall, the results of this study largely substantiate the earlier contentions of Christian Smith (2000, 9), who noted that when one analyzes ordinary evangelicals, one finds "more diversity, complexity, and ambivalence than conventional wisdom would lead us to expect."

In this concluding chapter, our focus is on the future of evangelical Protestantism in American public life. It first addresses issues related to continuity and change within evangelical Protestantism as well as issues related to what serves as the core of evangelicalism—for if there is to be any meaningful link between some future manifestation of the evangelical tradition and its past, then the core of evangelical Protestantism must continue to be largely present. Second, the chapter analyzes current divisions within evangelical Protestantism and what they may suggest about its ability to continue into the future. And, finally, the chapter concludes with a discussion of likely changes within American evangelicalism over the course of the next fifty years and the extent to which American evangelicalism will continue to be a vibrant force within American religious life.

Continuity and Change within Evangelical Protestantism

Over the past three-quarters of a century, there has been considerable continuity within American evangelicalism.[3] A number of different qualities continue to characterize American evangelicals today just as they did previously: "the quest to live lives pleasing to God in line with his purposes, the firm belief that God acts in individual lives and in human history, the preference to read the Bible literally whenever possible, the ambivalence toward churches belonging to the mainline denominations, the democratic bias toward grassroots authority" (Hatch and Hamilton 1995, 401–2).

Nevertheless, evangelicalism has also undergone considerable change over the past several centuries, as the tradition has been shaped by a variety of religious movements with differing emphases (e.g., revivalism, fundamentalism, Pentecostalism). Thus, despite its continuities, much is different. Three-quarters of a century ago, evangelicals were very much engaged in theological battles to thwart attempts by modernists to alter particular historic understandings of the Christian faith. Today, however, in both theology and worship, there has been a shift away from "the theological toward the relational"—from an emphasis on the knowledge of God toward a focus on the experience of God (Hatch and Hamilton 1995, 402). Previously, many evangelicals thought they needed to witness verbally to non-Christians at virtually every opportunity; now there is greater emphasis among evangelicals on less verbal, and more extended, lifestyle evangelism approaches. Likewise, changes have occurred with regard to association with non-Christians. Previously, many evangelicals viewed associations with non-Christians as "worldly"; now such associations are viewed within a more neutral or perhaps even a more positive framework.

These changes, of course, are open to different interpretations. Some see the new emphases as a return to an earlier, pre-fundamentalist past, whereas others view the changes as a break from traditional patterns. Thus, for some evangelicals, such changes suggest a "maturing" of American evangelicals in the aftermath of their "captivity" to fundamentalism during the era of the modernist-fundamentalist divide, whereas for others these shifts represent regression, if not apostasy.

Clearly, a tradition can continue despite changes within it. But whether such shifts reflect continuity within the tradition across different historical contexts or some significant departure from the tradition is dependent on identifying what constitutes the core of that tradition. Evangelical Protestants have been defined here in terms of their religious affiliations, but what originally served as the basis for the formation of these particular religious denominations? Given that denominations reflect human efforts to institutionalize particular theological movements and perspectives, the basis for their formation largely relates to theology, and theology has been central to the evangelical tradition (see chapter 1).

As a result, a major issue among evangelicals today relates to what particular theological perspective serves as the core or center of American evangelicalism. For some, it is Reformed theology, with its more cognitive, rational, and confessional approach. For such evangelicals, the current revival of Arminian influences within evangelicalism (with its greater emphasis on experience, emotion, and a more individualized faith) is viewed at best as a departure from the core of the evangelical faith and at worst "as heretical departures from the evangelical faith" (Horton 2001a, 16). But, for others, "much of what constitutes evangelicalism today is, historically and theologically, illuminated more by the 'Pentecostal' paradigm than the 'Presbyterian' paradigm" (Dayton 1991, 51). Accordingly, they see Reformed theology as a contributing stream within American evangelicalism, but never as its main defining current.

The Reformed perspective, in comparison to the "Pentecostal" perspective, places a greater emphasis on ideas and theological propositions, is more likely to see the rise of "neo-evangelicalism" in the 1940s and 1950s (through the formation of the National Association of Evangelicals and its related efforts) as originating primarily within Calvinist/Reformed circles, and more strongly advocates a vision that emphasizes cultural engagement and the transformation of contemporary culture (Krapohl and Lippy 1999, 7–8). The alternative view sees a much greater influence of John Wesley's theology, with the roots of modern evangelicalism being found largely within "Methodist denominations of the early nineteenth century and the Wesleyan-oriented Holiness and Pentecostal groups . . . of the late nineteenth and early twentieth centuries" (Krapohl and Lippy 1999, 9).

While we must leave it to others to answer which of the two interpretations most accurately reflects the historical record, several observations can be made. First, it is not surprising, in an era in which a shift has been made from the printed word to the visual image and from reason to experience, that a similar shift in emphasis would occur within the religious life of Americans. American evangelicals have participated fully in the increasing turn to images that is replacing "the historic Protestant reliance on the written word" (Noll and Kellstedt 1995, 156). Confessional evangelicalism is more likely to be evident and stronger when it is planted in the soil of a culture that places "a high value on the kind of logical, clear thinking that a print culture engenders" (Wells 1994, 403). In contrast, a more experiential evangelicalism is likely to be more evident in cultural contexts in which visual images are emphasized and where religious faith "is rooted not so much in ideas as in spiritual encounter" (Wells 1994, 403).

Second, seeking to discern which of the two theological perspectives has served, and continues to serve, as the core or center of American evangelicalism is not an easy task when different perspectives have been evident—and perhaps even fused together. Randall Balmer, for example, argues that American evangelicalism is based on "the fusion of two strains of Protestantism, Puritanism and Pietism" (Balmer 1999, 14).[4] And if the core is some fusion of the two, then it is far more difficult to discern just how, and in what ways, each element serves to define the larger whole.

The issue, then, is not so much whether there has been diversity within the evangelical tradition but whether the "center" of that tradition is more rooted in Reformed or Arminian theology. Just which of the two is deemed to be the core shapes how one views contemporary changes within American evangelicalism as to whether those modifications stand within, or outside, the mainstream of the tradition. For example, if American evangelicalism is rooted more fully in pietistic, revivalistic, and Arminian soil than in Reformed soil, then "the appearance of the church growth movement, seeker-driven worship, and the growing attractiveness of alternatives to classical (i.e., Protestant scholastic) views of God, sin, salvation, and judgment may be seen as a resurgence rather than a significant departure" from the evangelical tradition (Horton 2001a, 18). On the other hand, if it is rooted more fully in the Reformed tradition, then these changes may be viewed as departures from the foundational core.

Similarly, how the "core" of the tradition is viewed affects how one normatively assesses changes transpiring within the tradition today. Some are alarmed about certain changes that have transpired within American evangelicalism, and they seek to restore evangelicalism to what they perceive to be its historic roots. Not surprisingly, those who take this path view the heritage much differently than those who approve of such changes. And while evangelicals continue to subscribe to certain religious beliefs to the same extent as they did nearly a half century ago (see chapter 4), there are those who contend that these tenets of the faith have lost the power to shape thinking and motivate action, as these religious "beliefs have moved from the psychological center to its periphery" among evangelicals (Wells 1994, 405). Those of the Reformed tradition, with its emphasis on ideas and theological propositions, would likely view such changes far more negatively than evangelicals of the Wesleyan tradition, with their greater emphasis on experience and practice.

Divisions among Evangelical Protestantism

Certainly, evangelical Protestantism has long been composed of many separate and strikingly diverse pieces. Religiously, they are drawn from a variety of denominations, as well as many nondenominational churches, both large and small. Those attending such churches are drawn from different social strata, different ethnic and racial groups, and different theological heritages. In addition, a variety of religious movements, whether located largely within or outside evangelical Protestantism (e.g., fundamentalism, Pentecostalism, the charismatic movement), have influenced different segments of evangelicals, and these movements have generated, at times, substantial intergroup tensions and conflict.

However, for some evangelicals, differences within the tradition seem to be much greater today than in the past. If certain confessional statements of faith previously served as the core of the evangelical tradition, then any shift from intellectual assent to "spiritual discipline and affective religion" (Balmer 1999, 16) or even any decline in the power of such doctrinal positions to shape thinking or motivate action is likely to lead to a far greater diversity in thought and behavior among evangelicals today than in the past.

Evangelical Protestantism is composed of "a conglomeration of varied subgroups that differ on many issues and sometimes clash significantly (among themselves)" (Smith 2000, 13). For those located outside the tradition, these differences may be largely unseen or be viewed as relatively unimportant. But because they matter to evangelicals, they profoundly affect their ability "to think, speak, and act with one voice," thereby having "tremendous social and political consequences" (Smith 2000, 15).

In this study, we have examined divisions among evangelical Protestants in terms of four possible fault lines: racial/ethnic, generational, educational, and theological differences. What have we learned about the relative commonalities evident among evangelicals across these lines when examining religious beliefs and practices, social theological perspectives, and their civic and political engagement? And what do the current lines of cleavage within the ranks of evangelicals suggest about the future of evangelicalism in American public life?

Racial Differences

On some matters, there is considerable similarity among evangelicals across racial lines. Black evangelicals are much like white and Hispanic evangelicals on matters of religious beliefs and practices, and tend to be more "religious" than their fellow blacks who are affiliated with the Black Protestant tradition. Hispanic evangelicals are more like white and black evangelicals religiously than they are their fellow Hispanics affiliated with the Roman Catholic tradition. Where differences begin to emerge among evangelicals along racial and ethnic lines concern matters related to social theology (e.g., the preferred size of government) and politics (particularly in terms of partisan identification and voting patterns).

Given the similarities of religious beliefs among evangelicals across racial and ethnic lines, social context clearly matters in how those beliefs are applied to political life. Religion serves as a mediating factor among African Americans, as religious black Americans express different assessments of politicians than those blacks who are less religious (Harris-Lacewell 2008, 217–18; Cooper and Smidt 2012), and different social contexts and historical experiences lead black and white evangelicals, despite their similarities in religious beliefs, to move in different directions politically in terms of how they view government, assess threats, and cast their ballots.

Generational Differences

The overall findings of this study reveal generational differences among evangelicals in terms of religious beliefs and behavior, social theology, and civic and political life. On some matters, however, these generational differences are far smaller among evangelicals than among those affiliated with other religious traditions, so that millennial evangelicals remain far closer to older evangelicals in their attitudes and behavior than they do to the fellow millennials in other traditions. So, for example, though some substantial differences exist between the two generations of evangelicals in terms of religious belief and practice, far greater differences are evident with regard to these same religious beliefs and practices between millennial evangelicals and those millennials affiliated with other religious traditions.

And yet, on other matters, there is some evidence to suggest that a new generation of evangelicals may be emerging—one that is substantially different from older evangelicals in their thinking and behavior. Millennial evangelicals are far more likely than older evangelicals to favor an activist government and to believe that the government should do more to help the needy; on these points, millennial evangelicals more closely mirror their generational counterparts than they do their older evangelical brethren. Moreover, when compared to other religious traditions, evangelicals exhibit the greatest level of generational difference in relationship to social trust, perceptions of threat to one's values by the entertainment industry, and willingness to allow homosexuals to teach.

However, in terms of political life, the evidence is far more mixed. On the one hand, millennial evangelicals are less likely than their older co-religionists to believe that peace is best obtained through military strength, to consider oneself a political conservative, or to identify as a Republican. Still, a substantial gap continues to exist politically between evangelical millennials and millennials in the other religious traditions. Though younger evangelicals differ in many ways politically from their older co-religionists, the political differences within the millennial generation across the different religious traditions are frequently more substantial in magnitude than the corresponding differences between younger and older evangelicals.

Educational Differences

Education tends to function in a somewhat different fashion religiously among evangelicals than it does among those affiliated with other religious traditions: having a college education does not produce the kind of general liberalizing social and political effects typically associated with having such an education. Like those affiliated with other Christian faith traditions, evangelicals who have graduated from college are far more "religious" than their co-religionists who have not in terms of adherence to religious beliefs and engagement in such religious practices as church attendance and private prayer.

Moreover, different levels of educational attainment function in a similar fashion across all religious traditions with regard to civic life. College-educated evangelicals, like their counterparts in other religious traditions, are more likely to express trust in others, join voluntary associations, volunteer, and be willing to allow homosexuals to teach.

But in terms of political life, the opposite is the case. In contrast to the college educated in other traditions, college-educated evangelicals are just as likely as their non-college-educated co-religionists to state that abortion should be illegal in all or most instances and that homosexuality as a way of life should not be accepted by society. Further, college-educated evangelicals are more likely than their less educated co-religionists to classify themselves as political conservatives and as Republicans.

Theological Differences

At the mass level, religious traditionalism generally explained more variance in differences among evangelicals than did racial, generational, or educational differences. The measure employed in this study to tap religious traditionalism was whether respondents thought their church or denomination should "preserve its traditional beliefs and practices."

However, this theological division among evangelicals at the mass level is reflective of a corresponding division that has emerged among evangelical "elites," as there are now two opposing parties among evangelical theologians: a traditionalist party and a reformist party that divide along several lines (Olson 1998).[5] For traditionalists, evangelicalism has a clear confessional basis. This acceptance of particular historical confessional statements provides traditionalists with clear theological boundaries that enable them to specify who is, and who is not, an evangelical. Moreover, for such traditionalists, recognizing these boundaries is the "only way to avoid the slide into debilitating relativism and pluralism" (Olson 1998, 40). But, for reformists, such an emphasis on strict boundaries is viewed as being too restrictive, bordering on obsession with order. Instead, reformists contend that the theological boundaries between evangelicals and non-evangelicals can "remain relatively open and undefined so long as the center remains strong" (Olson 1998, 42).

Traditionalists and reformists also part company in terms of how they view doctrines of the faith.[6] For traditionalists, the basic core doctrines of the faith are drawn rather directly from what is taught in scripture. Accordingly, they view such core doctrines as reflecting a "first-order" language of revelation—God-revealed doctrines. For reformists, however, doctrines of the faith are viewed as "second-order" in nature, as they emphasize the human component that is involved in formulating doctrines of the faith.

Finally, traditionalists and reformists adopt different stances with regard to theologies outside the evangelical tradition as well as interaction with culture more generally. Because traditionalists establish clear boundaries for evangelicalism and believe their particular doctrinal formulations reflect the essence of the faith, they are more likely to view non-evangelical theological formulations as false and to contend that it is important for evangelical theologians to provide the necessary critique and exposure of such falsehoods. Reformists, on the other hand, are more inclined to be open to the contributions of those outside the evangelical tradition and more likely to emphasize dialogue with non-evangelical theologians and philosophers.

This openness to the insights and influences of non-evangelical theological perspectives, however, only convinces traditionalists that reformers are too open to doctrinal compromise. But, for reformists, the old guard among evangelical theologians has been simply sliding back toward fundamentalism (Olson 1995, 480). Moreover, according to reformists, the particular theological questions and issues that have been addressed by theologians over the past several centuries are issues primarily related to the modern mind, whereas the theological landscape of today is one of postmodernity. For reformists, therefore, the essence of both Christianity and theology does not entail certain "propositional truths enshrined in doctrines," but rather its essence as reflected in "narrative-shaped experience" (Olson 1995, 481).

Evangelical Protestantism at the Middle of the Twenty-First Century

So what does the future, then, hold for evangelical Protestants? Are their ranks likely to grow or diminish? Are they likely to become more divided and less unified politically? Here, we will explore some current social trends as a means by which to make some hazardous projections about possible changes that may transpire within evangelical Protestantism over the next half century. But, as Yogi Berra[7] once opined, "It is tough making predictions, especially about the future." It is far easier to analyze important social changes that are occurring than it is to project how those particular changes are likely to shape and influence human relationships, organizational structures, and institutional arrangements in the future.

The Declining Vitality of Evangelical Denominations

Given current trends, it is likely that evangelical denominations will decline in strength over the next half century. As human organizations, denominations were formed as a means to provide order, facilitate communication, and expedite ministry, but they are shaped by the cultural context in which they are found. And the theological, ritual, and social practices that once served to sustain distinct religious traditions are now being eroded.

Over the past several decades, there has been a growing decline in denominational loyalties that stem from a variety of forces at work both within and outside the denominations. First, larger cultural forces within American life are making it difficult for denominations to sustain themselves. Given social changes such as increased geographic mobility, weakening European ethnic communities, and rising levels of education, the cultural and social bases on which many denominations once built their domains have all but disappeared. In addition, the individualistic, subjective, and anti-institutional spirit of contemporary life has weakened members' denominational loyalty, as congregations increasingly chart their own course.

As a result, it is likely that congregations will become less preoccupied with denominational identity and less impressed with denominational delivery systems, leading an increasing number of congregations to go outside their own denominations to obtain pastors, church leaders, ministry and program modules, and curricula. Thus, in the years ahead, the ongoing decline of denominationalism that has already affected mainline Protestantism is likely to become more strongly encountered within evangelical Protestantism as well.

The Continuing Vitality of Evangelical Congregational Life

Though denominational loyalty within evangelical churches may continue to decline over the coming decades, it is far less clear to what extent this will have an adverse effect on the vitality of congregational life. Most congregations are able to chart their course apart from the denomination with which they may be affiliated. Monies once provided by local congregations for the operation of denominational programs may instead be kept at the local level to pay for additional church staff or to launch new programs. Thus, the vitality of congregations could well continue even with a decline in the vitality of the broader life of the denomination itself.

Yet it is also true that this same individualistic, subjective, and anti-institutional spirit of contemporary life that has weakened denominational loyalties could also lessen individual commitment to one's local congregation. However, local congregations are far less institutionalized and much more personal than denominational structures, and they may therefore be somewhat less subject to the anti-institutional sentiments that tend to prevail today.

The Continuing Salience of Religion among Evangelical Protestants

For religious groups that seek to maintain the vitality of their faith in a pluralistic world, the presence of a religious subculture can be of critical importance. A necessary, but not sufficient, condition for the emergence of a subculture is the perception among a group of people that their group exhibits some distinctiveness in relationship to "mainstream culture or other groups in society" (Olson 1993, 36). Thus, sociocultural pluralism can actually help to strengthen religious groups by providing them with "a greater variety of other groups and subcultures against which to 'rub' and feel distinction and tension, in a way that strengthens religious subcultural life internally" (Smith 1998, 116).

For a subculture to develop, there must be at least some level of contact with others—both within and outside one's religious group. Without the formation of social ties within the group itself, religious life would remain highly privatized in nature. In the effort to forge a subculture, resources are typically mobilized and structures created (e.g., organizations, clubs, service agencies, magazines, social events, meetings) that are intended to "facilitate subcultural interaction and help to maintain, shape, and transmit the shared identity" (Olson 1993, 37). The resulting increased interaction among subculture members strengthens ties within the group, while the conflict that can arise from cultural pluralism helps to clarify boundaries, solidify identity, increase cohesion, and augment resource mobilization within such groups (Smith 1998, 115).

Accordingly, the religious faith of evangelicals may well continue to remain relatively strong through the presence of a (perhaps weakened) evangelical subculture that continues to be sustained through a weakened denominational structure and relatively independent houses of worship. But the presence of such a subculture would seem to be highly dependent on the continued vitality of congregational life. If contact with other members of the group is necessary in order for subcultures to emerge and continue, then it would seem that local houses of worship would be the most likely context within which such subcultural contact would occur, thereby allowing personal friendships among co-religionists to be forged and religious social networks to be established. Thus, in the end, the extent to which religion is likely to remain highly salient in the social and political life of most evangelicals will largely depend on the extent to which local evangelical houses of worship are able to attract worshippers to attend on a somewhat regular basis.[8]

The Relative Size of Evangelical Protestantism

The relative size of evangelicals within American society in 2050 will likely continue to remain about the same size as that found today—and this is true despite the likely growth in the proportion of the religiously unaffiliated over the same period of time.

Several factors point to this conclusion. First, among those who are religious today, evangelicals tend to be younger than mainline Protestants, but somewhat older than Black Protestants and Catholics (see table 3.4). Consequently, over the next several decades, the relative size of evangelical Protestantism in relationship to mainline Protestantism should increase in that, based simply on current age differences and natural rates of morality within the ranks of the two traditions, a larger proportion of mainline than evangelical Protestants will be dying over the course of the next several decades. Moreover, replacement of those sitting within the pews of mainline Protestant churches will likely fail to keep pace with departures, as the levels of those joining mainline Protestant churches will likely be lower than the levels departing through death.

Catholics tend to be somewhat younger than evangelicals, but they currently exhibit a far lower level of retention among those reared in their faith than do evangelical Protestants (Pew Forum on Religion & Public Life 2009, 21).[9] And among those Catholics who have left the church, more have become Protestants than have become religiously unaffiliated—with nearly twice as many former Catholics joining the ranks of evangelical Protestants as those becoming mainline Protestants (Pew Forum on Religion & Public Life 2009, 21). Moreover, the influx of Hispanic Catholics may not necessarily help to sustain current levels of affiliation with the Catholic Church either, as the extent to which Latinos in the United States affiliate with the Catholic Church drops with every successive generation, with the largest drop occurring between the second and third generation, and with the majority of those converting to Protestantism doing so after arriving in the United States (Espinosa, Elizondo, and Miranda 2003, 15). Thus, despite the somewhat younger age of Catholics in comparison to evangelical Protestants, it is likely that evangelicals will continue to hold their religious market share in relationship to Catholicism as well.

Finally, during the 1990s, the overwhelming proportion of youth continued to claim a denominational affiliation of some kind, with approximately 85 percent of teens doing so (Smith and Faris 2002; Smith and Denton 2005). These young people were also relatively active religiously, as nearly one in three of all high schoolers indicated they attended religious services once per week or more (Smith and Faris 2002). But the level of religious salience and activity among young people varied by religious tradition, as those affiliated with more theologically conservative traditions (e.g., evangelical Protestants) tended to attend religious services more frequently and rate their faith as being more important to them (Smith et al. 2002; Smith 2003). All this suggests, therefore, that evangelical Protestantism is likely to continue to be a vital religious tradition over the course of the next several decades, as those who are more religiously committed as a youth are more likely to remain within the faith tradition in which they were reared (Pew Forum on Religion & Public Life 2009, 4).

However, it is also true that over the past decade that the proportion of young people who claim no religious affiliation has grown, as one-quarter of those between the ages of 18 and 24 now choose "unaffiliated" when asked about their religious affiliation (Markoe 2012).[10] Those who choose to leave their religious faith usually do so by their early twenties, while few change their religious affiliation after age fifty (Pew Forum on Religion & Public Life 2009, 4). And though there is a tendency for young adults to reconnect with church life as they marry and have children (Wuthnow 2007a, 54–56), it is likely that many of these religiously unaffiliated young adults will continue to remain unaffiliated as they grow older, marry, and raise their families. As a result, the proportion of the religiously unaffiliated will likely continue to grow in size within American society over the next several decades. But despite this growth among the unaffiliated, it is likely that about one-quarter of Americans will continue to be evangelical Protestants, given various demographic and cultural factors—namely, that evangelicals currently have somewhat larger families, that they are likely to retain religiously a higher proportion of their adolescents upon entering adulthood, and that they are likely to experience a overall net growth through religious switching from mainline Protestantism and Roman Catholicism.

The Continuing Public Engagement of Evangelicals

Evangelicals have exhibited a cyclical pattern of political engagement—with evangelicals being more politically engaged during some periods of American history than other periods. Since evangelicals have been rather active politically over the past several decades, it is possible that we may see a decline in the level of evangelical political involvement over the next several decades.

But, regardless of what happens politically, it is likely that evangelicals will continue to exhibit a relatively high level of involvement in civic life. Though engagement in political life may wax and wane among evangelicals over time, there is far less vacillation in the extent to which evangelicals are involved in civic life through volunteering and charitable contributions, whether through their local houses of worship or other nonprofit organizations in their endeavors to address community needs. Such endeavors are not only less divisive relationally with one's co-religionists, but commands to "feed the hungry," "clothe the naked," and "visit those in prison" are more clearly mandated by biblical texts than political efforts to pass specific public policies or elect particular candidates to public office.

The Expansion of the Evangelical Political Agenda

At the beginning of the twentieth century, the vast majority of Christians resided in the Northern Hemisphere, either in Europe or North America; today, approximately two-thirds of all Christians reside in the Southern Hemisphere, whether in Africa, Asia, or Latin America. Moreover, over the coming several decades, the proportion of Christians living in the Southern Hemisphere is only likely to increase based simply on differential birth rates among Christians across the two hemispheres. Given this numerical significance of churches in the Southern Hemisphere, along with the processes of globalization that forge connections between people in different countries (Wuthnow 2009b, 90), American churches are likely to become far more internationally conscious in the coming decades.

Not surprisingly, therefore, evangelicals have become increasingly aware of issues facing Christians scattered across the globe as well as having become increasingly engaged in international affairs. Whether through international travel, mission trips, or international church networks, American Christians (including evangelical Protestants) are "awakening more generally to the afflictions visited on the world's vulnerable" (Hertzke 2009, 237). As a result, Christian groups in the United States have supported efforts to provide international debt relief for developing countries, backed AIDS funding for African nations, and sought to end slave trafficking. In these, as well as in other ways, "the globalization of Christianity" has fostered "an influential constituency of advocacy for the world's destitute," including among evangelical Christians (Hertzke 2009, 237). And attention to matters of concern to Christians in the Southern Hemisphere will likely only grow among American evangelicals over the next half century.

The Weakening Political Cohesion of Evangelical Protestantism

In the coming decades, it is also likely that the political cohesion currently evident among evangelical Protestants will decline. This change will stem from three sources: the growing ethnic diversity among evangelicals, the expanded political agenda of evangelicals, and the shift in the way religion shapes American politics—namely, from religious votes being structured less on the basis of religious traditions and more on the basis of religious traditionalism.

First, evangelical Protestantism will exhibit even greater diversity in the future than it has in the past, as the proportion of whites within its ranks will further decline. With the growth of Hispanic and Asian immigrants in this country, evangelical Protestantism is being shaped in new and different ways. Many Hispanic Protestants attend Pentecostal churches that are rooted in the evangelical Protestant tradition, and many Asian Christians (particularly Koreans) have aligned their congregations with evangelical Protestantism (Ecklund 2006). Moreover, given current birth rates, the Hispanic composition of the American population will continue to grow—regardless of whether or not the flow of illegal immigrants from Latin America is completely stopped. Though most Latinos are affiliated with the Catholic faith, many are nevertheless attracted to evangelical Protestantism; as a result, the relative presence of Hispanics within the evangelical community will grow over the next several decades. Though this increasing ethnic and racial diversity within evangelical Protestantism can lead to a revitalization of the tradition religiously, such growing diversity will make it more difficult for it to retain its relatively high levels of political cohesion, given the racial and ethnic differences among evangelicals in relationship to preferences for a more activist government.

Second, it is quite likely the current evangelical political agenda (at least the one that is typically tied to such social issues as abortion and gay rights) will expand considerably over the coming decades. Part of this expanding political agenda is linked to the growing ethnic diversity among evangelicals. But other factors will likely contribute to this expanding agenda as well—namely, the growing international consciousness of evangelicals and the generational replacement of older, more socially conservative, evangelicals with younger evangelicals who are more likely to advance other issues as their primary concerns (e.g., securing jobs, protecting the environment, etc.). And with this expansion of issue agendas, it is far more likely that evangelicals will be less unified in their partisanship than they have been over the past several decades.

Finally, though affiliation with particular religious traditions continues to remain important politically today, it is less clear whether this will continue to be the case several decades from now. On the one hand, religious traditions have long endured within American society and even now continue to shape the political responses of those associated with different faiths. On the other hand, a new religious order in American politics may be emerging in which theological divisions within and across religious traditions are moving to create new political cleavages that transcend, though perhaps not fully replace, the old political divisions associated with membership in different faith groups. In other words, the way in which religion serves to structure the vote may well be shifting from the long-standing ethnoreligious foundation[11] undergirding the religious vote to one reflecting the restructuring that has been transpiring within American religious life, with traditionalists, regardless of their religious affiliation, generally pitted against modernists (see, for example, Green 2007; Smidt et al. 2010).

Conclusion

Thus, over the course of the next several decades, evangelical Protestants will continue to remain a sizable religious tradition in American public life. However, given the weakening of denominational identities and loyalties, evangelicals will confront some important challenges in maintaining their proportionate size. Evangelical Protestants are not alone in having to confront these challenges, as other religious faiths also must face the anti-institutional sentiments currently found within American religious life. Though evangelical Protestantism has survived previous challenges to the appeal and vitality of its faith tradition, past success is no guarantee that it will continue to do so in the future.

Much of the future strength of evangelical Protestantism will rest on the extent to which emerging generations of Americans continue to find value in gathering together for corporate worship, whether within some denominational structure or not. Without regular interaction with fellow believers, religious ties are likely to become less salient, religious beliefs to lose much of their relevance, and one's religious practices to diminish in regularity. Currently, somewhere between 15 to 20 percent of Americans practice a "privatized faith," characterized by reporting a religious affiliation, engaging in daily prayer, but only occasionally gathering together with others in public worship (Smidt et al. 2008, 63). Should increasing numbers of evangelicals exhibit such a "privatized faith" over the course of the next several decades, the form of evangelical Protestantism may continue, but likely with ever decreasing substance.

Over the next several decades, evangelicals may well continue to remain relatively engaged in public life. But even if evangelicals were to remain engaged politically, their relative political influence will likely diminish in proportion to any decline in their relative size, any expansion of their political agenda, and any decline in their cohesion politically. However, the extent to which evangelicals remain involved in public life is largely dependent on whether evangelicals continue to exhibit relatively high levels of regular worship attendance. To the extent that evangelicals come together for purposes of collective public worship, they will likely continue to contribute to the health and vitality of community life through their "acts of generosity." But should evangelicals increasingly exhibit a "privatized religion," they will increasingly become disengaged not only from political life but from civic life as well in that a privatized religion simply leads to a privatized life, largely devoid of engagement in either civic or political life.[12]

Notes

Introduction: When Morning Gilds the Sky?
Evangelicals in Contemporary American Society

1. These issues are discussed more fully in chapter 2.

2. The history of evangelicals in America is discussed more fully in the next chapter.

3. For a description of this survey, along with a discussion of some of the approaches used to identify evangelical respondents, see Gallup (1979).

4. There was one other early book on evangelicals, *The Evangelical Voter* (Rothenberg and Newport 1984), which focused more narrowly on the political characteristics of evangelicals. In addition, there is at least one book based on survey research that has examined "conservative Christians" (Greeley and Hout 2006), a designation that is sometimes employed as an equivalent label for evangelicals. However, as will be discussed at various points throughout the volume, this label is both misleading and problematic—as the designation leads to the inclusion of many religionists in the category who do not fall within the evangelical tradition (e.g., Latter-day Saints or Mormons, Christian Scientists, and Jehovah's Witnesses). See, for example, Greeley and Hout (2006, table 1.2). Of course, scholars have also produced a wealth of scholarly articles on evangelical Christians based on survey research, though these studies have been far more narrow in their focus and have used a variety of conflicting definitions and operational measures to identify American evangelicals.

5. Perhaps it was this lack of current information about the sociodemographic characteristics of evangelicals that led a *Washington Post* reporter some years ago to describe followers of Jerry Falwell and Pat Robertson as "largely poor, uneducated and easy to command" (Weisskopf 1993).

6. Mark Pinsky, who has long served as a religion writer at the *Orlando Sentinel*, has given a more regional cast to some of these differences among evangelicals, observing that "Sun Belt evangelicalism" differs from the "old Bible Belt evangelicalism." See Fitzgerald (2008).

7. For example, assume that evangelicals constitute 25 percent of the population; a survey of 1000 respondents would likely capture, therefore, about 250 evangelical respondents (1000 respondents x .25=250 evangelical respondents). Now assume that approximately 25 percent of all evangelicals are under the age of 35 and that Hispanics constitute about 7 percent of the group. If one wanted to examine differences among evangelicals (e.g., comparing younger with older evangelicals or comparing Hispanic evangelicals with white evangelicals), one would confront the problem of making assessments of differences based on relatively few cases. For example, given the approximately 250 evangelicals secured in a sample size of 1,000, there would only be about 63 evangelical respondents under the age of 35 (250 evangelical respondents x .25=62.5), and perhaps as many as 18 Hispanic evangelical respondents (250 evangelical respondents x .07=1.75). On the other hand, with a survey sample of 35,000 respondents, the same proportions would yield approximately 8,750 evangelical respondents surveyed—including over 2,175 "young" evangelical respondents and over 600 Hispanic evangelicals.

8. For example, younger evangelicals may be more likely to have obtained a college education and may be more likely to be found within the ranks of "modernist evangelicals" than older evangelicals.

9. The terms "Hispanic" and "Latino" will be used interchangeably here. There are different approaches to the definition of who constitutes an Hispanic. One approach labels Hispanics as "a member of an ethnic group that traces its roots to the 20 Spanish-speaking nations of Latin America and Spain itself," whereas the other approach is to allow people simply to classify themselves as Hispanics when asked (Passel and Taylor 2009). Note that Hispanics represent an ethnic group rather than a racial category, as Hispanics can be of any race.

10. Throughout this volume the religious tradition Black Protestant will be capitalized, whereas the religious traditions of evangelical Protestant and mainline Protestant will not. This convention is adopted as a means to remind the reader that the Black Protestant tradition does not constitute a racial category per se, as some whites choose to affiliate with churches in the Black Protestant tradition, and not all black Protestants necessarily choose to be affiliated with churches in the Black Protestant tradition (see, for example, table 3.3). So the difference in capitalization seeks to avoid this potential ambiguity by capitalizing Black Protestant when referring to those who are affiliated with churches in the Black Protestant tradition but not doing so when simply referring to blacks who are Protestants in their religious affiliations (whether evangelical Protestant, mainline Protestant, or Black Protestant).

11. Thus, although blacks comprise only 6 percent and Hispanics only 7 percent of evangelical Protestants (see table 3.4), the Pew Religious Landscape Survey captures 461 blacks and 476 Hispanics who are affiliated with evangelical Protestant churches—providing sufficient numbers to examine the extent to which evangelical

Protestants may diverge ethnically and racially in terms of their beliefs, attitudes, and behavior.

12. References to the Baby Boom generation typically refer to those born between 1946 and 1965. Millennials are those who came to adulthood (age 18) after the turn of the millennium (hence they were born sometime in 1982 or thereafter). Generation X is here defined as those who were born after 1965 but before 1982.

13. As will be noted later, the argument that there are two opposing worldviews all too easily leads analysts to think that individuals must choose either one or the other perspective; in reality, there are certainly some who might be labeled "centrists" who fall between the two opposing positions.

14. For some theorists, the growing number of secular Americans is a natural extension of the "liberal" or "progressive" side—and may even be the product of struggles over restructuring. See, for example, Hout and Fischer (2002).

15. In later analyses, "traditionalists" will be compared to "non-traditionalists," with this latter category composed of "centrists" and "modernists."

Chapter 1: Oh God, Our Help in Ages Past? The Evangelical Tradition in American Religious Life

1. Given that the use of the label "religious tradition" in this study is based on affiliation with particular religious denominations, the words "religious tradition" and "religious affiliation" may be used interchangeably for stylistic purposes.

2. The word "myth" is not used here to refer to either the truth or falsehood of such an interpretation, but rather to refer to a simplification that helps to interpret historical facts. Myths assist in highlighting, but can also distort, such historical events.

3. For more thorough treatments of the history of evangelicalism in America, see Balmer (1999), Noll (2001), and Sweeney (2005).

4. For an argument that historians should abandon the term "the Great Awakening" because "it distorts the character of eighteenth-century religious life and misinterprets its relationship to prerevolutionary American society and politics," see Butler (1982).

5. The early Puritans drew upon a Calvinistic heritage that emphasized that the doctrine of election or predestination, believing that God did the choosing with regard to salvation (as opposed to the idea that people choose whether or not to accept God's gracious offer of salvation through Jesus Christ, an idea associated with Arminianism). Nevertheless, in response to the anxieties produced by the doctrine of election, the desire for some form of assurance that one was among the elect became existentially central within Puritanism (Ahlstrom 1975, 272), and so the Puritans insisted that every believer was marked by a conversion experience (Brauer 1976, 9; Brauer 1978, 230). But the greater importance attached to personal experience of conversion during the First Great Awakening meant that the Arminian understanding of salvation began to undermine the prevailing Calvinist understanding, because "if each individual should have some inner experience, then each must be actively involved in the process of salvation, not just a passive bystander" (Krapohl and Libby 1999, 18).

6. Conversion within Puritanism was largely volitional in nature as it represented human consent of the reality of divine election. It was not something that came upon an individual like a thunderbolt, but was something that involved "a self-conscious decision to consent to God's will for forgiveness." See Brauer (1976, 9) and Brauer (1978).

7. For a more critical analysis of the linkage between the First Great Awakening and the American Revolution, see Noll, Hatch, and Marsden (1983, chapter 3).

8. Sweet (1976) is an exception. He has argued that the forces of the First Great Awakening were still strong enough, both during and after the American Revolution, to provide continued evangelical presence during the period in which other historians argue that religion was in decline or stagnation. Thus, Sweet links the First and Second Great Awakenings as being part of the same phenomenon.

9. Actually, the First Amendment simply left the establishment of religion to local option, and three New England states did retain a form of established religion for several decades after the adoption of the amendment. However, by 1833, all forms of establishment had ceased in the three New England states as well.

10. Finke and Stark (1992, 15) suggest a slightly higher figure, but still well below 20 percent. In part, this low level of church affiliation was due to the fact that too few churches existed in many parts of the country to provide for the religious needs of the people. However, this figure is also "depressed" because the social meaning of church membership has changed over time.

11. Revivalism and democracy were interrelated phenomena during both the eighteenth and nineteenth centuries, as "each asserted popular claims against those of the elite, pluralism against orthodoxy, charisma against rationalism" (Howe 2007, 125).

12. The moral foundation undergirding republican thought was largely tied to two distinct assumptions—namely, that "morality was necessary to create the virtuous citizens without which a republic could not survive, and that churches should contribute to the promotion of that morality" (Noll 2001, 196).

13. While most historians probably view revivalism as giving rise to voluntary societies, others have argued that it was the lay voluntary societies that sparked the Second Great Awakening (e.g., Birdsall 1970; Shiels 1980). Similarly, it is not clear whether such societies represented an accommodation to the constitutional principle of separation of church and state or a strategy to resist it (Maclear 1959; Shiels 1980). But whatever the historical sequence or motivational basis, the challenges of the time were viewed to require the widest possible cooperation—and such societies, by defining themselves in purposive rather than creedal terms, were designed as instruments for cooperative action (Hudson 1961, 83).

14. Another grouping of denominations also achieved prominence during this period of time—those of the Restorationist tradition. Restorationists held that "Christians could and should recapture in their lives and in their Christianity exactly what was common to believers of the apostolic age" (Krapohl and Lippy 1999, 20).

15. See, for example, Dieter (1975).

16. Actually, the Holiness movement had two distinct wings. The second wing was embodied in the Keswick movement, located primarily within the Reformed tradition. The movement began in the mid-1870s with the specific purpose to promote "a

deeper Christian life." Keswick "holiness" argued that sanctification occurred gradu-ally, over the course of a believer's life. Thus, within the Keswick movement, holi-ness/sanctification was not viewed in the Wesleyan terms of "eradication" but more in terms of "an enduement of power." It did, however, constitute a distinct work of grace in which the Holy Spirit empowered an individual for Christian existence, but the anticipated experience associated with sanctification was not so much understood in terms of cleansing as in terms of anointing. Further, sanctification constituted not so much a second, instantaneous, religious experience that established a state of holi-ness, but a "maintained condition" reflecting a process that embodied willful behavior (Menzies 1975, 86).

17. It can be argued, however, that the social gospel was tied to evangelical view-points and that its message, at least as initially formulated by Rauschenbusch (1907), was not directly opposed to evangelical understanding. See, for example, Bowman (2007).

18. Postmillennialists hold that through Christian action the millennium (literally a thousand years, but a symbolic figure used to refer to an extended period of time in which humans flourished and peace prevailed) could be established and that Jesus Christ would return to earth only after the establishment of the millennium. Hence, human action could hasten the day of Christ's return.

19. Premillennialism holds that Jesus Christ must return first prior to any realiza-tion of the millennium.

20. For well over a century, premillennial views had been held by a minority of evangelicals. But during and after the Civil War, premillennial views had grown in popularity. Both premillennialists and postmillennialists saw history as involving a cosmic struggle between good and evil, both permitted literal interpretations of cer-tain biblical passages, and both tended to think that certain prophesies concerning the nature of time immediately preceding the millennium were being fulfilled in current events. Pre- and postmillennialists disagreed, however, on whether Christ would re-turn before or after the millennium—with premillennialists tending to be somewhat less optimistic concerning human progress and more prone to adopt a more literal interpretation of scripture (Marsden 1980, 51).

21. *The Fundamentals* was published in twelve volumes between 1910 and 1915. When the term "fundamentalist" was coined in 1920, the title of these volumes brought to mind the kind of opposition to modernism characterized by these "widely known, if little studied, volumes" (Marsden 1980, 119).

22. The infallibility of the Bible suggests that the Bible is the inspired Word of God and that it is true in all that it teaches. But what does it teach? Namely, the way unto salvation. Hence, this understanding does not require a defense of every "jot and tittle" found in the text.

23. German Higher Criticism was an approach or method of studying the Bible. Though the intent of the method was to free the study of the text from starting theo-logical presuppositions, it came to be viewed as desacralizing the Bible.

24. Black churches, though theologically conservative in nature, did not become significantly involved in this controversy. For black Protestants and those hungry for liberation, it was "cultural praxis, not correct doctrine" that was important. Black

Protestants, while appealing to biblical authority, have remained largely outside the fundamentalist-modernist fray and have not tended to develop rigid doctrines of inerrancy (Sernett 1991, 142).

25. For a detailed analysis of this development, see Carpenter (1980).

26. Since fundamentalism arose out of the larger evangelical body of Christians, all fundamentalists are evangelicals—but not all evangelicals are fundamentalists.

27. These excesses were viewed in terms of fundamentalism's tendencies toward anti-intellectualism, its unwillingness to work cooperatively with other Christian bodies, and its strong emphasis on cultural isolation.

28. In fact, in the late 1960s, the national media even brought the work of "God is Dead" theologians to the attention of the American people.

29. Moreover, the inclusion and growth of Pentecostals (and later the inclusion and growth of charismatics) within the evangelical fold helped to shape evangelical Protestantism in new, and more diverse, ways.

30. For an alternative interpretation, see Daniel Williams's *God's Own Party* (2010).

31. Though it was not the only factor involved, the decisions and actions of Vatican II certainly played an important role in this growing reconciliation.

32. Many evangelicals have also noted that the lack of a "pope" and hierarchical structure within their tradition results in various other consequences. For example, the lack of any hierarchical structure enables anyone to claim the mantle of evangelical and promote whatever theological interpretations (e.g., a "health and wealth" gospel) they may wish. Moreover, "success" within the evangelical traditions sometimes tends to be associated more with audience size than with fidelity to the gospel.

33. See note 12.

34. Though much of contemporary media coverage of politics today emphasizes differences between the "left" and the "right," or between conservative and liberals, throughout much of our history Americans were viewed as being more pragmatic than ideological in their orientation—being more concerned about whether something worked in practice than whether a particular perspective was the "correct idea" or approach.

Chapter 2: Seek and You Shall Find?
The Bases of Analyzing Evangelicals Today

1. However, categorical groups can become social groups. Suppose that some rising politicians associated with a growing political party began to argue that people with brown eyes were genetically inferior, that they should have their political rights restricted, and that they should even be eliminated from the gene pool. Under such circumstances, one might anticipate that people with brown eyes would begin to recognize themselves as belonging to the same group, would start developing similar political attitudes (at least in relationship to their survival), and might begin to interact with each other in a more systematic and regular basis in order to prevent the influence of such politicians and political parties from growing and being socially accepted.

2. Evangelicalism has also been defined as an ethos and as a mood. See, for example, Marsden (1984, xiv, xv; 1991, 1–6). If defined as a movement (or even as an ethos or a mood), then certain Roman Catholics, for example, might be properly labeled "evangelicals."

3. Typically, but depending upon one's particular research purposes, the major religious traditions examined within the American context are evangelical Protestants, mainline Protestants, black Protestants, Roman Catholics, Jews, and the religiously unaffiliated. These six categories, however, do not capture the full range of all religious faiths, as there are others (e.g., Latter-day Saints, Jehovah's Witnesses, Muslims, Hindus, etc.) who do not fall within these six categories. Depending on how many categories the analyst wishes to employ, these "other faiths" are combined together, differentiated, or dropped. Together, however, these "other faiths" typically comprise less than 10 percent of all respondents surveyed. Hart (2004, 82) has contended that to label evangelical Protestantism as a tradition is somewhat ironic, in that it is a form of Christianity that has been quite hostile to tradition. Thus, it is a tradition that is generally hostile to tradition *qua* tradition.

4. For a more thorough discussion of the various assumptions and different measurement approaches related to religion, see Smidt, Kellstedt, and Guth (2009).

5. The specific question used by Gallup in 1979 was this: "Have you ever had a religious experience—that is, a particular powerful religious insight or awakening that changed the direction of your life?" A couple of years later, Gallup simply asked, "Would you say that you have been 'born again' or have had a 'born again' experience—that is, a turning point in your life when you committed yourself to Christ?"

6. However, even Gallup recognized this (see note 7 below).

7. Actually, Gallup (1979) did initially differentiate between "conversionalist evangelicals" and "confessional evangelicals" (which he labeled "orthodox evangelicals")—with the latter group not having to respond positively to having had a born-again experience. Though the overlap between the two groups was relatively large (in that many conversionalist evangelicals also met the criteria for being a confessional evangelical), it was by no means complete, as there were some important differences between the two groups. However, because they were so close in agreement on most items, Gallup found it easier to speak of the two as one group; subsequently, Gallup has generally employed a born-again question in operationally identifying evangelicals.

8. These data are publicly available from the Association of Religion Data Archives. For a summary of the broader survey results, see http://pbs.org/wnet/religion-andethics/week534/specialreport.html (accessed December 12, 2011).

9. There are many types of religious groups with which respondents can claim an attachment, for example, a local congregation, a particular denomination (the Southern Baptist Convention, the Disciples of Christ), a broader religious family (Baptist, Lutheran, Methodist), or even some religious movement (charismatic renewal movement or the fundamentalist movement).

10. Affiliation has both objective and subjective components: one can be a formal member of a religious congregation and a denomination, but one can also claim "affiliation" with, or identify with, such organizations without actually "joining."

11. Though not all respondents can necessarily reveal the specific denominational affiliation of the local congregation with which they are affiliated, most respondents are able to do so.

12. Certain objective criteria can be used in making such assignments (e.g., denominations associated with the National Association of Evangelicals are deemed to be evangelical denominations, while denominations associated with the National Council of Churches are deemed to be "mainline" Protestant denominations).

13. Sometimes in an effort to identify evangelical respondents, the question is posed as "Do you consider yourself to be a born-again or evangelical Christian?" But this too is problematic, for two distinct phenomena are being assessed in one question. If someone answers affirmatively, it is unclear whether the response is in reference to "born again" or to "evangelical." As noted earlier in the discussion above, "born again" could connote a particular experience (a religious conversion experience) or a status (being born again in the sight of God on the basis of an individual recognizing his or her shortcomings and asking Jesus for forgiveness and future direction). But "born again" could also connote an *identification* with a movement or group of people, "the born-again crowd." Such ambiguities make this a poor measure for capturing evangelical respondents.

14. At times, both affiliation and movement identification are conceptualized as religious identities (Alwin et al. 2006), and certainly it is possible that some claims of affiliation may reflect little more than identification. Nevertheless, most respondents who claim an affiliation also report some level of worship attendance. Hence, it is generally better to conceptualize affiliation as reflecting primarily a sociological phenomenon, similar to gender or race, rather than as a psychological phenomenon (though obviously there are psychological facets related to these types of variables).

15. This ambiguity has three important results: (1) the meaning of religious movement labels is likely to vary considerably from one individual to another, (2) individuals experience much greater latitude in personal assessments of their association with these movements than they do with congregations or denominations, and (3) there is likely to be much greater measurement error in responding to movement labels than to denominational affiliation.

16. Given that Barna's measurement approach is based on complete adherence to particular religious beliefs rather than on religious affiliation, the proportion of the population who are evangelicals is much smaller and much more racially diverse when using Barna's approach, as many African Americans are willing to stand in agreement with his specified religious beliefs.

17. For a discussion of some of the differences between evangelical and mainline Protestants, see Smidt (2007a).

18. This discussion of religious tradition is drawn directly from my earlier discussion of the nature of religious traditions found in Smidt (2007a).

19. For example, in a typical survey of 1,200 cases, there may be around 300 evangelicals surveyed, of which half or more (e.g., 160) may be women. If one wanted to examine the attitudes and behavior of young evangelical women (e.g., below 34 years or younger), you might capture a total of 40 evangelical women of such age. In contrast, the number of evangelical women 34 years of age or younger captured

in the Pew Religious Landscape Survey is 770. Clearly, patterns based on 770 young evangelical women are far more likely to reflect the true characteristics of young evangelical women than the patterns based on a total of 40 such women.

20. The Pew Religious Landscape Survey will serve as the primary data source, and the Henry Institute National Survey on Religion and Public Life and the Fifth National Survey of Religion and Politics will serve as secondary sources. On occasion, several other surveys will be used to answer questions that these three primary surveys do not address.

21. However, it should be noted that surveys can be weighted in such a manner to reflect particular demographic characteristics to ensure that the survey is reflective of the population as a whole. This was done in each of the three surveys. Of course, the weighting of respondents in terms of one variable (e.g., gender) shifts the frequency of respondents falling within categories of the other sociodemographic categories (e.g., assuming one needs to weight in order to increase the proportion of males in the survey, then all the other social characteristics associated with being a male will increase proportionally as a result of that weighting process). The one sociodemographic characteristic in which such weighting was not conducted for any of the three surveys was marital status. Here, however, there are issues related to the fact that different surveys used different categories in terms of capturing the marital status of respondents (with the Pew Religious Landscape Survey providing a "living with partner" option that the other two surveys did not include within their response options), with the additional response option altering the potential percentage distribution for the remaining categories. Nevertheless, the results once again confirm the relative comparability of the three surveys in terms of the respondents captured by each survey.

Chapter 3: Let the Weak Say I Am Strong?
The Size and Social Characteristics of Evangelicals

1. See, for example, the discussion of the postwar religious boom in America found in Ellwood (2000).

2. Surveys have consistently shown that married couples are more likely to attend church than those who have never been married, and that married couples with no children are the least likely of married couples to attend church, while those with more than one child are more likely to attend than couples with only one child. See, for example, the discussion found in Wuthnow (2007a, 54–58).

3. This was also a period of time in which there were growing conversations about denominational mergers—particularly among mainline Protestant denominations—as the Consultation on Church Union (COCU) was in full swing, seeking to bring together all major Protestant denominations under one denominational umbrella. Such talk and efforts tended to divide members of such denominations, as some favored the continuation of the historical denominational structures while others questioned their viability in a changing, and anticipated increasingly secular, society.

4. Analysts advanced different explanations in attempting to account for this apparent growth in numbers among evangelical compared to mainline Protestant churches. Some scholars stressed institutional factors as the bases for such change, while others stressed various contextual factors. Kelley (1972), for example, focused almost entirely upon institutional characteristics in accounting for conservative church growth. Simply stated, Kelley argued that "strong" churches grow, while "weak" churches decline, with strong churches exhibiting an absolutism in religious beliefs, conformity in the lifestyles of its members, a willingness to exercise discipline over the members' beliefs and lifestyles, an expectation of high commitment from its members, and a zeal for proselytizing those outside the faith. On the other hand, weak churches were characterized by the converse: a relativism in religious beliefs, a tolerance of diversity in the lifestyle of its members, a lack of enforcement of church doctrines or canons, an emphasis upon dialogue with outsiders rather than proselytism, and a limited commitment to the church. Other analysts, however, focused primarily upon structural changes in American society as the explanatory factors for evangelical growth. Bibby (1978), for example, suggested that differences in birth rates among evangelical and mainline Protestants helped to account for the growing numbers of evangelicals.

5. As noted in chapter 2, questions such as the one used in the Religious Landscape Survey to inquire whether people consider themselves to be "born-again or evangelical Christians" are poorly constructed and do not provide a very reliable means by which to classify respondents as evangelicals.

6. Unfortunately, analysts frequently use the terms "biblical inerrancy" and "biblical literalism" synonymously, and, at times, analysts have even equated the position of biblical infallibility with biblical literalism (e.g., Rothenberg and Newport 1984, 16). Given such confusion, it is not surprising that questions tapping respondents' views of the Bible can vary considerably in what the items measure.

7. In other words, each of these positions constitutes a subset of a broader perspective that the Bible is the infallible Word of God. While all inerrantists subscribe to biblical infallibility, not all who subscribe to the infallible nature of the Bible are necessarily biblical inerrantists. Similarly, while all biblical literalists subscribe to biblical inerrancy, not all inerrantists are biblical literalists.

8. Almost invariably, social surveys have included Bible measures that provide relatively few response options and provide very unequal gradations of assessment of biblical authority—almost forcing respondents to choose between some assessment of the Bible as "the Word of God" or as a "book of fairy tales and myths." These limitations can lead to the impression that Americans hold very high views of scriptural authority. While these highly skewed distributions may reveal something of the high regard Americans have for the Bible, it limits its use for explanatory purposes. In order to explain variation, one needs measures that vary. Given such measures, the resultant distribution of views of biblical authority does not vary greatly, and its value as an explanatory variable is thereby diminished (Smidt, Kellstedt, and Guth 2009, 20).

9. Though the Religious Landscape Survey does employ a different approach to assessing a respondent's view on biblical authority by first asking Christian respondents whether he/she considers the Bible to be "the Word of God" or simply "a book written

by men and not the Word of God." Providing this choice is certainly better than the common survey practice of largely offering respondents a choice between "the Bible is the Word of God" or "the Bible is a book of myths and fairy tales." Still, overall, it would be better to provide respondents with some options that would reflect some kind of middle ground between the Landscape options.

10. This study was conducted by the University of Akron Survey Research Center: 4,000 respondents were surveyed.

11. An alternative interpretation might be that the rather precise denominational affiliations employed in the 1964 survey still were not sufficiently refined to capture all differences in denominational affiliations; as a result, some people who appear to be mainline Protestants by their assigned denominational affiliations are, in fact, part of evangelical denominations. Then, if this were the case, the apparent growth in evangelical Protestantism over the past forty years would be far less than what these data reveal.

12. For the rest of this book, the category of "other" will not be analyzed, in that it is composed of diverse elements and any resultant social characteristics of the group would lack meaning.

13. Technically speaking, Hispanics constitute an "ethnic" group rather than a distinct "racial" group. However, in practice, Hispanics are frequently differentiated from whites and blacks in terms of analysis of the racial composition of Americans. Hence, in the analysis here, Hispanics are included in the analysis of race.

14. In fact, such differences in marital status are even greater when the age of the respondents is analyzed in terms of 18 to 29 years of age, with 34 percent of all evangelicals of that age bracket reporting that they are married. The next closest percentage found among the other religious traditions is 29 percent for Roman Catholics (data not shown).

15. The South is defined here in terms of the states included within the designation of southern states employed by the U.S. Census and not in terms of the former eleven states of the old Confederacy.

16. Only two of the nine volumes published by AltaMira Press in their Religion by Region series are cited here. Clearly, the publication of this nine-volume series suggests there continue to be important regional differences in terms of American religion.

17. These educational differences across different religious traditions are not a function of a higher percentage of evangelicals living in small communities and rural areas. Even when controlling for community size, evangelicals continue to trail other religious traditions in terms of their educational attainment.

18. Analysis of changes in the social characteristics of evangelicals over time is limited to only a couple of factors due to the far smaller sample size associated with the 1964 survey. For example, changes in the racial composition of evangelicals are not examined here due to the relatively small number of non-whites found among evangelical Protestants in 1964. As a result, it is unclear whether the greater percentage of non-whites among evangelical Protestants found in 2007 reflects real change in the social composition of evangelical Protestants or is simply a function of the much smaller number of respondents initially surveyed in 1964.

19. Though it is sometimes cited that half of all marriages end in divorce, it is also true that the new American Census data reveal that 76 percent of Americans marry just once, with almost 20 percent having been married twice and 5 percent three or more times. www.usatoday.com/news/nation/census/2009-09-21-marriage-gay_Nhtm?loc=interstitialskip (accessed September 22, 2009).

Chapter 4: How Firm a Foundation?
The Theological Beliefs and Religious Behavior of Evangelicals

1. Since this chapter focuses on religious beliefs and behavior, only racial/ethnic, generational, and educational differences will be examined in how this may divide evangelicals in terms of their particular religious thoughts and practices. Beginning with the chapter on social theology, each chapter will also examine the extent to which evangelicals are divided in terms of theological, as well as racial/ethnic, generational, and educational, differences.

2. The other options were "somewhat agree," "somewhat disagree," and "completely disagree."

3. Actually, among those who do believe in heaven (whether "completely" or "mostly" so), almost all (98 percent or more) indicate that they believe in hell as well (whether "completely" or "mostly" so). This is true regardless of one's religious tradition.

4. Perhaps this is because respondents might be inclined to view religious teachings to be more the result of human creation than the Bible itself.

5. Nevertheless, accepting the role of evolution in the process of the creation of human beings can be viewed through a theistic lens. Within some Christian traditions, particularly the Catholic Church, there has been an acceptance that God may well have used evolution as part of the creative process; as a result, Catholics do not necessarily see evolution as something that denies the divine process of creation.

6. Part of that history involves a famed evangelical participant in the so-called Scopes Monkey Trial. In a highly publicized legal trial that captured national attention, a high school public school teacher, John Scopes, was accused of violating a Tennessee state law that prohibited the teaching of evolution. Clarence Darrow, the famed defense lawyer, spoke for Scopes, while William Jennings Bryan, the evangelical who was a three-time Democratic candidate for president during the turn of the nineteenth to twentieth centuries, argued for the prosecution.

7. However, there are also some evangelicals who argue that the scientific evidence for evolution is lacking; they choose, instead, to advance notions of "scientific creationism."

8. Other evangelicals, particularly those in the more Reformed wings of the tradition, have held that God speaks through "two books"—namely, scripture and nature—and that because God is the author of both books, there cannot be, at least in principle, any real conflict between the two.

9. Wuthnow (2005, 76) cites three long-standing assumptions in American culture that serve to undergird this tendency to view diversity positively: (1) the respect for

human rights; (2) the commonsense view of morality that people can readily distinguish good from evil on the basis of their common experience, regardless of race, ethnicity, or nationality; and (3) just like diversity of goods in the marketplace is a good thing, so too is diversity in the marketplace of ideas something to be valued.

10. In a more recent survey, Putnam and Campbell (2010, 520) found that 84 percent of Americans agreed that "religious diversity has been good for America."

11. Of course, not all religions necessarily posit that the ultimate goal of religious life is salvation. Salvation is something far more tied to the Abrahamic faiths.

12. In his analysis of these data, Wuthnow (2005, 190) combined responses to "Christianity is the best way to understand God" and "All major religions . . . are equally good ways of knowing about God" to create categories that he designated as "Spiritual Shoppers," "Christian Inclusivists," and "Christian Exclusivists." Based on his classification system, nearly one-half of evangelical Protestants (49 percent) constitute Christian inclusivists, while one-third (34 percent) could be labeled Christian exclusivists—with the remaining constituting spiritual shoppers.

13. Books directed toward a more popular audience include William Paul Young's *The Shack* (written in 2007) and Rob Bell's *Love Wins: A Book about Heaven, Hell, and the Fate of Every Person Who Ever Lived* (published in 2011). *The Shack* was originally self-published, but became a *USA Today* bestseller. By January 2010, it had sold over ten million copies and had been on the *New York Times* bestsellers list for 84 consecutive weeks, mostly at number one (Beal 2010). In *Love Wins*, which gathered considerable national media attention at the time of its release, Bell questions the idea that hell is a place in which certain people are assigned to an eternity of punishment for their sins and suggests instead that, given the loving nature of God, everyone will in the end be forgiven of their sins and be saved. For more scholarly efforts by evangelicals, see Anderson (1984), Newbigin (1989), Pinnock (1992), and Okholm and Phillips (1995).

14. An alternative, and frequently employed, approach to capturing religious traditionalism is to factor analyze a number of religious beliefs and religious behavior measures to identify which respondents might best be classified as "traditionalists" (e.g., Green 2007; Smidt et al. 2010).

15. These particular contentions are likely to be evident, for example, among those who claim to be "spiritual but not religious." For most, if not all, such individuals, religion is something associated with "organized religion," in which people participate in some organized social structure; "spiritual but not religious" people choose not to do so. Yet though such individuals may hold particular religious beliefs, their religious beliefs are not likely to play a central role in their lives.

16. This perspective on the formation of subcultures is not limited to religious phenomena. Subcultures can be generated through a variety of social bases, whether it be related to ethnicity (Irish), age (the "youth culture"), sexual preference (the gay community), or religion.

17. But these subcultures do not simply comprise interpersonal phenomena. As interpersonal relationships develop, institutional structures (e.g., associations, regular meeting places, special events, newsletters and specialized newspapers, etc.) may be created that further facilitate subcultural interaction and that, in turn, serve to main-

tain, shape, and strengthen the subculture. Thus, the strength of subcultures varies in terms of both the level of within-group ties and the level of institutionalization evident within the subculture (Olson 1993, 37).

18. Multiple answers were permitted in response to the question, with 60 percent reporting theology or religious beliefs being "very important." Other responses included liturgy or style of worship (45 percent), spouse or other family members (roughly 40 percent), and location (32 percent); being with friends and "political and social views" were cited only infrequently (both around 20 percent). See figure 6.2 in Putnam and Campbell (2010, 170).

19. For stylistic purposes, the terms "church" and "congregation" will be used interchangeably in this book.

20. Though the terms *religious behavior* and *religious practice* will be used interchangeably here, it should be noted that "the concept of practice has proven increasingly attractive in discussions of religion" because the term denotes a greater "learned and sequential character of action" than that associated with the term *behavior* (Wuthnow 2007b, 352).

21. This lack of membership, despite affiliation, may be the result of a variety of factors. For some, given our mobile society, it may simply reflect the fact that one has moved into a new community and has not, as yet, found a local congregation that one wishes to join. Others, however, may choose not to join and are unlikely ever to do so because they perceive that becoming a church member provides relatively few benefits while creating certain expectations they wish to avoid (e.g., expectations related to both time and money to be contributed to the local congregation). And for still others, it may be simply a failure to take the time to go through the particular steps required to join the church.

22. Given the wording of several of these items in these surveys, it is unclear to what extent some of these activities are relatively private (e.g., reading the Bible on one's own) or more communal in nature (e.g., reading the Bible within a Bible study group). Hence, though scholars frequently make a distinction between public and private religious activities, I do not make that distinction here as there are ambiguities as to whether certain of the behaviors analyzed are essentially private or public religious practices.

23. This pattern of a monotonic increase holds true even when controlling for the religious tradition of the respondent, except among Black Protestants.

24. The original survey options enabled respondents to specify: none, less than one-quarter, one-quarter to one-half, one-half to three-quarters, and three-quarters or more. For the sake of simplicity, responses were coded in terms of "none," "less than one-half," and "more than one-half" of one's friends. Collapsing the results in this fashion does not alter the basic patterns that were evident when the fuller version of response options was provided.

25. Perhaps one reason why Catholics exhibit the largest percentage of friendships among weekly church attendees is that Latino Catholics exhibited the highest level of religious social network homogeneity in the Putnam and Campbell survey (2010, 525). In table 5.2, Latino and non-Latino Catholics are combined together within the Catholic religious tradition category.

26. One reason why Black Protestant responses here may differ somewhat from those found by Putnam and Campbell relates to the narrower basis of the question in calculating religious homogeneity of one's social networks. Putnam and Campbell used family, friends, and neighbors together as a means of calculating their religious homogeneity index, whereas the measure examined here specifies the proportion of friends drawn from the house of worship one attends. Many black congregations tend to be relatively small in size, while many Black Protestants live in neighborhoods in which other blacks (largely Black Protestants) also reside. As a result, many Black Protestants may report that a greater proportion of their close friends (who may live in close proximity to them) actually attend some other congregation. Given the use of these alternative approaches to assessing social network homogeneity, the results may vary. Nevertheless, other than this discrepancy related to Black Protestants, the basic patterns that emerge for the major Christian traditions are quite similar in nature.

27. It is also possible that particular theological beliefs may also play a role in this matter, as their content may encourage some religious group members to form friendships primarily within the group itself to the exclusion of other relationships outside the group. In particular, it might be anticipated that "the more an individual holds exclusive theological beliefs, the more his or her friends will come from his or her congregation" (Scheitle and Adamczyk 2009, 25).

28. One's social network is broader than one's friends. And though people are relatively free to choose with whom they wish to form friendships, the composition of an individual's social networks is constrained by the context in which such networks are embedded (Huckfeldt and Sprague 1988). Studies have shown that one's social networks have various effects: (1) they can influence religiosity, as one's embeddedness within congregational social networks shapes a variety of religious activities and beliefs (Stroope 2012); (2) religious people are generally more satisfied and happier with their lives than are nonbelievers (Hadaway 1978; Ferris 2002; Greeley and Hout 2006; Inglehart 2010), and it seems that it is one's social contacts within religious life, rather than one's religious beliefs per se, that fosters this general life satisfaction (Lim and Putnam 2010); and (3) the political influence of the weak ties linked to one's broader social network are just as important as personal friendships in their effects in shaping individual attitudes and behavior (Levine 2005, 141–46; Djupe and Gilbert 2009, 10).

29. The Second Vatican Council met between 1962 and 1965. Among the changes made by the Council included conducting Mass in the vernacular language of the people rather than in Latin, exhibiting greater openness to other expressions of the Christian faith, and placing less emphasis on the church as an institution and more as the people of God.

30. Moreover, as is also evident in table 3.4, some whites also report affiliation with congregations within the Black Protestant tradition.

31. This is done, in part, for several reasons. First, to keep these few respondents within the evangelical and mainline Protestant categories would reduce the already smaller number of survey participants who fall within the Black Protestant tradition. Second, were such blacks to be retained within their more proper evangelical and mainline Protestant categories, no meaningful comparisons could be made racially across religious traditions given their very small numbers within both the evangelical

and mainline Protestant traditions. Finally, as was noted in the introduction to this volume, religious tradition is a sociological concept based, in part, on typical patterns of social interaction, and since most churchgoers report that their local congregation tends to be relatively homogeneous in terms of race, patterns of social interaction among blacks may not diverge greatly regardless of the particular Protestant tradition of which they may be a part.

32. Despite the perceived negative relationship between increased education and religious commitment and practice, religious attendance in the United States has been relatively more frequent among those with higher levels of education; this has been the case since at least the 1970s (Wuthnow 2007a, 61).

33. Since this chapter focuses on religion, only generational and educational differences will be examined in terms of how these variables divide evangelicals in terms of their particular thoughts and practices. Subsequent chapters will examine the extent to which evangelicals are also divided theologically in terms of their social theology and their engagement in civic and political life.

34. Just why this is the case cannot be ascertained here. It could be, for example, that college education provides evangelicals with greater information and resources by which to continue to adhere to certain aspects of their faith. It is also possible that evangelicals, overall, tend to graduate from different kinds of colleges or universities than do graduates of other religious faiths. Other explanations can be advanced as well.

Chapter 5: Living for Jesus? The Social Theology of Evangelicals

1. For stylistic purposes, the terms "government" and "state" will be used interchangeably in this chapter. Though the two terms are related, they can nevertheless be used to convey slightly different meanings.

2. Still, at the same time, even those passages that contain specific instructions for a particular time and place may, nevertheless, provide certain general political principles that hold across time and space.

3. This is largely true regardless of whether such Christians view governments arising only as the result of the fall or arising through natural development even without the fall. There are, however, different ways to think about the purposes of the state. For example, Douglas (2010, 73–82) delineates three different answers that Christians have given to the question of the state's purposes: order, distinctiveness, and training.

4. For example, even in a sinless garden, there may well be a need for some kind of state authority that would, for example, make decisions as to where to install traffic lights and determine how those at such intersections should proceed in some orderly fashion.

5. In fact, when respondents were asked in the University of Akron Fifth National Survey of Religion and Politics whether they agreed with the statement that "because of Christ's commands, Christians have a special obligation to solve social problems," evangelicals were much more likely than those of other religious traditions to respond affirmatively to the statement. More than two-thirds of evangelicals (71 percent)

agreed, compared to less than two-thirds of Black Protestants (64 percent) and less than three-fifths of mainline Protestants and Catholics (58 percent).

6. Likewise, the responses of Catholics found in table 5.1 are also likely shaped, in large part, by the presence of a large proportion of Latinos within their ranks. In fact, when one examines responses to preferences for a government with fewer services among whites only, religious differences nearly disappear, while within religious traditions there are substantial differences in opinion on the basis of race (see table 5.5).

7. But how does one explain the results evident among Black Protestants (who are far more prone than evangelicals to look to government for addressing needy Americans)? (See table 5.1.) As mentioned earlier, Black Protestantism largely emerged out of evangelical Protestantism prior to the Civil War, and on this matter of the primacy of religion we likely see the legacy of this heritage within Black Protestantism.

8. These philosophical perspectives of republicanism and liberalism are related to, yet distinct from, political philosophies that emphasize individualism and communitarianism.

9. Other differences in perspectives are also linked to these two philosophies. For example, the liberal tradition generally conceives "persons as independent selves, 'unencumbered' by moral or civic ties they have not chosen" (Tipton 2007, 37), with freedom being conceived largely in terms of the absence of restraint and the capacity to choose one's own values and ends. In contrast, the republic tradition sees people born and embedded into different moral communities in which freedom represents "the fruit of sharing in self-government whose public-spirited character is cultivated by these very practices of deliberating together over common goods and sharing responsibility for the destiny of the political community" (Tipton 2007, 37).

10. For example, the difference between millennial evangelicals and millennial Black Protestants in expressing favor for the government to do more is 11 percent, but for non-millennial evangelicals and Black Protestants the difference is 24 percent. When examining generational components within the two traditions, the difference between millennial and non-millennial evangelicals on this matter stands at 9 percent, whereas the difference between millennial and non-millennial Black Protestants stands at 4 percent.

11. Previous research has generally focused on differences among traditionalists, centrists, and modernists within the three largest traditions: evangelical Protestant, mainline Protestant, and Roman Catholic traditions (excluding the unaffiliated). Due to the relatively small number of respondents surveyed, such differentiations have not been made among Black Protestants. With the larger Pew Religious Landscape Survey, differences among Black Protestants are examined here.

12. Whereas previous analyses have employed a centrist category, "centrists" are combined here with "modernists" into a non-traditional category. Given that generational and educational differences were dichotomized, the utilization of a dichotomous measure for traditionalism was done in order to make these various analyses more comparable by not artificially creating greater religious differences through the use of three categories (see comments in note 13 below).

13. Most previous analyses have constructed the tripartite measure of traditionalism based on a combination of religious belief and religious behavior measures (see,

for example, Smidt et al. 2010, 237). For purposes of comparison, I did construct a similar composite measure, and the results revealed highly similar patterns. Of course, when one uses three categories for this composite measure, the differences between traditionalists and modernists become greater in magnitude than when, as was done here, centrists are combined with modernists into a "non-traditionalist" category. However, when "centrists" and "modernists" are combined into a "non-traditionalist" category when employing the former approach, the resulting patterns shown in table 5.7 do not differ significantly from the patterns that are obtained when one uses the single question employed here to measure "traditionalism" within each tradition. This dichotomous measure also divides the religious population roughly in half (the religiously unaffiliated were not asked the "traditionalist" question)—with 51 percent being non-traditionalist and 49 percent traditionalist.

14. Multiple classification analysis (MCA) first provides the mean score on the dependent variable for each category of the independent variable. This procedure yields a bivariate measure of association (*eta*) between the independent and dependent variable. In addition, MCA provides deviations from the mean score on the dependent variable for each category of the independent variable after controls for each of the other independent variables have been entered into the analysis, with the statistic *beta* being the multivariate equivalent of *eta*—revealing the relative strength of the relationship once the effects of the other variables in the analysis have been taken into account.

15. Several factors account for the relatively low level in the amount of variance explained (the values for R^2). First, the analysis is limited to evangelicals only, rather than a full range of respondents. Second, to the extent that evangelicals provide relatively similar answers to these questions, there is less variation to explain. Third, the independent variables are basically dichotomous in nature (except for the racial/ethnic variable).

Chapter 6: They Will Know We Are Christians by Our Love? The Civic Life of Evangelicals

1. This statement reflects more a general quality of civic engagement than some universal causal property of such involvement, as the statement is partially dependent on the nature of the activity (e.g., vandalism) or the association involved (e.g., Hitler youth organization).

2. To state this point in Putnam's terminology, some religious traditions or modes of religious expression may "bond" co-religionists to each other without "bridging" them to outsiders, thereby leaving those co-religionists without a "generalized" social trust.

3. It is likely that evangelical Protestants exhibit a greater tendency to subscribe to the doctrine of original sin (with all human beings born in a state of sin) than those within other religious traditions. This is evident, in part, in its greater emphasis on revivalism (and the need for individual salvation). Those who subscribe to the doctrine may well be more cautious in terms of placing higher levels of trust in others.

4. Differences in perceived cultural tensions across religious traditions become even more pronounced when one examines responses to these two questions among weekly church attendees within each religious tradition—with evangelicals continuing to exhibit the highest percentage reporting cultural tensions; moreover, differences between evangelical and Black Protestants also become more pronounced when one examines weekly church attendees only (data not shown).

5. In many ways, this propensity of Americans to join and form associations might not be expected. As the noted historian Arthur Schlesinger (1944, 1) has stated, "It seems paradoxical that a country famed for being individualistic should provide the world's greatest example of joiners."

6. For a comparison of the variation evident in both the substance and range of categories employed to capture associational involvement, see appendix B in Smidt et al. (2010, 237–39).

7. Though scholars rarely indicate why they choose to exclude church membership, some (e.g., Smith 1975, 249) have indicated that they have done so because such membership is largely ascriptive and involuntary in nature. But, given the nature of American religious life, it is hard to understand how religion can be viewed in such a fashion; not only can people choose not to affiliate with a church, they are also relatively free, and frequently do choose, to change their religious affiliation. Some surveys do ask about membership in "church-affiliated groups" (e.g., the Knights of Columbus), without addressing why membership in a religious congregation should not be considered as a form of membership in a voluntary association.

8. Actually, members of religious congregations constitute the core of memberships in voluntary associations more generally (Smidt et al. 2008, 77–81). Though church members are more likely to report membership in religious voluntary associations than in associations located outside of religious life, they nevertheless still join nonreligious voluntary associations at a higher rate than the population as a whole—despite their existing level of engagement in religious life.

9. A similar pattern emerges when respondents were asked in the GSS 2010 survey whether or not they had helped the homeless during the past year. When responses of "a lot" or "some" are combined together, evangelical Protestants and Black Protestants are the most likely to report such (57 percent and 60 percent, respectively), with mainline Protestants and Catholics trailing somewhat further behind (at 45 and 47 percent, respectively), with the religiously unaffiliated being the least likely to have done so (41 percent).

10. Putnam and Campbell (2010, 448) note that "as a fraction of annual income, the average person in the most religious fifth of Americans is more than four times as generous in the least religious fifth, roughly 7 percent vs. roughly 1.5 percent." Since evangelical Protestants and Black Protestants generally exhibit, as a group, the highest levels of religiosity, one would anticipate that their giving as a proportion of annual income would rank at, or near, the top.

11. Still, when one examines tolerance more fully, the concept becomes murkier. First, there are limits to tolerance. For example, no one tolerates everything under every circumstance. People may support some ideas (agree), oppose other ideas but believe they should be allowed to be expressed (tolerate), yet oppose still other ideas or

actions and hold that they should not be allowed to be expressed or permitted (do not tolerate). And, clearly, not all expressions or actions are to be tolerated or permitted (e.g., murder or rape). Moreover, practicing tolerance may well be circumstantial. For example, what ought to be tolerated in one context (e.g., an illustrated debate among adults about pornography) should not necessarily be tolerated in another context (e.g., in an unsupervised middle school classroom). Nor does tolerance necessarily reflect the lack of *prejudice*. Gibson (2006) distinguishes between social tolerance and political tolerance. He proposes that survey questions related to prejudice and social distance are more precisely measures of *social* tolerance. Gibson finds that social intolerance and political intolerance are not necessarily closely connected empirically (Gibson 2006, 25), as his analyses revealed that *prejudice* against a group and intolerance of that group's *political* activities are fairly independent of each other.

12. The GSS frequently utilized a procedure in which all respondents are asked certain questions, while only half of the sample may be asked other questions or even a quarter of the sample asked other questions. The battery of questions related to membership in voluntary associations was asked of only a quarter of the respondents surveyed in the 2010 survey. Black Protestants comprise the smallest religious tradition and, as a religious tradition, exhibit a relatively low level of college graduates. Consequently, given that only a quarter of the sample were asked these questions, the resultant number of college-educated Black Protestants who were asked these questions were too few to provide "valid" estimates of the level of voluntary organizational memberships within their ranks.

13. Because the 2010 General Social Survey did not employ the Pew Religious Landscape Survey measure used to differentiate traditionalists and non-traditionalists, the traditionalism measure used for the GSS is based on a factor analysis of three items: frequency of church attendance, frequency of private prayer, and views related to whether engaging in premarital sex is morally wrong. Factor scores were then divided into traditionalist and non-traditionalist categories based on the relative frequency of traditionalists found among evangelicals using the Pew Religious Landscape Survey measure.

14. A brief description of this procedure is found in the previous chapter related to the discussion of table 5.8.

15. Because the race/ethnicity variable is employed in analyzing evangelicals, it is necessary to restrict the analysis to the Pew Religious Landscape Survey data.

16. The *beta* coefficient reveals the relative strength of the relationship once the effects of the other variables in the analysis have been taken into account.

Chapter 7: We're Marching to Zion? The Politics of Evangelicals

1. Green (2005, 15), however, notes that evangelical Protestants also engaged in certain forms of movement politics during this period of time—particularly in terms of their opposition to the teaching of evolution.

2. In fact, Karl Rove, the chief political strategist for President Bush, contended that four million fewer evangelicals voted in the 2000 presidential election than in

the previous election, a statement that received massive and repeated coverage in the national media. What data Rove used as the basis for his contention is not clear. Some have argued that it was based on a 4 percent drop in the percentage who claimed to be members of the Christian Right in the exit polls of the 2000 election from that in the 1996 election. However, as will be discussed in a later section of the chapter, evangelical Protestants and those who claim to be part of the Christian Right are two distinct, though partially overlapping, groups.

3. Scholars have advanced different theories related to the origin of social movements. One long-standing perspective has argued that grievances and discontent lead to the formation of social movements; the major alternative perspective advances the notion of resource mobilization as the basis for the origin of social movements (Jenkins 1983).

4. While the economic vulnerability of evangelicals as a whole does not match that of Black Protestants as a whole, their lower overall income levels (see table 3.8) suggest that evangelical Protestants as a whole more closely share such vulnerability with Black Protestants than do members of the other religious traditions.

5. Nevertheless, those who call themselves liberals are more likely to take liberal positions on specific issues, whereas self-classified conservatives are more inclined to adopt conservative stances on the same policies (Federico 2012, 80).

6. It might be noted that the 2010 Pew Religion and Public Life Survey asked respondents whether they agreed with "the conservative Christian movement sometimes known as the Religious Right." The percentage of evangelical respondents who responded positively was 46 percent. However, this figure was calculated on the basis of those who had heard of the movement. When one takes into account the fact that some evangelicals report not having heard of the movement (see note 8 below), the resultant percentage of evangelicals agreeing with the Christian Right movement would be 30 percent.

7. Despite the fact that Black Protestants (and blacks more generally) vote overwhelmingly Democratic (roughly around 90 percent vote Democratic), a substantial proportion of blacks (generally between one-quarter and one-third) nevertheless respond in exit polls that they feel close to the Christian Right. Just how to reconcile these two facts is not totally clear. While there are likely to be some blacks who do feel close to the Christian Right and support its efforts, it is also likely that at least some are simply responding to the word "Christian" without fully understanding what the term "Christian Right" attempts to designate.

8. It was contended in chapter 2 that it was far preferable to measure evangelical Protestants by means of one's reported denominational affiliation than through the use of the question "Do you consider yourself to be a born-again or evangelical Christian?" However, because it is seemingly easier to use such an identification question, many survey organizations choose not to employ the denominational approach. Hence, in table 7.4, respondents are classified by this alternative approach, with those labeled as evangelical Protestants being white Protestants who indicated that they considered themselves either a born-again or an evangelical Christian.

9. Interestingly, the 2010 Pew Religion and Public Life Survey also asked respondents whether or not they had heard of the "conservative Christian movement sometimes known as the Religious Right"; despite its presence on the American political scene for several decades, evangelical Protestants exhibited the highest level of recognition of the movement, with 66 percent of those within its ranks reporting that they had heard of the movement. Clearly, in the months prior to the 2010 congressional elections, far more Americans reported that they had heard of the Tea Party movement than had heard of the "Religious Right."

10. This statement is based on an analysis of data from the 2010 Pew Religion and Public Life Survey.

11. These are the resultant figures when those who have not heard of the Tea Party and/or have not heard of the "conservative Christian movement sometimes known as the Religious Right" are included in the analysis. When respondents who report not having heard of these movements are removed from the analysis, the resultant percentage found among evangelicals jumps from 20 percent to 34 percent (with corresponding increases for the other religious traditions as well). Though analysts frequently drop those who have not heard about the movement from their computations, it can easily distort the results and the implications of their analyses. Consider the following example: Only 10 percent of Group A has heard of X, and among those who have heard of X, 75 percent approve of X. The conventional practice, then, would suggest that 75 percent of Group A approve of X. However, given that the bulk of Group A has not even heard of X, one could easily contend that, in fact, only 7.5 percent of Group A approve of X (the result when one multiplies the percentage who have heard of X by the percentage who approve of X).

12. Several different explanations have been advanced to account for these differences. Probably the most commonly accepted explanation is that voting is perceived to be a social norm and people do not wish to reveal that they have not conformed to social expectations.

13. If anything, social norms related to voter turnout were probably stronger in 1964 than today; as a result, if anything, there is likely a higher level of overreporting in 1964 than presently.

14. In 2008, mainline Protestants moved once again in a more Democratic direction, as a majority of mainline Protestants cast their ballots for Obama in 2008 (Smidt et al. 2010, 196–200).

15. However, due to the candidacy of Democrat and Catholic John F. Kennedy, the level of Republican voting among Catholics in 1960 may have been somewhat depressed from its more typical patterns in 1952 or 1956.

16. The exceptions to these generalizations occur among Black Protestants in relationship to peace through strength and Republican partisan identification, where basically no political differences exist between the two generational groups of Black Protestants.

17. In 2011, the Public Religion Research Institute found that "Forty-four percent of white evangelical Millennials (18–29 years old) favor allowing gay and lesbian people to marry" (Public Religion Research Institute 2011, 5).

18. It will be recalled that members of each religious tradition are classified into traditionalist and non-traditionalist categories based on the answer the respondents provided to the question of whether they thought that their church or denomination should "preserve its traditional beliefs and practices," "adjust [them] in light of new circumstances," or "adopt modern beliefs and practices." Those who offered the first answer ("should preserve") were classified as "traditionalists," whereas those who provided one of the other two answers ("adjust" or "adopt") were classified as "non-traditionalists."

19. It will be recalled that those who indicated they were not affiliated with any particular denomination or house of worship were not asked the question on which the measure of religious traditionalism is based. Hence, when examining religious traditionalism, those who are religiously unaffiliated are dropped from the analysis.

20. A brief description of this procedure is found in the previous chapter related to the discussion of table 5.8.

21. Because the race/ethnicity variable is employed in analyzing evangelicals, it is necessary to restrict the analysis to the Pew Religious Landscape Survey data.

22. The *beta* coefficient reveals the relative strength of the relationship once the effects of the other variables in the analysis have been taken into account.

Chapter 8: In the Sweet By and By? Evangelicals and the Future

1. There are a number of issues related to conducting surveys. These include decisions as to which topics are to be addressed, the framing of the survey questions, and the selection of the particular response options to such questions. Each of these factors can ultimately shape one's resultant findings.

2. The decision as to which elites supposedly represent any social group is quite subjective in nature. Certainly, there may be grounds for choosing certain elites over others. But, regardless, it is difficult to know the extent to which particular statements made by elites necessarily reflect the view of the rank-and-file members of the group—or, if they do not, the extent to which they may have any persuasive effects in shifting attitudes of group members. Moreover, when the media are involved in selecting a spokesperson for a group, they are more prone to seek out contentious and extreme spokespersons for the group than those who may be less flashy or controversial, as conflict helps to build audiences and attract more public attention, thereby boosting media ratings, sales, and subscriptions.

3. This section of the chapter draws heavily from the discussion found in Penning and Smidt (2002, 167–74).

4. Pietistic evangelicals are part of the Reformation tradition, but pietists sought to balance heart and mind by incorporating the experiential elements of the faith and stressing private religious practices and holy living. What pietists emphasized, therefore, was "spiritual discipline and affective religion rather than intellectual assent" (Balmer 1999, 16).

5. This discussion of traditionalists and reformists among contemporary evangelical theologians draws heavily from the description provided by Olson (1998, 40–49).

6. On this point, there is some overlap between Calvinist and Wesleyan perspectives on matters of theology.

7. Yogi Berra is a former catcher for the New York Yankees who played major league baseball largely in the 1950s and 1960s. Phrases such as "I really didn't say everything I said," or "It ain't over 'til it's over" have become known as "Yogi-isms."

8. Clearly, reciprocal causation is at work here. Some level of religious salience is likely necessary in order for someone to decide to attend church, but attending church helps attendees to meet others, forge friendships with other congregational members, and build religious social networks, which, in turn, enhances the salience of religion for such individuals.

9. Technically, the study makes no exact comparison between evangelical Protestantism and Catholicism—only between Protestantism and Catholicism. But, given that evangelicals comprise the largest proportion of all Protestants, the fact that Protestantism has a lower rate of defection suggests that this is likely to be the case among evangelical Protestants.

10. It should be noted that with the decline of denominationalism, many who are affiliated with some local congregation may nevertheless report that they are religiously unaffiliated (in light of the fact that they are not affiliated with some particular denomination). Consequently, one must also take this seeming growth in the religiously unaffiliated somewhat cautiously when no follow-up questions are asked in relationship to affiliation with some local church. See, for example, Dougherty, Johnson, and Polson (2007) and Johnson (2011).

11. According to this understanding, religion shapes American politics primarily through religious belonging (as opposed to religious belief or behavior). As developed by historians, American party politics is seen as largely involving competing alliances of ethnoreligious groups. Thus, when one talks of "the Catholic vote" or "the Jewish vote," one is implicitly employing an ethnoreligious approach to understanding American politics. For a more extended discussion, see Smidt, Kellstedt, and Guth (2009).

12. This assertion is substantiated by the analysis found in Smidt et al. (2010), which examines a variety of surveys and compares those who exhibit a "privatized religion" with those who exhibit a "public religion" or an "integrated religion."

References

Abell, Aaron. 1983. *The Urban Impact on American Protestantism*. Cambridge, MA: Harvard University Press.

Ahearn, David Oki. 2003. "Aliens and Citizens: Competing Models of Political Involvement in Contemporary Christian Ethics." In *Faith, Morality, and Civil Society*, eds. Dale McConkey and Peter Augustine Lawler, 197–208. Lanham, MD: Lexington Books.

Ahlstrom, Sidney. 1972. *A Religious History of the American People*. New Haven, CT: Yale University Press.

——. 1975. "From Puritanism to Evangelicalism: A Critical Perspective." In *The Evangelicals*, eds. David Wells and John Woodbridge, 269–89. Nashville, TN: Abingdon Press.

Albanese, Catherine. 1981. *America: Religions and Religion*. Belmont, CA: Wadsworth.

Alwin, Duane F., Jacob L. Felson, Edward T. Walker, and Paula Tufis. 2006. "Measuring Religious Identities in Surveys." *Public Opinion Quarterly* 70 (4): 530–64.

Ammerman, Nancy. 2009. "American Evangelicals in American Culture: Continuity and Change." In *Evangelicals and Democracy in America*. Vol. 1, *Religion and Society*, eds. Steven Brint and Jean Reith Schroedel, 44–73. New York: Russell Sage Foundation.

Anderson, Sir James Norman. 1984. *Christianity and World Religions: The Challenge of Pluralism*. Downers Grove, IL: InterVarsity Press.

Anti-Semitism in the United States, 1964. www.thearda.com/Archive/Files/Descriptions/ANTSEMUS.asp.

Askew, Thomas, and Peter Spellman. 1984. *The Churches and the American Experience*. Grand Rapids, MI: Baker Books.

Balmer, Randall. 1999. *Blessed Assurance: A History of Evangelicalism in America.* Boston: Beacon.

Balmer, Randall, and Mark Silk, eds. 2006. *Religion and Public Life in the Middle Atlantic Region: The Fount of Diversity.* Walnut Creek, CA: AltaMira Press.

Beal, Timothy. 2010. "Theology for Everyone." *The Chronicle of Higher Education* 56 (January 10). http://chronicle.com/article/Theology-for-Everyone/63452 (accessed March 3, 2012).

Bean, Lydia. 2014. *The Politics of Evangelical Identity: Local Churches and Partisan Divides in the United States and Canada.* Princeton, NJ: Princeton University Press.

Beatty, Kathleen, and Oliver Walter. 1984. "Religious Preference and Practice: Reevaluating Their Impact on Political Tolerance." *Public Opinion Quarterly* 48 (Spring): 318–29.

Bebbington, David W. 1989. *Evangelicalism in Modern Britain: A History from the 1730s to the 1980s.* London: Unwin Hyman.

Bell, Rob. 2011. *Love Wins: A Book about Heaven, Hell, and the Fate of Every Person Who Ever Lived.* New York: HarperOne.

Bellah, Robert, and Philip Hammond. 1980. *Varieties of Civil Religion.* San Francisco, CA: Harper & Row.

Berger, Peter. 1967. *The Sacred Canopy: Elements of a Sociological Theory of Religion.* New York, NY: Doubleday.

Beyerlein, Kraig. 2004. "Specifying the Impact of Conservative Protestantism on Educational Attainment." *Journal for the Scientific Study of Religion* 43 (4): 505–18.

Bibby, Reginald. 1978. "Why Conservative Churches *Really* Are Growing: Kelly Revisited." *Journal for the Scientific Study of Religion* 17:129–37.

Bielo, James. 2009. *Words upon the Word: An Ethnography of Evangelical Group Bible Study.* New York: New York University Press.

Birdsall, Richard. 1970. "The Second Great Awakening and the New England Social Order." *Church History* 39 (September): 345–64.

Black, Amy E. 2008. *Beyond Left and Right: Helping Christians Make Sense of American Politics.* Grand Rapids, MI: Baker Books.

Bowman, Matthew. 2007. "Sin, Spirituality, and Primitivism: The Theologies of the American Social Gospel, 1985–1917." *Religion and American Culture* 17 (1): 95–126.

Brauer, Jerald. 1976. "Puritanism, Revivalism, and the Revolution." In *Religion and the American Revolution*, ed. Jerald Brauer, 1–28. Philadelphia: Fortress Press.

——. 1978. "Conversion: From Puritanism to Revivalism." *Journal of Religion* 58 (July): 227–43.

——. 1982. "Revivalism and Millennialism in America." In *In the Great Tradition*, eds. Joseph D. Ban and Paul R. DeKar, 147–59. Valley Forge, PA: Judson Press.

Brehm, John, and Wendy Rahn. 1997. "Individual-Level Evidence for the Causes and Consequences of Social Capital." *American Journal of Political Science* 41:999–1023.

Bretherton, Luke. 2010. *Christianity & Contemporary Politics.* Malden, MA: Wiley-Blackwell.

Brint, Steven, and Seth Abrutyn. 2010. "Who's Right about the Right? Comparing Competing Explanations of the Link between White Evangelicals and Conservative Politics in the United States." *Journal for the Scientific Study of Religion* 49 (2): 328–50.

Brint, Steven, and Jean Reith Schroedel. 2009. "Introduction." In *Evangelicals and Democracy in America.* Vol. 1, *Religion and Society,* eds. Steven Brint and Jean Reith Schroedel, 1–23. New York: Russell Sage Foundation.

Brokaw, Tom. 1998. *The Greatest Generation.* New York: Random House.

Brooks, Arthur C. 2003. "Religious Faith and Charitable Giving." *Policy Review* 121 (October–November): 39–50.

Butler, Jon. 1982. "Enthusiasm Described and Decreed: The Great Awakening as Interpretative Fiction." *Journal of American History* 69 (2): 305–25.

Campbell, David. 2004. "Community Heterogeneity and Participation." Paper presented at the annual meeting of the American Political Science Association, Chicago, IL.

Campbell, David, and Steven Yonish. 2003. "Religion and Volunteering in America." In *Religion as Social Capital: Producing the Common Good,* ed. Corwin Smidt, 87–106. Waco, TX: Baylor University Press.

Caplovitz, Darren, and Fred Sherrow. 1977. *The Religious Drop-outs: Apostasy among College Graduates.* Beverly Hills, CA: Sage.

Carpenter, Joel. 1980. "Fundamentalist Institutions and the Rise of Evangelical Protestantism, 1929–1942." *Church History* 49 (March): 62–75.

———. 1984a. "From Fundamentalism to the New Evangelical Coalition." In *Evangelicals and Modern America,* ed. George Marsden, 3–16. Grand Rapids, MI: Eerdmans.

———. 1984b. "The Fundamentalist Leaven and the Rise of an Evangelical United Front." In *The Evangelical Tradition in America,* ed. Leonard Sweet, 257–88. Macon, GA: Mercer University Press.

———. 1997. *Revive Us Again: The Reawakening of American Fundamentalism.* New York: Oxford University Press.

———. 2004. "The Fellowship of Kindred Minds: Evangelical Identity and the Quest for Christian Unity." In *Pilgrims on the Sawdust Trail: Evangelical Ecumenism and the Quest for Christian Identity,* ed. Timothy George, 27–42. Grand Rapids, MI: Baker Academic.

Cavendish, James, Michael Welch, and David Leege. 1998. "Social Network Theory and Predictors of Religiosity for Black and White Catholics: Evidence of a 'Black Sacred Cosmos'?" *Journal for the Scientific Study of Religion* 37 (3): 397–410.

Chaplin, Jonathan. 2009. "Conclusion: Christian Political Wisdom." In *God and Government,* eds. Nick Spencer and Jonathan Chaplin, 205–37. London: Theos.

Chaves, Mark. 2004. *Congregations in America.* Cambridge, MA: Harvard University Press.

Clement, Scott, and John Green. 2011. "The Tea Party, Religion and Social Issues." Pew Research Center Publications (February 23). http://pewresearch.org/pubs/1903/tea-party-movement-religion-social-issues-conservative-christian (accessed April 4, 2012).

Clydesdale, Tim. 2007. *First Year Out: Understanding American Teens after High School.* Chicago: University of Chicago Press.

Cochran, Clarke. 1990. *Religion in Public and Private Life*. New York: Routledge.

Cohen, Jean. 1999. "Does Voluntary Association Make Democracy Work?" In *Diversity and Its Discontents: Cultural Conflict and Common Ground in Contemporary American Society*, eds. Neil Smelser and Jeffrey Alexander, 263–91. Princeton, NJ: Princeton University Press.

Coleman, Richard. 1980. *Issues of Theological Conflict*. rev. ed. Grand Rapids, MI: Eerdmans.

Conyers, A. J. 2001. "Rescuing Tolerance." *First Things*, August/September, 43–46.

Cooper, Valarie C., and Corwin E. Smidt. 2012. "African-Americans, Religion, and the 2008 Election." In *Religion, Race, and Barack Obama's New Democratic Pluralism*, ed. Gaston Espinosa, 185–212. New York: Routledge.

Cornwall, Marie. 1989. "The Determinants of Religious Behavior: A Theoretical Model and Empirical Test." *Social Forces* 68 (2): 572–92.

Dalton, Russell. 2002. *Citizen Politics: Public Opinion and Political Parties in Advanced Industrial Democracies*. 3rd ed. New York: Chatham House.

D'Antonio, Michael. 1989. *Fall from Grace: The Failed Crusade of the Christian Right*. New York: Farrar, Straus & Giroux.

Davie, Grace. 1994. *Religion in Britain since 1945: Believing without Belonging*. New York: Wiley-Blackwell.

Dayton, Donald. 1991. "The Limits of Evangelicalism: The Pentecostal Tradition." In *The Variety of American Evangelicalism*, eds. Donald Dayton and Robert Johnson, 36–56. Knoxville: University of Tennessee Press.

Dayton, Donald, and Robert Johnson, eds. 1991. *The Variety of American Evangelicalism*. Knoxville: University of Tennessee Press.

Deymaz, Mark. 2014. "Evangelicals and Politics." *Christian Post* (July 11). http://www.christianpost.com/news/evangelicals-and-politics-championing-political-positions-as-if-written-in-biblical-stone-hurting-churchs-purpose-123162/ (accessed September 25, 2014).

Diamond, Sara. 1989. *Spiritual Warfare: The Theo-Politics of the Christian Right*. Boston: South End Press.

Dieter, Melvin. 1975. "Wesleyan-Holiness Aspects of Pentecostal Origins." In *Aspects of Pentecostal-Charismatic Origins*, ed. Vinson Synan, 55–80. Plainfield, NJ: Logos International.

Dillon, Michele. 2007. "Age, Generation, and Cohort in American Religion and Spirituality." In *The Sage Handbook of the Sociology of Religion*, eds. James Beckford and N. J. Demerath III, 526–46. Thousand Oaks, CA: Sage.

Djupe, Paul, and Christopher Gilbert. 2002. "The Political Voice of Clergy." *Journal of Politics* 64 (2): 596–609.

———. 2009. *The Political Influences of Churches*. New York: Cambridge University Press.

Dougherty, Kevin, Byron Johnson, and Edward Polson. 2007. "Recovering the Lost: Remeasuring U.S. Religious Affiliation." *Journal for the Scientific Study of Religion* 46 (December): 483–99.

Dougherty, Kevin, and Andrew L. Whitehead. 2011. "A Place to Belong: Small Group Involvement in Religious Congregations." *Sociology of Religion* 72 (1): 91–111.

Douglas, Mark. 2010. *Believing Aloud: Reflections on Being Religious in the Public Square.* Eugene, OR: Cascade Books.

Ecklund, Elaine Howard. 2006. *Korean American Evangelicals: New Models for Civic Life.* New York: Oxford University Press.

Ellwood, Robert. 2000. *1950: Crossroads of American Religious Life.* Louisville, KY: Westminster John Knox Press.

Emerson, Michael, and Christian Smith. 2000. *Divided by Faith: Evangelical Religion and the Problem of Race in America.* New York: Oxford University Press.

Espinosa, Gaston, Virgilio Elizondo, and Jess Miranda. 2003. "Hispanic Churches in American Public Life: Summary of Findings." http://latinostudies.nd.edu/publica tions/pubs/HispChurchesEnglishWEB.pdf (accessed April 3, 2012).

Federico, Christopher. 2012. "Ideology and Public Opinion." In *New Directions in Public Opinion*, ed. Adam Berinsky, 79–100. New York: Routledge.

Faith Matters Survey. 2006. www.thearda.com/Archive/Files/Descriptions/FTH-MATT.asp.

Feldman, Kenneth, and Theodore Newcomb. 1969. *The Impact of College on Students.* Vol. 2. San Francisco, CA: Jossey-Bass.

Ferris, Abbot L. 2002. "Religion and Quality of Life." *Journal of Happiness Studies* 3:199–215.

Fifth National Survey of Religion and Politics. 2008. Akron, OH: University of Akron Survey Research Center.

Finke, Roger, and Rodney Stark. 1992. *The Churching of American 1976–1990.* New Brunswick, NJ: Rutgers University Press.

Fiorina, Morris, Samuel Abrams, and Jeremy Pope. 2005. *Culture War? The Myth of a Polarized America.* New York: Pearson Longman.

Fischer, Claude. 1977. *Networks and Places: Social Relations in the Urban Setting.* New York: Free Press.

Fitzgerald, Frances. 2008. "The New Evangelicals." *New Yorker* 84 (June 30): 28–34.

Flanigan, William, and Nancy Zingale. 1983. *Political Behavior of the American Electorate.* 5th ed. Newton, MA: Allyn & Bacon.

———. 1998. *Political Behavior of the American Electorate.* 9th ed. Washington, DC: CQ Press.

Fowler, Robert Booth. 1982. *A New Engagement: Evangelical Political Thought, 1966–1976.* Grand Rapids, MI: Eerdmans.

Fowler, Robert, Allen Hertzke, Laura Olson, and Kevin den Dulk. 2004. *Religion and Politics in America.* 3rd ed. Boulder, CO: Westview.

Free, Lloyd, and Hadley Cantril. 1967. *The Political Beliefs of Americans.* New Brunswick, NJ: Rutgers University Press.

Gallup, George. 1979. "The *Christianity Today*–Gallup Poll: An Overview." *Christianity Today* 23 (December 21): 1666–73.

General Social Survey. 2010. Chicago, IL: National Opinion Research Center. www.thearda.com/Archive/Files/Descriptions/GSS10PAN.asp.

Gibbs, Nancy, and Michael Duffy. 2007. *The Preacher and the Presidents: Billy Graham in the White House.* New York: Center Street.

Gibson, James L. 2006. "Enigmas of Intolerance: Fifty Years after Stouffer's *Com-munism, Conformity, and Civil Liberties.*" *Perspectives on Politics* 4:1 (March): 21–34.

Glenn, Norval. 1987. "The Trend in 'No Religion' Respondents to U.S. Surveys, Late 1950s to Early 1980s." *Public Opinion Quarterly* 51 (Fall): 293–314.

Glock, Charles, and Rodney Stark. 1966. *Christian Beliefs and Anti-Semitism.* New York: Harper & Row.

Goodstein, Laurie. 2008. "Obama Made Gains among Younger Evangelical Voters, Data Show." *New York Times* (Nov. 7). http:www.nytimes.com/2008/11/07/us/politics/07religion.html (accessed April 6, 2011).

Gray, Don. 2008. "Beyond Orthodoxy: Social Theology and the Views of Protestant Clergy on Social Issues." *Review of Religious Research* 50 (2): 221–40.

Greeley, Andrew, and Michael Hout. 2006. *The Truth about Conservative Christians.* Chicago: University of Chicago Press.

Green, John C. 2005. "Seeking a Place." In *Toward an Evangelical Public Policy: Political Strategies for the Health of the Nation*, eds. Ronald Sider and Diane Knippers, 15–34. Grand Rapids, MI: Baker Books.

———. 2007. *The Faith Factor: How Religion Influences American Elections.* Westport, CT: Praeger.

———. 2009. "Exploring the Traditionalist Alliance: Evangelical Protestants, Religious Voters, and the Republican Presidential Vote." In *Evangelicals and Democracy in America.* Vol. 1, *Religion and Society*, eds. Steven Brint and Jean Reith Schroedel, 117–58. New York: Russell Sage Foundation.

———. 2010. "Religious Diversity and American Democracy." In *Religion and Democracy in the United States: Danger or Opportunity?*, eds. Alan Wolfe and Ira Katznelson, 46–88. Princeton, NJ: Princeton University Press.

Green, John C., Lyman A. Kellstedt, Corwin E. Smidt, and James L. Guth. 2007. "How the Faithful Voted: Religious Communities and the Presidential Vote." In *A Matter of Faith: Religion in the 2004 Presidential Election*, ed. David Campbell, 15–36. Washington, DC: Brookings.

Griffiths, Paul J., and Jean Bethke Elshtain. 2002. "Proselytizing for Tolerance: Parts I and II." *First Things*, November, 30–36.

Gushee, David. 2008. *The Future of Faith in American Politics: The Public Witness of the Evangelical Center.* Waco, TX: Baylor University Press.

Guth, James L., John C. Green, Corwin E. Smidt, Lyman A. Kellstedt, and Margaret Poloma. 1997. *The Bully Pulpit: The Politics of Protestant Clergy.* Lawrence: University Press of Kansas.

Guth, James L., Lyman A. Kellstedt, Corwin E. Smidt, and John C. Green. 2006. "Religious Influences in the 2004 Presidential Election." *Presidential Studies Quarterly* 36 (June): 223–42.

Hackett, Conrad, and D. Michael Lindsay. 2008. "Measuring Evangelicalism: Consequences of Different Operationalization Strategies." *Journal for the Scientific Study of Religion* 47 (3): 499–514.

Hadaway, C. Kirk. 1978. "Life Satisfaction and Religion: A Reanalysis." *Social Forces* 57:636–43.

Hadaway, C. Kirk, and Wade Clark Roof. 1988. "Apostasy in American Churches: Evidence from National Survey Data." In *Falling from the Faith: Causes and Consequences of Religious Apostasy*, ed. David G. Bromley, 29–46. Newbury Park, CA: Sage.

Hadden, Jeffrey. 1969. *The Gathering Storm in the Churches: The Widening Gap between Clergy and Laymen*. Garden City, NY: Doubleday.

Hammond, John. 1979. *The Politics of Benevolence: Revival Religion and American Voting Behavior*. Northwood, NJ: Ablex.

Handy, Robert. 1955. "Fundamentalism and Modernism in Perspective." *Religion in Life* 24 (3): 381–94.

———. 1967. *The Protestant Quest for a Christian America, 1830–1930*. Philadelphia: Fortress Press.

———. 1971. *A Christian America: Protestant Hopes and Historical Realities*. New York: Oxford University Press.

———. 1977. *A History of Churches in the United States and Canada*. New York: Oxford University Press.

Hankins, Barry. 2008. *American Evangelicals*. Lanham, MD: Rowman & Littlefield.

Harris-Lacewell, Melissa. 2008. "African-Americans, Religion, and the American Presidency." In *Religion, Race, and the American Presidency*, ed. Gaston Espinosa, 205–28. Lanham, MD: Rowman & Littlefield.

Hart, D. G. 2004. *Deconstructing Evangelicalism: Conservative Protestantism in the Age of Billy Graham*. Grand Rapids, MI: Baker Books.

Hatch, Nathan. 1980. "The Christian Movement and the Demand for a Theology of the People." *Journal of American History* 67 (December): 545–67.

———. 1982. "*Sola Scriptura* and *Novus Ordo Sectorum*." In *The Bible in America: Essays in Cultural History*, eds. Nathan Hatch and Mark Noll, 59–78. New York: Oxford University Press.

———. 1984a. "Millennialism and Popular Religion in the Early Republic." In *The Evangelical Tradition in America*, ed. Leonard I. Sweet, 113–30. Macon, GA: Mercer University Press.

———. 1984b. "Evangelicalism as a Democratic Movement." In *Evangelicalism and Modern America*, ed. George Marsden, 71–82. Grand Rapids, MI: Eerdmans.

———. 1989. *The Democratization of American Christianity*. New Haven, CT: Yale University Press.

Hatch, Nathan, and Michael Hamilton. 1995. "Taking the Measure of the Evangelical Resurgence, 1942–1992." In *Reckoning with the Past: Historical Essays on American Evangelicalism from the Institute for the Study of American Evangelicals*, ed. D. G. Hart, 395–412. Grand Rapids, MI: Baker Books.

Hauerwas, Stanley, and William Willimon. 1989. *Resident Aliens: Life in the Christian Colony*. Nashville, TN: Abingdon Press.

Henry Institute National Survey on Religion and Public Life. 2008. Grand Rapids, MI: The Henry Institute, Calvin College.

Hertzke, Allen. 2009. "Emerging Trends in Religion, Society, and Politics." In *The Future of Religion in American Politics*, ed. Charles Dunn, 229–55. Lexington: University Press of Kentucky.

Hodgkinson, Virginia A., Murray S. Weitzman, Eric A. Crutchfield, Aaron J. Heffron, and Arthur D. Kirsch. 1996. *Giving and Volunteering in the United States.* Washington, DC: Independent Sector.

Hodgkinson, Virginia, Murray Weitzman, and Arthur Kirsch. 1990. "From Commitment to Action: How Religious Involvement Affects Giving and Volunteering." In *Faith and Philanthropy in America: Exploring the Role of Religion in America's Voluntary Sector,* eds. Robert Wuthnow and Virginia Hodgkinson, 93–114. San Francisco, CA: Jossey-Bass.

Hoge, Dean. 1979. "A Test of Theories of Denominational Growth and Decline." In *Understanding Church Growth and Decline: 1950–1978,* eds. Dean Hoge and David Roozen, 179–97. New York: The Pilgrim Press.

Hoge, Dean, Benton Johnson, and Donald Luidens. 1994. *Vanishing Boundaries: The Religion of Mainline Protestant Baby Boomers.* Louisville, KY: Westminster John Knox Press.

Hoge, Dean, and Ernesto de Zulueta. 1985. "Salience as a Condition for Various Social Consequences of Religion." *Journal for the Scientific Study of Religion* 24:21–38.

Hollinger, Dennis. 1983. *Individualism and Social Ethics: An Evangelical Syncretism.* Lanham, MD: University Press of America.

Horton, Michael S. 2001a. "The Battles over the Label 'Evangelical.'" *Modern Reformation* 10 (March/April): 15–21.

———. 2001b. "Reflection: Is Evangelicalism Reformed or Wesleyan? Reopening the Marsden-Dayton Debate." *Christian Scholar's Review* 31 (Winter): 131–55.

Hout, Michael, and Claude Fischer. 2002. "Explaining the Rise of Americans with No Religious Preference." *American Sociological Review* 67:165–90.

Hout, Michael, Andrew Greeley, and Melissa Wilde. 2001. "The Demographic Imperative for Religious Change." *American Journal of Sociology* 107:468–500.

Howe, Daniel Walker. 2007. "Religion and Politics in the Antebellum North." In *Religion and American Politics: From the Colonial Period to the Present,* eds. Mark A. Noll and Luke E. Harlow, 121–43. New York: Oxford University Press.

Huckfeldt, Robert, and John Sprague. 1988. "Choice, Social Structure, and Political Information: The Informational Coercion of Minorities." *American Journal of Political Science* 32:467–82.

Hudson, Winthrop. 1961. *American Protestantism.* Chicago: University of Chicago Press.

Hunter, James Davison. 1981. "Operationalizing Evangelicalism: A Review, Critique and Proposal." *Sociological Analysis* 42 (Winter): 363–72.

———. 1983. *American Evangelicalism.* New Brunswick, NJ: Rutgers University Press.

———. 1987. *Evangelicalism: The Coming Generation.* Chicago: University of Chicago Press.

———. 1991. *Culture Wars: The Struggle to Define America.* New York: Basic.

Hutchison, William. 1976. *The Modernist Impulse in American Protestantism.* Cambridge, MA: Harvard University Press.

Inglehart, Ronald. 2010. "Faith and Freedom: Traditional and Modern Ways to Happiness." In *International Differences in Well-Being,* eds. E. Diener, J. F. Helliwell, and D. Kahneman, 351–59. New York: Oxford University Press.

Isaac, Rhys. 1974. "Evangelical Revolt: The Nature of the Baptists' Challenge to the Traditional Order in Virginia, 1765 to 1775." *William and Mary Quarterly* 31 (July): 345–68.

Jackman, Robert, and Ross A. Miller. 1998. "Social Capital and Politics." *Annual Review of Political Science* 1:47–73.

Jenkins, J. Craig. 1983. "Resource Mobilization Theory and the Study of Social Movements." *Annual Review of Sociology* 9:527–53.

Johnson, Byron. 2011. "The Good News about Evangelicalism." *First Things*, no. 210 (February): 12–14.

Johnson, Daniel. 1997. "Formal Education vs. Religious Belief: Soliciting New Evidence with Multinomial Logit Modeling." *Journal for the Scientific Study of Religion* 36 (2): 231–46.

Kelley, Dean. 1972. *Why Conservative Churches Are Growing*. New York: Harper & Row.

Kellstedt, Lyman, and John C. Green. 1993. "Knowing God's Many People: Denominational Preference and Political Behavior." In *Rediscovering the Religious Factor in American Politics*, eds. David C. Leege and Lyman A. Kellstedt, 53–71. Armonk, NY: M. E. Sharpe.

Kellstedt, Lyman A., John C. Green, James L. Guth, and Corwin E. Smidt. 1996. "Grasping the Essentials: The Social Embodiment of Religion and Political Behavior." In *Religion and the Culture Wars*, eds. John C. Green, James L. Guth, Corwin E. Smidt, and Lyman A. Kellstedt, 174–92. Lanham, MD: Rowman & Littlefield.

Kellstedt, Lyman A., John C. Green, Corwin E. Smidt, and James L. Guth. 2007. "Faith Transformed: Religion and American Politics from FDR to George W. Bush." In *Religion and American Politics: From the Colonial Period to the Present*, 2nd ed., eds. Mark A. Noll and Luke E. Harlow, 269–95. New York: Oxford University Press.

Kellstedt, Lyman A., Corwin E. Smidt, and Paul M. Kellstedt. 1991. "Religious Tradition, Denomination, and Commitment: White Protestants and the 1988 Election." In *The Bible and the Ballot Box: Religion and Politics in the 1988 Election*, eds. James L. Guth and John C. Green, 139–58. Boulder, CO: Westview.

Killen, Patricia O'Connell, and Mark Silk, eds. 2004. *Religion and Public Life in the Pacific Northwest: The None Zone*. Walnut Creek, CA: AltaMira Press.

Kincheloe, Joe, Jr. 1980. "European Roots of Evangelical Revivalism: Methodist Transmission of the Puritanistic Socio-Religious Tradition." *Methodist History* 18 (July): 262–71.

King, Jr., Neil. 2013. "Evangelical Leader Preaches Pullback from Politics, Culture Wars." *Wall Street Journal* (Oct. 21). http://online.wsj.com/news/articles/SB10001424127887324755104579072722223166570 (accessed September 26, 2014).

Knoke, David. 1986. "Associations and Interest Groups." *Annual Review of Sociology* 12:1–21.

Kohut, Andrew, John C. Green, Scott Keeter, and Robert Toth. 2000. *The Diminishing Divide: Religion's Changing Role in American Politics*. Washington, DC: Brookings.

Krapohl, Robert, and Charles Lippy. 1999. *The Evangelicals: A Historical, Thematic, and Biographical Guide*. Westport, CT: Greenwood.

Kyle, Richard. 2006. *Evangelicalism: An Americanized Christianity.* New Brunswick, NJ: Transaction.

Kymlicka, Will, and Wayne Norman. 1995. "Return of the Citizen: A Survey of Recent Work on Citizenship Theory." In *Theorizing Citizenship*, ed. Ronald Beiner, 283–322. Albany: University of New York Press.

Layman, Geoffrey. 2001. *The Great Divide: Religion and Cultural Conflict in American Party Politics.* New York, NY: Columbia University Press.

Layman, Geoffrey, and John C. Green. 2005. "Wars and Rumors of Wars: The Contexts of Cultural Conflict in American Political Behavior." *British Journal of Political Science* 36 (1): 61–89.

Lenski, Gerhard. 1963. *The Religious Factor: A Sociological Study of Religion's Impact on Politics, Economics, and Family Life.* Rev. ed. Garden City, NJ: Anchor Books.

Levi, Margaret, and Laura Stoker. 2000. "Political Trust and Trustworthiness." *Annual Review of Political Science* 3:475–507.

Levine, Jeffrey. 2005. "Choosing Alone? The Social Network of Modern Political Choice." In *The Social Logic of Politics: Personal Networks as Contexts for Political Behavior*, ed. Allen Zuckerman, 132–51. Philadelphia: Temple University Press.

Lindsay, D. Michael. 2007. *Faith in the Halls of Power.* New York: Oxford University Press.

Lim, Chaeyoon, and Robert Putnam. 2010. "Religion, Social Networks, and Life Satisfaction." *American Sociological Review* 75 (6): 914–33.

Long, Michael. 2008. "Introduction." In *The Legacy of Billy Graham: Critical Reflections on America's Greatest Evangelist*, ed. Michael Long, xi–xiv. Louisville, KY: Westminster John Knox Press.

Longley, Clifford. 2009. "Government and the Common Good." In *God and Government*, eds. Nick Spencer and Jonathan Chaplin, 159–79. London: Theos.

Maclear, James. 1959. "'The True American Union' of Church and State: The Reconstruction of the Theocratic Tradition." *Church History* 28 (1): 41–61.

Markoe, Lauren. 2012. "Young 'Millennials' Losing Faith in Record Numbers." www.washingtonpost.com/national/on-faith/2012/04/19/gIQA9QoxTT_story.html (accessed April 20, 2012).

Marsden, George. 1975. "From Fundamentalism to Evangelicalism: An Historical Analysis." In *The Evangelicals*, eds. David Wells and John Woodbridge, 122–42. Nashville, TN: Abingdon Press.

——. 1980. *Fundamentalism and American Culture: The Shaping of Twentieth-Century Evangelicalism, 1870–1925.* New York: Oxford University Press.

——. 1982. "Everyone One's Own Interpreter? The Bible, Science, and Authority in Mid-Nineteenth-Century America." In *The Bible in America: Essays in Cultural History*, eds. Nathan Hatch and Mark Noll, 79–100. New York: Oxford University Press.

——. 1983. "Understanding Fundamentalist Views of Society." In *Reformed Faith and Politics*, ed. Ronald Stone, 65–75. Washington, DC: University Press of America.

——. 1984. "Introduction: The Evangelical Denomination." In *Evangelicalism and Modern America*, ed. George Marsden, vii–xix. Grand Rapids, MI: Eerdmans.

———. 1991. *Understanding Fundamentalism and Evangelicalism*. Grand Rapids, MI: Eerdmans.

Marty, Martin. 1970. *Righteous Empire: The Experience in America*. New York: Dial Press.

———. 1977. *Religion, Awakening and Revolution*. Wilmington, NC: Consortium Books.

———. 1981. "The Revival of Evangelicalism and Southern Religion." In *Varieties of Southern Evangelicalism*, ed. David Harrell Jr., 7–21. Macon, GA: Mercer University Press.

———. 1982. "Religion in America since Mid-Century." *Daedalus* 111 (Winter): 149–63.

Massengill, Rebekah Peeples. 2008. "Educational Attainment and Cohort Changes among Conservative Protestants, 1972–2004." *Journal for the Scientific Study of Religion* 47 (4): 545–62.

———. 2011. "Why Evangelicals Like Wal-Mart: Education, Region, and Religious Group Identity." *Sociology of Religion* 72 (1): 50–77.

Mathews, Donald. 1969. "The Second Great Awakening as an Organizing Process, 1780–1830: An Hypothesis." *American Quarterly* 21:23–43.

Mayrl, Damon, and Freeden Oeure. 2009. "Religion and Higher Education: Current Knowledge and Directions for Future Research." *Journal for the Scientific Study of Religion* 48 (2): 260–75.

McKim. Donald. 1985. *What Christians Believe about the Bible*. Nashville, TN: Thomas Nelson.

McLoughlin, William. 1968. "Introduction, The American Evangelicals: 1800–1900." In *The American Evangelicals, 1800–1900*, ed. William McLoughlin, 1–27. New York: Harper & Row.

———. 1977. "Enthusiasm for Liberty: The Great Awakening as the Key to the Revolution." In *Preachers and Politicians: Two Essays on the Origins of the American Revolution*, eds. Jack Greene and William McLoughlin, 47–73. Worcester, MA: American Antiquarian Society.

———. 1982. "Religious Freedom and Popular Sovereignty." In *In the Great Tradition*, eds. Joseph Ban and Paul DeKar, 173–92. Valley Forge, PA: Judson Press.

McPherson, Miller, Lynn Smith-Lovin, and James M. Cook. 2001. "Birds of a Feather: Homophily in Social Networks." *Annual Review of Sociology* 27:415–44.

McPherson, Miller, and Thomas Totolo. 1996. "Testing a Dynamic Model of Social Composition: Diversity and Change in Voluntary Groups." *American Sociological Review* 61 (2): 179–202.

Menzies, William. 1975. "The Non-Wesleyan Origins of the Pentecostal Movement." In *Aspects of Pentecostal-Charismatic Origins*, ed. Vinson Synan, 81–98. Plainfield, NJ: Logos International.

Miller, Melissa K. 2003. "The Joiners: Voluntary Organizations and Political Participation in the United States." PhD diss., Northwestern University.

Miller, Steven P. 2014. *The Age of Evangelicalism: America's Born-Again Years*. New York: Oxford University Press.

Moorhead, James. 1979. "Social Reform and the Divided Conscience of Antebellum Protestantism." *Church History* 48:4 (December): 416–30.

———. 1984. "The Erosion of Postmillennialism in American Religious Thought, 1865–1925." *Church History* 53 (March): 61–77.

Nazworth, Napp. 2014. "Do Evangelical Churches Have to Accept Gay Marriage to Attract Millennials? *Christian Post* (July 11). http://www.christianpost.com/news/do-evangelical-churches-have-to-accept-gay-marriage-to-attract-millennials-123119 (accessed September 25, 2014).

Nemeth, Roger, and Donald Luidens. 2003. "The Religious Basis of Charitable Giving in the United States." In *Religion as Social Capital: Producing the Common Good*, ed. Corwin Smidt, 107–20. Waco, TX: Baylor University Press.

Newbigin, Lesslie. 1989. *The Gospel in a Pluralist Society*. Grand Rapids, MI: Eerdmans.

Nie, Norman, Jane Junn, and Kenneth Stehlik-Barry. 1996. *Education and Democratic Citizenship in America*. Chicago: University of Chicago Press.

Nivoli, Pietro, and David Brady, eds. 2006. *Red and Blue Nation*. Vol. 1. Washington, DC: Brookings.

Noll, Mark. 1977. *Christians in the American Revolution*. Grand Rapids, MI: Eerdmans.

———. 1983. "From the Great Awakening to the War for Independence: Christian Values in the American Revolution." *Christian Scholar's Review* 12 (2): 99–110.

———. 1994. "Revolution and the Rise of Evangelical Social Influence in North American Societies." In *Evangelicalism: Comparative Studies of Popular Protestantism in North America, the British Isles, and Beyond, 1700–1900*, eds. Mark Noll, David Bebbington, and George Rawlyk, 113–36. New York: Oxford University Press.

———. 2001. *American Evangelical Christianity: An Introduction*. Oxford: Blackwell.

———. 2002. *America's God: From Jonathan Edwards to Abraham Lincoln*. New York: Oxford University Press.

Noll, Mark, Nathan Hatch, and George Marsden. 1983. *The Search for Christian America*. Westchester, IL: Crossway Books.

Noll, Mark, and Lyman Kellstedt. 1995. "The Changing Face of Evangelicalism." *Pro Ecclesia* 4 (Spring): 146–64.

Nunn, Clyde, Henry Crockett, and J. Allen Williams. 1978. *Tolerance for Conformity: A National Survey of Americans' Changing Commitment to Civil Liberties*. San Francisco, CA: Jossey-Bass.

Okholm, Dennis, and Timothy Phillips, eds. 1995. *More Than One Way? Four Views on Salvation in a Pluralist World*. Grand Rapids, MI: Zondervan.

Olmstead, Clifton. 1961. *Religion in America: Past and Present*. Englewood Cliffs, NJ: Prentice Hall.

Olson, Daniel. 1989. "Church Friendships: Boon or Barrier to Church Growth?" *Journal for the Scientific Study of Religion* 28 (4): 432–47.

———. 1993. "Fellowship Ties and the Transmission of Religious Identity." In *Beyond Establishment: Protestant Identity in a Post-Protestant Age*, eds. Jackson Carroll and Wade Clark Roof, 32–53. Louisville, KY: Westminster John Knox Press.

Olson, Roger. 1995. "Postconservative Evangelicals Greet the Postmodern Age." *Christian Century* 112 (May 3): 480–83.

————. 1998. "The Future of Evangelical Theology." *Christianity Today* 42 (February): 40–49.

Pally, Marcia. 2011. *The New Evangelicals: Expanding the Vision of the Common Good.* Grand Rapids, MI: Eerdmans.

Pascarella, Ernest, and Patrick Terenzini. 2005. *How College Affects Students.* Vol. 2, *A Third Decade of Research.* San Francisco, CA: Jossey-Bass.

Passel, Jeffrey, and Paul Taylor. 2009. "Who's Hispanic?" http://www.pewhispanic .org/2009/05/28/whos-hispanic (accessed December 28, 2011).

Penning, James, and Corwin Smidt. 2002. *Evangelicalism: The Next Generation.* Grand Rapids, MI: Baker Academic.

Petersen, Larry. 1994. "Education, Homogamy, and Religious Commitment." *Journal for the Scientific Study of Religion* 33 (2): 122–34.

Pew Forum on Religion & Public Life. 2009. "Faith in Flux: Changes in Religious Affiliation in the U.S." www.pewforum.org/uploadedfiles/Topics/Religious_Affili ation/fullreport.pdf (accessed May 11, 2012).

Pew Forum on Religion & Public Life. 2012. "How the Faithful Voted: 2012 Pre-liminary Analysis." www.pewforum.org/Politics-and-Elections/How-the-Faith ful-Voted-2012-Preliminary-Exit-Poll-Analysis.aspx#rr (accessed November 19, 2012).

Pew U.S. Religious Landscape Survey (Continental Data Set). 2007. Washington, DC: Pew Forum on Religion & Public Life. www.thearda.com/Archive/PewResearch.asp.

Pinnock, Clark. 1992. *A Wideness in God's Mercy: The Finality of Jesus Christ in a World of Religions.* Grand Rapids, MI: Zondervan.

Poloma, Margaret. 1982. *The Charismatic Movement: Is There a New Pentecost?* Bos-ton: Twayne.

Public Religion Research Institute. 2011. "Generations at Odds: The Millennial Generation and the Future of Gay and Lesbian Rights." http://publicreligion.org/ research/2011/08/generations-at-odds (accessed June 15, 2012).

Public Religion Research Institute. 2012. "'Teaevangelicals': Alignments and Tensions between Tea Party and White Evangelical Protestants." http://publicreligion.org/ research/2011/11/fact-sheet-alignment-of-evangelical-and-tea-party-values/ (ac-cessed November 15, 2011).

Putnam, Robert. 1995. "Tuning In, Tuning Out: The Strange Disappearance of Social Capital in America." *PS: Political Science and Politics* 28 (December): 631–43.

————. 2000. *Bowling Alone: The Collapse and Revival of American Community.* New York: Simon & Schuster.

Putnam, Robert, and David Campbell. 2010. *American Grace: How Religion Divides and Unites Us.* New York: Simon & Schuster.

Quebedeaux, Richard. 1974. *The Young Evangelicals.* New York: Harper & Row.

Queen, Edward. 2002. "Public Religion and Voluntary Associations." In *Religion, Politics, and the American Experience: Reflections on Religion and American Public Life,* ed. Edith L. Blumhofer, 86–102. Tuscaloosa: University of Alabama Press.

Rauschenbusch, Walter. 1907. *Christianity and the Social Crisis.* New York: Hodder and Stoughton.

Regnerus, Mark, Christian Smith, and David Sikkink. 1998. "Who Gives to the Poor? The Influence of Religious Tradition and Political Location on the Personal Generosity of Americans toward the Poor." *Journal for the Scientific Study of Religion* 37 (3): 481–93.

Reimer, Sam, and Jerry Z. Park. 2001. "Tolerant (In)civility? A Longitudinal Analysis of White Conservative Protestants' Willingness to Grant Civil Liberties." *Journal for the Scientific Study of Religion* 40 (December): 735–45.

Religion and Diversity Survey, 2002–2003. www.thearda.com/Archive/Files/Descriptions/DIVERSTY.asp.

Roof, Wade Clark. 1982. "America's Voluntary Establishment: Mainline Religion in Transition." *Daedalus* 111 (Winter): 165–84.

Roof, Wade Clark, and William McKinney. 1987. *American Mainline Religion: Its Changing Shape and Future.* New Brunswick, NJ: Rutgers University Press.

Rothenberg, Stuart, and Frank Newport. 1984. *The Evangelical Voter.* Washington, DC: Free Congress Research & Education Foundation.

Ryden, David, ed. 2010. *Is the Good Book Good Enough? Evangelical Perspectives on Public Policy.* Lanham, MD: Lexington Books.

Sacerdote, Bruce, and Edward Glaeser. 2001. "Education and Religion." *Harvard Institute of Economic Research Paper No. 1913.* http://www.economics.harvard.edu/pub/hier/2001/HIER1913.pdf.

Sandeen, Ernest. 1970. *Roots of Fundamentalism: British and American Millenarianism, 1800–1930.* Chicago: University of Chicago Press.

Scheitle, Christopher, and Amy Adamczyk. 2009. "It Takes Two: The Interplay of Individual and Group Theology on Social Embeddedness." *Journal for the Scientific Study of Religion* 48 (1): 16–29.

Schlesinger, Arthur. 1944. "Biography of a Nation of Joiners." *American Historical Review* 50 (1): 1–25.

Second National Survey of Religion and Politics. 1996. Akron, OH: University of Akron Survey Research Center.

Sernett, Milton. 1991. "Black Religion and the Question of Evangelical Identity." In *The Variety of American Evangelicalism*, eds. Donald Dayton and Robert Johnson, 135–47. Knoxville: University of Tennessee Press.

Shiels, Richard. 1980. "The Second Great Awakening in Connecticut: Critique of the Traditional Interpretation." *Church History* 49 (December): 401–15.

Sider, Ron, and Dianne Knippers, eds. 2005. *Toward an Evangelical Public Policy: Political Strategies for the Health of the Nation.* Grand Rapids, MI: Baker Books.

Singleton, Gregory. 1975. "Protestant Voluntary Organization and the Shaping of Victorian America." *American Quarterly* 27 (December): 549–60.

Skerkat, Darren. 1998. "Counterculture or Continuity? Competing Influences on Baby Boomers' Religious Orientations and Participation." *Social Forces* 76 (3): 1087–114.

Smidt, Corwin E. 1989. "Identifying Evangelical Respondents: An Analysis of 'Born Again' and Bible Questions Used across Different Surveys." In *Religion and Political Behavior in the United States*, ed. Ted G. Jelen, 23–43. New York: Praeger.

———. 2007a. "Evangelical and Mainline Protestants at the Turn of the Millennium: Taking Stock and Looking Forward." In *From Pews to Polling Places in the American Religious Mosaic*, ed. Matthew Wilson, 29–51. Washington, DC: Georgetown University Press.

———. 2007b. "The Christian Faith and Politics: The Principled Pluralist Perspective." In *Church, State and Public Justice: Five Views*, ed. Paul Kemeny, 127–53. Downers Grove, IL: InterVarsity Press.

———. 2008. "Evangelicals and the American Presidency." In *Religion, Race, and the American Presidency*, ed. Gaston Espinosa, 1–15. Lanham, MD: Rowman & Littlefield.

Smidt, Corwin E., Kevin den Dulk, Bryan Froehle, James Penning, Stephen Monsma, and Douglas Koopman. 2010. *The Disappearing God Gap? Religion in the 2008 Presidential Election*. New York: Oxford University Press.

Smidt, Corwin E., Kevin R. den Dulk, James M. Penning, Stephen V. Monsma, and Douglas L. Koopman. 2008. *Pews, Prayers, and Participation: Religion and Civic Responsibility in America*. Washington, DC: Georgetown University Press.

Smidt, Corwin E., and Lyman A. Kellstedt. 1987. "Evangelicalism and Survey Research: Interpretive Problems and Substantive Findings." In *The Bible, Politics, and Democracy*, ed. Richard J. Neuhaus, 81–102. Grand Rapids, MI: Eerdmans.

Smidt, Corwin E., Lyman A. Kellstedt, and James L. Guth. 2009. "The Role of Religion in American Politics: Explanatory Theories and Associated Analytical and Measurement Issues." In *The Oxford Handbook of Religion and American Politics*, eds. Corwin E. Smidt, Lyman A. Kellstedt, and James L. Guth, 3–42. New York: Oxford University Press.

Smidt, Corwin, and James Penning. 1982. "Religious Commitment, Political Conservatism, and Political and Social Tolerance in the United States: A Longitudinal Analysis." *Sociological Analysis* 43:231–46.

Smith, Christian. 1998. *American Evangelicalism: Embattled and Thriving*. Chicago: University of Chicago Press.

———. 2000. *Christian America? What Evangelicals Really Want*. Berkeley: University of California Press.

———. 2003. "Theorizing Religious Effects among American Adolescents." *Journal for the Scientific Study of Religion* 42:17–30.

Smith, Christian, and Melinda L. Denton. 2005. *Soul Searching: The Religious and Spiritual Lives of American Teenagers*. Oxford: Oxford University Press.

Smith, Christian, Melinda L. Denton, Robert Faris, and Mark Regnerus. 2002. "Mapping American Adolescent Religious Participation." *Journal for the Scientific Study of Religion* 41:597–612.

Smith, Christian, and Robert Faris. 2002. "Religion and American Adolescent Delinquency, Risk Behaviors and Constructive Social Activities: A Research Report of the National Study of Youth and Religion." No. 1. Chapel Hill, NC: The National Study of Youth and Religion. www.youthandreligion.org.

Smith, David Horton. 1975. "Voluntary Action and Voluntary Groups." *Annual Review of Sociology* 1:247–70.

Smith, Timothy. 1967. "Protestant Schooling and American Nationality, 1800–1850." *Journal of American History* 53 (March): 679–95.

Snow, David, Louis Zurcher, and Shelden Ekland-Olson. 1980. "Social Networks and Social Movements: A Microstructural Approach to Differential Recruitment." *American Sociological Review* 45 (5): 787–801.

Stackhouse, Max. 1982. "Religious Right: New? Right?" *Commonweal* 109 (January): 52–56.

Stark, Rodney, and Charles Glock. 1968. *American Piety: The Nature of Religious Commitment.* Berkeley: University of California Press.

Steensland, Brian, Jerry Park, Mark Regnerus, Lynn Robinson, W. Bradley Wilcox, and Robert Woodberry. 2000. "The Measure of American Religion: Toward Improving the State of Art." *Social Forces* 79:291–318.

Stetson, Brad, and Joseph G. Conti. 2005. *The Truth about Tolerance: Pluralism, Diversity, and the Culture Wars.* Downers Grove, IL: InterVarsity Press.

Stetzer, Ed. 2014. "Evangelicals and Same-Sex Marriage." *The Exchange* (August 27) http://www.christianitytoday.com/edstetzer/2014/august/evangelicals-and-same-sex-marriage-interview-with-john-ston.html (accessed September 24, 2014).

Stouffer, Samuel. 1955. *Communism, Conformity, and Civil Liberties: A Cross-Section of the Nation Speaks Its Mind.* New York: Doubleday.

Stout, Harry S. 1977. "Religion, Communications, and the Ideological Origins of the American Revolution." *William and Mary Quarterly* 34 (October): 519–41.

Stroope, Samuel. Forthcoming. "Social Networks and Religion: The Role of Congregational Social Embeddedness in Religious Belief and Practice." *Sociology of Religion* 73 (3): 273–98.

Stump, Roger. 1984a. "Regional Divergence in Religious Affiliation in the United States." *Sociological Analysis* 45 (Winter): 283–99.

———. 1984b. "Regional Migration and Religious Commitment in the United States." *Journal for the Scientific Study of Religion* 23 (September): 292–303.

Sullivan, John L., James Pierson, and George E. Marcus. 1982. *Political Tolerance and American Democracy.* Chicago: University of Chicago Press.

Swaim, Barton. 2014. "Book Review: *The Age of Evangelicalism* by Stephen P. Miller." *Wall Street Journal* (July 3). http://online.wsj.com/articles/book-review-the-age-of-evangelicalism-by-steven-p-miller-1404433658?cb=logged0.4266485464759171 (accessed September 27, 2014).

Sweeney, Douglas A. 1991. "The Essential Evangelical Dialectic: The Historiography of the Early Neo-Evangelical Movement and the Observer-Participant Dilemma." *Church History* 60 (March): 70–84.

———. 2005. *The American Evangelical Story: A History of the Movement.* Grand Rapids, MI: Baker Academic.

Sweet, Douglas. 1976. "Church Vitality and the American Revolution: Historiographical Consensus and Thoughts toward a New Perspective." *Church History* 45 (September): 341–57.

Sweet, Leonard. 1984a. "The Evangelical Tradition in America." In *The Evangelical Tradition in America*, ed. Leonard Sweet, 1–86. Macon, GA: Mercer University Press.

———. 1984b. "The 1960s: The Crises of Liberal Christianity and the Public Emergence of Evangelicalism." In *Evangelicalism and Modern America*, ed. George Marsden, 29–45. Grand Rapids, MI: Eerdmans.

Swierenga, Robert. 1990. "Ethno-Religious Political Behavior in the Mid-Nineteenth Century." In *Religion & American Politics: From the Colonial Period to the 1980s*, ed. Mark Noll, 146–71. New York: Oxford University Press.

Synan, Vinson. 1971. *The Holiness-Pentecostal Movement in the United States*. Grand Rapids, MI: Eerdmans.

Theiss-Morse, Elizabeth, and John R. Hibbing. 2005. "Citizenship and Civic Engagement." In *Annual Review of Political Science*, 8:227–49. Palo Alto, CA: Annual Reviews.

Thomas, Cal, and Ed Dobson. 1999. *Blinded by Might: Can the Religious Right Save America?* Grand Rapids, MI: Zondervan.

Tipton, Steven. 2007. *Public Pulpits: Methodists and Mainline Churches in the Moral Argument of Public Life*. Chicago: University of Chicago Press.

Tocqueville, Alexis de. 1969. *Democracy in America*. Garden City, NY: Doubleday.

Tyack, David. 1966. "The Kingdom of God and the Common School." *Harvard Educational Review* 36:447–69.

Ulzurrun, Laura Morales Diez de. 2002. "Associational Membership and Social Capital in Comparative Perspective: A Note on the Problems of Measurement." *Politics & Society* 30 (September): 497–523.

Valentine, Katie. 2014. "Evangelical Group: Climate Change is a 'Pro-Life' Issue." ClimateProgress (May 20). http://thinkprogress.org/climate/2014/05/20/3439695/evangelical-environmental-network-rick-scott-petition (accessed September 26, 2014).

Wacker, Grant. 1984. "Uneasy in Zion: Evangelicals in Postmodern Society." In *Evangelicalism and Modern America*, ed. George Marsden, 17–28. Grand Rapids, MI: Eerdmans.

———. 1985. "The Holy Spirit and the Spirit of the Age in American Protestantism, 1880–1910." *Journal of American History* 72 (1): 45–62.

Wadsworth, M. E. J., and S. R. Freeman. 1983. "Generational Differences in Beliefs: A Cohort Study of Stability and Change in Religious Beliefs." *British Journal of Sociology* 34 (3): 416–37.

Wald, Kenneth D., and Allison Calhoun-Brown. 2007. *Religion and Politics in the United States*. 5th ed. Lanham, MD: Rowman & Littlefield.

Wald, Kenneth D., and Corwin E. Smidt. 1993. "Measurement Strategies in the Study of Religion and Politics." In *Rediscovering the Religious Factor in American Politics*, eds. David C. Leege and Lyman A. Kellstedt, 26–49. Armonk, NY: M. E. Sharpe.

Wallis, Jim. 2005. *God's Politics: Why the Right Gets It Wrong and the Left Doesn't Get It*. San Francisco, CA: HarperSanFrancisco.

———. 2008. *The Great Awakening: Reviving Faith & Politics in a Post–Religious Right America*. New York: HarperOne.

Warner, R. Stephen. 1979. "Theoretical Barriers to the Understanding of Evangelical Christianity." *Sociological Analysis* 40 (1): 1–9.

———. 1994. "The Place of Congregation in the Contemporary American Religious Configuration." In *American Congregations: New Perspectives in the Study of Congregations*, eds. James Wind and James Lewis, 54–100. Chicago: University of Chicago Press.

Weber, Timothy. 1983. *Living in the Shadow of the Second Coming: American Premillennialism, 1875–1982*. Enlarged ed. New York: Oxford University Press.

———. 1991. "Pentecostalism and the Branches of Evangelicalism." In *The Variety of American Evangelicalism*, eds. Donald W. Dayton and Robert K. Johnson, 5–21. Downers Grove, IL: InterVarsity Press.

Wehner, Peter. 2007. "Among Evangelicals, a Transformation." *National Review* 59 (December 31): 30–32.

Weisskopf, Michael. 1993. "Energized by Pulpit or Passion, the Public Is Calling." *Washington Post* (February 1): A1. www.lexisnexis.com/hottopics/lnacademic/?verb=sr&csi=8075 (accessed September 5, 2011).

Welch, Kevin. 1981. "An Interpersonal Influence Model of Traditional Religious Commitment." *Sociological Quarterly* 22 (Winter): 81–92.

Welch, Michael, and David C. Leege. 1991. "Dual Reference Groups and Political Orientations: An Examination of Evangelically Oriented Catholics." *American Journal of Political Science* 35:28–56.

Wells, David. 1994. "On Being Evangelical: Some Theological Differences and Similarities." In *Evangelicalism*, eds. Mark Noll, David Bebbington, and George Rawlyk, 389–410. New York: Oxford University Press.

Wentz, Richard. 1998. *The Culture of Religious Pluralism*. Boulder, CO: Westview.

White, R. H. 1969. "Toward a Theory of Religious Influence." *Pacific Sociological Review* 11 (1): 23–28.

Whitehead, Andrew L. 2010. "Financial Commitment within Federations of Small Groups: The Effect of Cell-Based Congregational Structure on Individual Giving." *Journal for the Scientific Study of Religion* 49 (4): 640–56.

Wilcox, Clyde. 1992. *God's Warriors: The Christian Right in 20th Century America*. Baltimore, MD: Johns Hopkins University Press.

Wilcox, Clyde, and Ted Jelen. 1990. "Evangelicals and Political Tolerance." *American Politics Quarterly* 18 (January): 25–46.

Wilcox, Clyde, and Carin Larson. 2006. *Onward Christian Soldiers? The Religious Right in American Politics*. 3rd ed. Boulder, CO: Westview.

Williams, Daniel. 2010. *God's Own Party: The Making of the Christian Right*. New York: Oxford University Press.

Williams, Rhys, ed. 1997. *Cultural Wars in American Politics: Critical Reviews of a Popular Myth*. New York: Aldine DeGruyter.

Wilson, John. 2000. "Volunteering." *Annual Review of Sociology* 26:215–40.

Woodberry, Robert, and Christian Smith. 1998. "Fundamentalism et al.: Conservative Protestants in America." *Annual Review of Sociology* 24:25–56.

Worthen, Molly. 2013. *Apostles of Reason: The Crisis of Authority in American Evangelicalism*. New York: Oxford University Press.

Wuthnow, Robert. 1988. *The Restructuring of American Religion*. Princeton, NJ: Princeton University Press.

———. 1991. *Acts of Compassion: Caring for Others and Helping Ourselves.* Princeton, NJ: Princeton University Press.

———. 1993. "Small Groups Forge New Notions of Community and the Sacred." *Christian Century* (December 8): 1236–40.

———. 1994a. *"I Come Away Stronger": How Small Groups Are Shaping American Religion.* Grand Rapids, MI: Eerdmans.

———. 1994b. *Sharing the Journey: Support Groups and America's Quest for Community.* New York: Free Press.

———. 1998a. *After Heaven: Spirituality in America since the 1950s.* Berkeley: University of California Press.

———. 1998b. *Loose Connections: Joining Together in America's Fragmented Communities.* Cambridge, MA: Harvard University Press.

———. 1999. "Mobilizing Civic Engagement: The Changing Impact of Religious Involvement." In *Civic Engagement in American Democracy,* eds. Theda Skocpol and Morris Fiorina, 331–63. Washington, DC: Brookings.

———. 2003. "Overcoming Status Distinctions? Religious Involvement, Social Class, Race, and Ethnicity in Friendship Patterns." *Sociology of Religion* 64 (4): 423–42.

———. 2004a. "The Religious Factor Revisited." *Sociological Theory* 22 (June): 205–18.

———. 2004b. *Saving America? Faith-Based Services and the Future of Civil Society.* Princeton, NJ: Princeton University Press.

———. 2005. *America and the Challenges of Religious Diversity.* Princeton, NJ: Princeton University Press.

———. 2007a. *After the Baby Boomers: How Twenty- and Thirty-Somethings Are Shaping the Future of American Religion.* Princeton, NJ: Princeton University Press.

———. 2007b. "Cognition and Religion." *Sociology of Religion* 68:341–60.

———. 2009a. "The Cultural Capital of American Evangelicalism." In *Evangelicals and Democracy in America.* Vol. 1, *Religion and Society,* eds. Steven Brint and Jean Reith Schroedel, 27–43. New York: Russell Sage Foundation.

———. 2009b. *Boundless Faith: The Global Outreach of American Churches.* Berkeley: University of California Press.

Young, William Paul. 2008. *The Shack.* Newbury Park, CA: Windblown Media.

Zimmerman, Earl. 2007. *Practicing the Politics of Jesus.* Telford, PA: Cascadia.

Index

abolition of slavery, 27, 29
abortion: as common fight for evangelicals, 38; as measure of ideological position, 193; opinions based on race, 203–4; Supreme Court decision to legalize, 37; views based on educational attainment, 206–8, 220; views based on generation, 205–8; views based on religious traditionalism, 189, 191–92, 208–12, 227
absolute standards of right and wrong, 140–43, 150–55
African American evangelicals, 7, 29, 114, 230n11, 243n31. *See also* Black Protestants
age: within denominational affiliations, 74, 80; among various religious traditions, 74, 81–82, 224–25, 227. *See also* generational differences
American Revolution. *See* Revolutionary War
Arminianism, 215, 217, 231n5
attention to politics. *See* political attention

Baby Boom generation, 8, 63, *73*, 74, 81, *87*, 231n12. *See also* generational differences
Barna Research Group, 50–51, 55, 236n16
Bebbington, David, 50, 51
believers but not belongers, 4, 110, 228. *See also* privatized religion; spiritual but not religious
biblical authority, nature of: as defining characteristic of evangelicals, 64–67; survey questions regarding, 238n8, 238n9; views of various religious traditions, 64, 92–95, 127. *See also* inerrancy of scripture; infallibility of scripture
black. *See* African American evangelicals; Black Protestants
Black Protestants: belief differences based on educational attainment, 120–26, 147–49; belief differences based on generation, 118–24, 126, 146, 149; beliefs compared to black evangelicals, 115–17, 144–46; charitable giving, 165–66, 247n10;

223–24, 228; among various religious traditions, 90, 111–13, 120–21, 123

religious tolerance. *See* tolerance of other opinions

religious tradition: within American culture, 227; evangelicalism categorized as, 6, 48–50, 56–58, 213

Republicans: affiliation differences based on educational attainment, 206–8, 220; affiliation differences based on generation, 205–8, 219; affiliation differences based on race, 204; affiliation differences based on religious traditionalism, 208–11; evangelical Protestant self-identification as, 194–95, 198–212, 219, 220; party relationship to evangelicals, 6

republicanism, 137, 245n8, 245n9

Restorationist tradition, 232n14

revivalism: as basis for social reform, 26, 28, 32; as means to increase church membership, 22, 246n3; as movement, 19, 25, 40, 135, 215, 217, 232n11, 232n13

Revolutionary War, 18, 19, 20, 24–25, 232n7, 232n8

Robertson, Pat, 229n5

Roman Catholics. *See* Catholics

Romney, Mitt, 195

Rove, Karl, 248n2, 249n2

sacraments, 38

salvation by faith/belief, 51, 95–96, 111–13

salvation by works/behavior, 95–96

saved for service, 22, 32

Scopes Monkey Trial, 33, 35, 184, 240n6

Second Great Awakening, 21–26, 36, 232n8, 232n13

secularization thesis, 35. *See also* educational attainment

separation of church and state, 18, 23, 135, 183, 232n13

sexual revolution, 37

Silent Generation, 8, 74, *87*. *See also* generational differences

smaller government. *See* government with fewer services

small group activities within church: among evangelical Protestants, 104–5, 124–28, 223; level of participation in, 11, 102–3; participation in as means of solidifying community, 103–5, 223; and perceived similarity of beliefs within group, 107–8; among various religious traditions, 104–5, 124–27

Smith, Christian, 3, 54, 158, 159, 214

social gospel, 28, 30, 32, 131, 233n17

social justice, 6

social trust, in others, 159–61, 171–72, 175–77, 179–80, 219, 220

sola scriptura, 22, 31

spiritual but not religious, 110, 241n15. *See also* believers but not belongers; privatized religion

spiritual world, belief in, 92

Sweet, Leonard, 16

Tea Party movement: evangelical Protestants identifying with, 196–98, 212; as extension of Republican Party, 196–97; survey questions regarding, 197, 250n11; various religious traditions identifying with, 196–98

theological training, 25. *See also* education of clergy

Tocqueville, Alexis de, 161

tolerance of other opinions, 10, 140–41; among evangelical Protestants, 168–70, 171–73, 176–80, 219, 220; religiosity and, 166–67; survey questions regarding, 167–69, 248n11; among various religious traditions, 167–70, 172–73, 176–77, 179–80. *See also* equality before law

traditionalism, religious: among evangelical Protestants, 11, 101,